Reflections of an American Composer

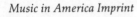

Reflections of an American Composer

ARTHUR BERGER

University of California Press

BERKELEY   LOS ANGELES   LONDON

*The publisher gratefully acknowledges the generous
contribution to this book provided by Sukey and Gil
Garcetti, Michael Roth, and the Roth Family Foundation.*

Excerpts from Aaron Copland's "Into the Streets May First" and from
Copland's letter to Arthur Berger, 10 April 1943, are reprinted by permission of the Aaron Copland Fund for Music, Inc., copyright owner.
Arthur Berger's article "Copland's Piano Sonata" first appeared in *Partisan Review* 10, no. 2 (March–April 1943). Excerpt from Arnold Isenberg, "Critical Communication," is from *Aesthetics and Language*, ed.
William Elton (Oxford: Basil Blackwell, 1959). Chapter 14 originally
appeared in different form in *Perspectives of New Music* 3, no. 1 (fall–
winter 1964), and is used by permission.

Excerpt from Third Symphony (In One Movement), by Roy Harris,
© 1939 (Renewed) by Associated Music Publishers, Inc. (BMI). International Copyright Secured. All Rights Reserved. Reprinted by
Permission.

Excerpt from Aaron Copland, Piano Variations, © Copyright 1932 by
the Aaron Copland Fund for Music, Inc. Copyright Renewed. Boosey
& Hawkes, Inc., Sole Licensee. Reprinted by permission.

Excerpts from Igor Stravinsky, *Symphony of Psalms*, © Copyright 1931
by Hawkes & Son (London) Ltd. Copyright Renewed. Revised version
© Copyright 1948 by Hawkes & Son (London) Ltd. Copyright Renewed. Reprinted by permission of Boosey & Hawkes, Inc.

University of California Press
Berkeley and Los Angeles, California

University of California Press, Ltd.
London, England

© 2002 by the Regents of the University of California

Library of Congress Cataloging-in-Publication Data

Berger, Arthur, 1912–.
    Reflections of an American composer / Arthur Berger.
        p.   cm.
Includes index.
    ISBN 0–520-23251-8 (alk. paper)
    1. Music—United States—History and criticism.   2. Berger, Arthur,
1912–.   I. Title.
    ML200.5 .B47   2002
    780'.973—dc21   2002006432

Manufactured in the United States of America
10   09   08   07   06   05   04   03   02   01
10 9 8 7 6 5 4 3 2 1

The paper used in this publication is both acid-free and totally chlorine-
free (TCF). It meets the minimum requirements of ANSI/NISO Z39.48-
1992 (R 1997) (*Permanence of Paper*). ♾

Contents

Illustrations follow page 138.

Acknowledgments

I should like to express my thanks to Maria Jane Loizou, Rosalie Calabrese, and Elliott Gyger for their prompt and efficient response to my requests for material requiring research. I am also indebted to Carroll Chomsky, David Kopp, and Grant Covell for helping me navigate what were to me, when I started writing this book, the strange waters of computer territory. Caldwell Titcomb was always available to me and obliging whenever I had any questions; and I hope that it will be obvious from the results that I am also indebted to my editor, Kay Scheuer, as well as to my project managers at the University of California Press, David Gill and Jacqueline Volin. For a variety of reasons, from their reading and commenting on parts of the manuscript to easing my way in undertaking and completing the entire writing project, I should like to acknowledge the cooperation of Joseph Kerman, Robert Bachrach, Martin Boykan, Benjamin Boretz, Rodney Lister, Gunther Schuller, and David Del Tredici. Not least of all I want to express my gratitude to my wife, Ellen, for her patience and sympathy during the period when I remained riveted to the computer, unavailable to her when she needed me and could have profited from my assistance or companionship.

Introduction

The decision to write conventional memoirs is something I have scarcely ever had to contend with. To make interesting reading out of one's personal life requires the craft and skill of a fiction writer, which I am not sure I possess. Also I am not convinced that my origins, childhood, and amorous pursuits would be of sufficient interest to most readers even if they were to be conveyed through the most elegant writing. I do however believe that as an actual participant much of the time since about 1930 (more specifically, 1929, the year of the notorious Wall Street Crash) and as a composer and critic who has been a zealous observer all of the time, I am in a good position to have a story to tell.

I had not anticipated to what extent a book of essays on subjects out of my past that had to do with music would burst at the seams with anecdotes, many of which involve me personally, as if those memoirs were vying to come out. This brought me around to the idea of having chapter 18, which is devoted solely to capsule items reporting isolated incidents frankly out of context. These are items that would be in my diary had I kept one, so I hope I am not out of line notwithstanding in using the title "From My Diary: Brief Encounters" for that chapter.

It may be a needless precaution but I feel I should remind the reader that my approach is not from the historian's vantage point. If the trends in composition are presented in somewhat chronological order, that is because to observe each one as a reaction to its predecessor can be illuminating. But this chronological approach is limited to the first of the four sections. More important, if this book is approached as a survey or chronicle it will occasion a field-day for the sleuths who make it their business to track down facts and events that "should have been" included. I have written about my own experience from the angle of vision from which I saw it, as well as about any matters that stand out in my memory or that came back to me as I looked through the clippings of my reviews in my scrapbooks (a few thousand daily reviews and contributions to periodicals). In selecting what to use I have been guided by a sense of a given circumstance's importance as well as by my projection of how much it would be of interest now. Still, I should make it clear to readers who may occasionally feel I am flogging a dead horse that within our lifetime and not long ago the issues in question may have been burning issues and, while in the judgment of the most informed readers they no longer are such, it could very well be that to others they may still pose problems. Also, as a consequence of my effort to project myself into the past I may very well be more sensitive than others to any residue of a thing today that had currency then.

It should become clear from my observations that I have been a resident of the Eastern Seaboard of the United States, which will place a boundary on what I have experienced firsthand. I spent the first half of my days as a New Yorker and have been a Bostonian (more specifically, a Cantabrigian) the rest of the time though there have been side trips to the West Coast and Western Europe. My period as a New Yorker (interrupted by a spell as a Harvard graduate student, including a fellowship for study abroad, and by a brief tenure teaching at Mills College in California) was the period during which I was most active on the musical scene. By the time I turned sixteen, which was when I entered the College of the City of New York, I was well aware of what was transpiring in the New York music world, and I became a participant when I moved over to New York University to complete my undergraduate studies. Almost from the beginning I knew that my orientation would be in the direction of contemporary music, as composer or musicologist.

My career in the professional music world started quite early with a job that fell into my lap while I was still engaged in completing my requirements for the bachelor degree. Even though it was a modest job as a stringer on a lowdown New York Hearst tabloid, the *Daily Mirror*, it was enough to launch me in 1931 on my twenty-year career (with some interruptions) as influential newspaper music reviewer—briefly in Boston while a Harvard graduate student, but mostly on the *New York Herald Tribune*—and to establish me as an individual very much involved in current music events.

Though at my age of course memory is not altogether reliable, I do not feel comfortable taking refuge behind the dictates of the school of thought that accepts with equanimity the circumstance that our recollections, being siphoned through our knowledge of the present, are inevitably emended by what we now know. According to Ned Rorem, "The past exists only inside the head. . . . attempts to retrieve it are *current* impulses which distort, of necessity, since we know now more than we knew then; so the past is by definition embellished."[1] I have taken precautions that have enabled me to make the imaginary journey back to the past by using my old reviews and articles to jog my memory where I may have forgotten things and to verify facts (including dates) and ideas. Also, chapter 14, "New Linguistic Modes and the New Theory," incorporates quite a bit of the thinking that determined the approach to an article of the same name that appeared in *Perspectives of New Music,* and chapter 8, "Postmodern Music," is a version of an article published in *The Boston Review* under the title "Is There a Postmodern Music?" The reader will also encounter references of a more modest nature to other of my publications. In chapter 15, "The Octatonic Scale," I have leaned rather heavily on a lecture I gave at Harvard University in a series sponsored by the music department.

I should like to think that my readership will include not only musicians but those who are dedicated listeners—to contemporary music in particular—but lack the professional tools (the ability to decode musical notation, for example) for coping with technical discourse on music. To address both types of reader is very difficult, and I must beg those who are interested in what I have to say to approach the following pages with indulgence. The informed reader may be offended by the condescension, for example, when I suggest that anyone who does not know what a pentatonic scale sounds like can easily find out by playing the black keys of the piano or any keyboard instrument. The uninformed reader will find some (not many) pages hard going, especially in the few instances where there are musical illustrations. Such pages will be found in the last part of chapter 4. They may be glossed over, but I would hope that uninformed readers would get what they can out of chapter 15 as a way of becoming aware of the kind of internecine political conflicts in which music theorists become engaged. I would also hope they would seriously consider a suggestion once made by the British novelist E. M. Forster. Speaking at the opening of the Harvard University Symposium on Music Criticism in May 1947, he said the talks that were to be given "promised particular examinations and I look forward to following these so far as an amateur can. It is delightful and profitable to enter into technicalities to the limit of one's poor ability, to continue as far as one can in the wake of an expert mind, to pursue an argument till it passes out of one's grasp."[2]

I trust it is not an unwarranted assumption that people interested in music as listeners are likely also to be interested as part of general knowledge in those who make it—the artistic movements in which they are involved and all kinds of things on the periphery. I say "likely" because it is not absolutely necessary to a proper appreciation of music. If I ask my readers to address themselves to passages that dwell on the anecdotal, the nature of different tendencies, or the relation of composers to the world around them, and then shift abruptly to the entirely different intellectual level of aesthetics or music theory, I am not proposing, as some might be inclined to do, that they are all equally important to our apprehension of music. The distinguished critic of architecture Charles Jencks in *The Language of Post-Modern Architecture*, even before he reached his chapters on postmodernism, advised us, referring to a fascinating Australian structure, "It is virtually impossible to perceive the building without knowing about the notorious 'Sydney Opera House Case,' the firing of the architect, the cost, and so forth. So these local, specific meanings also become symbolised in the 'extravagant' shells."[3] Thank god for the qualifier "virtually." What I have in mind is not at all like that. This should become obvious from the passages on aesthetics that insist what is required for apprehension of music is all *within* the work as presented to an unanaesthetized and attentive listener—something not to be confused with "art for art's sake" and its advocacy of pure form.

While the essays in this book may be read separately or in a different order without causing any problem, there is a semblance of organization of a kind that is very much the same as what it would have been if they were a collection of previously published articles. This is especially true of the first part which, as I remarked above, is an almost chronological presentation of the tendencies in which American composers were engaged as they seemed to evolve on my horizon. (Chapter 3, "Is Music in Decline?" is a kind of side trip assessing the developments.) This takes us up to chapter 9 which opens the second section with the self-explanatory title, "Writing about Music," the approach being from the point of view of reviewing and editing. The third section contains the book's most challenging writing on music but it is mixed in with aesthetic discussion that should be of general interest. Finally in the fourth part there is reading of more general, anecdotal character.

A final word: it will be observed that my reflections are mostly in the form of memories of a time gone by. Perhaps it is because the current scene is too crowded and undifferentiated for the most striking moments to stand out as yet, or is it that at my advanced age I am less involved than I used to be?

I

TRENDS IN TWENTIETH-CENTURY
AMERICAN COMPOSITION

1 Composers and Their Audience in the Thirties

When Arnold Schoenberg, having fled Nazi Germany, came to Boston in 1933 to teach at the short-lived Malkin Conservatory of Music, a story made the rounds to the effect that Richard Burgin, concertmaster and assistant conductor of the Boston Symphony Orchestra, had had a conversation with the celebrated composer in which he proudly announced that some years earlier he had given the first Boston performance of *Pierrot Lunaire*. Schoenberg expressed surprise that so difficult and "advanced" a composition had been played in Boston. But there was not the slightest display of gratitude or pleasure; instead, Schoenberg looked perturbed. It seems he had somehow got the impression that the performance had taken place in Symphony Hall, which was the only Boston concert venue he knew, and all he could say was that it was much too large for a work like that. Burgin attempted to relieve his anxiety by explaining that Boston had a smaller place for major concerts, the New England Conservatory's Jordan Hall, seating about a thousand, and it was only natural that the work should have been played there. "Yes," said Schoenberg, "but even that is too large for *Pierrot*." "I know," replied Burgin, "but maestro, the hall was not full." "That's much better," was Schoenberg's response and he was obviously relieved.

The anecdote may very well have been the fabrication of some pundit. But this would not affect its appeal to musicians as a metaphor for Schoenberg's claim that he was addressing a small and intellectually elite audience, and true or false, it gave them an opportunity to air their conviction that there was something a bit foolish about an individual disdaining a large and conceivably adoring public. I wonder if it occurred to anybody that in those days Schoenberg was well aware that among a thousand people there would be a sufficient number who despised atonality and would accordingly manifest their impatience in ways (coughing, fidgeting, etc.) that would interfere with the evanescence and translucent balance of the music.

Nobody likes being excluded from anything, and to be excluded from something that is purported to be a universal art naturally breeds resentment. There is a further factor that enters into the equation, a factor of a political nature that exacerbates and seems to justify resentment. In the old days when the aristocracy was in power, they were the ones who cultivated and supported the fine arts. The arts were theirs just as in a previous era the arts had been what has often been referred to as the "handmaiden" of the church. When the age of the aristocracy had passed, the concept of "art for the few" became a mark of privilege, a means for the bourgeoisie to identify itself with aristocracy.[1] If there is any residue today of this propensity of the wealthy to use the arts to advertise their wealth, it is more likely to take the peripheral form of buying costly twentieth-century paintings or purchasing a box (where they still exist) at the symphony, or opera seats at today's stratospheric prices, though we still sometimes find wealthy individuals, big corporations, or foundations supporting artistic ventures from square one.

It is not surprising that your average member of the audience for serious music should be inclined to assimilate to the rich man's "art for the few" the exclusivity fostered by the kind of difficulty that much innovative twentieth-century music imposes on the listener. This was a factor particularly to be reckoned with during the administration of Franklin Delano Roosevelt in the thirties, when democracy in America was at its peak and a new liberalism cast its spell over thinkers and artists of many persuasions who were also responding to the dialectical materialism and Marxist ideology emanating from Soviet Russia and still at a stage when they were found promising.

Many of us started to feel embarrassed at excluding the masses when we wrote music that they found inaccessible or accessible with difficulty. We need not have been card-carrying Party members, and we had no wish to overthrow the American government. We had our infighting as followers of either Leon Trotsky or Joseph Stalin, but during the mid-thirties many of us viewed Socialism in Russia through rose-colored glasses. We were known as "fellow-travelers," and we mingled with the faithful at endless meetings where the subject of how to communicate to the masses was ardently thrashed out and the tendency of the artist to take refuge in "escapism" was bitterly reviled. Around that time the intellectuals were quite concerned about being accused of escapism. Even that businessman-poet Wallace Stevens, who you would think was beyond such things, felt he had

Ex. 1. "Into the Streets May First," *New Masses*, 1 May 1934

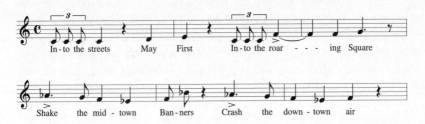

to come to grips with the problem when he gave a lecture at Harvard to which my good friend and neighbor, the poet Delmore Schwartz, urged me to accompany him. ".... the greater the pressure of the contemporaneous," Stevens preached in the staid voice of a minister, "the greater the resistance. Resistance is the opposite of escape."[2]

Occasionally someone would assume a more active role, as when Aaron Copland wrote a song for the picket line, "Into the Streets May First," which won a prize in a contest sponsored by the Communist-controlled Composers Collective and was published in the Communist mouthpiece *New Masses* in its May Day issue (1 May 1934). It is very surprising indeed that a composer who, as everyone knows, soon afterwards developed a manner that was so wide in its appeal and at the same time of such fine workmanship should so miscalculate the musical capacities of a worker on a picket line. The modulation to E-flat major in the fourth bar before the singer has had a chance to get into the song would give your worker quite a bit of trouble on an actual picket line where there might be no accompaniment (Ex. 1). Later there is a stretch in E major. Note also the peculiar syncopation in the second bar, giving the effect of a meter change from four-four to three-four. It was not Copland's finest hour, but the good intentions were there.

Since my book on Copland[3] appeared during a reactionary turn in political sentiment and at the height of what was known as a "witch hunt" for Communist sympathizers, namely in 1953, I thought it prudent not to mention the picket-line song. I also omitted any reference to the Young Composers Group that had formed with Copland as its mentor, since there were strong cleavages within it between Trotskyites and Stalinists that led to violent clashes, and only someone with the equanimity of a Copland could restore peace. In protecting Copland by being cautious in this matter,

I was merely being mindful that the authorities were expecting to find a Communist under every bed, as the saying went. The furthest thing from my mind was the prospect that the very same year as the publication of my book Copland would be called before the indomitable Joseph McCarthy and his House Un-American Activities Committee on charges of alleged Communist Party affiliations and that his existence would be rendered pretty intolerable for quite a while.[4]

After being inured to the music of composers like Karlheinz Stockhausen, Pierre Boulez, and Elliott Carter in the decades since its composition, we may find it difficult to understand how Copland's seminal Piano Variations of 1930 could have been found so disturbing and excessively demanding for listeners all through the decade. The distance between what was considered his very percussive and austere manner of the early thirties and the accessible manner he would shortly afterward assume was a long one indeed, and it is remarkable that he negotiated it so quickly. Even within the more enlightened artistic ambience of Germany, when the masterly pianist Walter Gieseking looked at the Piano Variations with the idea of programming it on his recitals, he decided that his audiences would not tolerate a work of such "crude dissonances."

Two more works in the category of Copland's tougher music were to follow in the next few years, *Statements* and *Short Symphony*, the latter and earlier of the two a work so much beyond the capacities of the orchestras of the time that though it was scheduled by both Serge Koussevitzky and Leopold Stokowski shortly after its completion, they both were obliged to shelve it when they came face to face with its technical difficulties, especially its jagged lines and rhythmical demands. (Copland arranged it for sextet because of the problems he had over it with orchestras, and the result has been a truly powerful chamber work.) Koussevitzky could not even start to consider it owing to his limited technique, though he was otherwise dedicated to bringing all of Copland's orchestral music to light. Stokowski made some attempt to study it, but was discouraged by its demands, returning to it, however, a decade later to give its U.S. premiere with his NBC Symphony, broadcasting from studio 8-H (more recently renowned for its Toscanini days). The players, Stokowski said, still found it very difficult. The first performance anywhere was conducted by Copland's close friend and fellow composer Carlos Chavez in Mexico (23 November 1934) with his Orquesta Sinfònico, over which he had sufficient authority to exact the unusual number of ten rehearsals.[5]

By the middle of the decade the more "popular" Copland that most audiences now know emerged virtually without any transition—the composer of *Lincoln Portrait, Billy the Kid,* and the like. Indeed those audiences to this day are usually quite unaware he has written any other kind of music, and some listeners who are aware of this other music have never quite forgiven him for the periods when he abandoned his less accessible approach for a highly accessible one. They even sometimes tend to view his more solid achievements with a certain suspicion, wondering whether the composer of the more popular works could really have been up to meeting the demands.[6]

It was not until 1941 that Copland returned to the compositional approach that most discriminating composers admired in him. We had attended debates at the leftist cultural groups on the subject of what proletarian music should be without being in any way convinced that his workaday music was any solution of the problem. The naughty E-word which I mentioned earlier was "escapism." That path had to be avoided at all costs. My own way of coping with the dilemma as a good leftist sympathizer, who according to the directive from above should have been writing music for the "masses," was to stop composing altogether in 1934, devoting myself instead to my other vocations of musicology and criticism until 1939. As for Copland, when he returned to his more exacting music he did not abandon the practice he had cultivated to win the attention and admiration of a wider audience, pursuing the two approaches for a while in tandem. Looking back in the forties he defended his appeal to a wider audience by pointing out: "an entirely new public for music had grown up around the radio and phonograph. It made no sense to ignore them and continue writing as if they did not exist."[7] In the forties one no longer spoke of a political motivation to reach the "masses." It was pretty obvious that by then Marxist sympathies considered benign in the Roosevelt era were being frowned upon. It is not certain what made Copland return to his earlier manner. Perhaps he never intended to abandon it altogether. But cause and effect are almost never a simple matter, one thing traceable to the other as a unique source.

In 1941 Copland's reversion to his abstract and tougher style of the early thirties took the form of a piano sonata. I was delighted when I saw the score and immediately dispatched an article discussing it to *Partisan Review:*

About nine years ago, Aaron Copland added to an "austere," somewhat uncompromising style of musical composition, an alternate style appropriate to "music for use"—music for cinema, radio, schools, and the picket-line. This new preoccupation was not to exclude other "more serious" work, but some of us were apprehensive of the effect on the future of the remarkable idiom expressed by the Piano Variations (1930) and the *Short Symphony* (1933), both of which indicated so many possibilities as yet but partially fulfilled. The Piano Sonata (1941), which has finally been presented in New York, is, however, reassurance of the fact that the other Copland not only continues to function, but assumes further significance. If anything is to be deplored, it is that the demands for "occasional" music stand in the way of the completion of more than one work like the Sonata in the course of several years. But this condition may be altered. An obliging forecaster of his musical intentions, Copland now advocates a musical language which would realize the implications of radio and phonograph by addressing a larger audience without "writing down" and, after the manner of Shostakovich when his "obvious weaknesses" have been discounted, without sacrificing seriousness. The Sonata may thus be a step towards concentrating in one form what Copland has been accomplishing separately in two fairly discrete series of efforts (to the partial exclusion of one of them). For while the allegedly "very severe" style of the Variations is much in evidence to discourage many listeners on their first acquaintance, there is also an admixture of the wholesome atmosphere of the music for the movie *Our Town* to soften the effect.

The exaggerated determinism of a certain glib school of "sociological" criticism is recalled when Copland insists: "More and more we shall have to find a style which satisfies both us and them"—i.e., the composers who now constitute one another's audience and the radio-phonograph public. Nevertheless, it is interesting in this regard to consider Mozart's confession (in one of his letters) that he put certain effects in his music to please his patrons and he expected approval of these effects to be manifested in a way, moreover, that would currently be considered barbaric anywhere but at the ballet—namely, by applause *during the music* as each effect is heard, just as we now applaud a pirouette.[8]

Copland was in Hollywood working on the score to the movie *North Star* when the article appeared, so I was surprised to receive a prompt response from him in a letter dated 10 April 1943. "Dear Arthur," it began, "The other night while walking down Hollywood Blvd., I happened on a copy of the *Partisan Review*. Imagine my surprise when I came across your piece on the Piano Sonata. I wonder what made you not tell me about it—

just neglect? Or was it 'fright' at my reaction?" As the letter continued he confronted me with his main reservations:

> When I call for a "style that satisfies both us and them," I am mostly trying to goad composers on toward what I think is a healthy direction. . . . I think also that for the sake of drawing sharp distinctions you rather overdo the dichotomy between my "severe" and "simple" styles. The inference is that only the severe style is really serious. I don't believe that. What I was trying for in the simpler works was only partly a larger audience; they also gave me a chance to try for a home-spun musical idiom, similar to what I was trying for in a more hectic fashion in the earlier jazz works. In other words, it was not only musical functionalism that was in question, but also musical language.[9]

I have never been able to share the view that there was no sharp dichotomy between the two approaches, and Copland, notwithstanding the warm friendship that developed between us and that diminished only late in his life when he was afflicted with Alzheimer's disease, was to persist in the belief that I was one of the commentators responsible for his being cast forever in the role of Dr. Jekyll and Mr. Hyde. I have come to appreciate the fine qualities of his ballet and movie scores and to recognize that these qualities go well beyond what is required to fulfill their function. But works that lean heavily, for example, on compiled folk music—even those of Stravinsky and Bartók—are liable to give up their secret too easily. This music can have its appeal to a discriminating listener, but some of us also want music that is tougher and more challenging. Henry James put it so well in his preface to *The Wings of the Dove* in a comment quite in passing and between parentheses:

> (The enjoyment of a work of art, the acceptance of an irresistible illusion, constituting, to my sense, our highest experience of "luxury," the luxury is not greatest, by my consequent measure, when the work asks for as little attention as possible. It is greatest, it is delightfully, divinely great, when we feel the surface, like the thick ice of the skater's pond, bear without cracking the strongest pressure we throw on it. The sound of the crack one may recognise, but never surely to call it a luxury.)[10]

Just what the nature of proletariat music should be—not only the worker songs but also the concert music for the masses—was a moot point in the early thirties. One of the leading spokesmen for the proposed genre was ironically one of our most far-out composers, the experimentalist Henry

Cowell, who had acquired an international reputation in the twenties (one might almost say "notoriety") for his employment of the fist and fore-arm on the keyboard (what that produced was called "tone cluster") and, at other times, fingers on the strings. (Later his student John Cage must have gotten the idea of the prepared piano from this.) It was not too surprising that a modernist like Cowell should become involved in the proletarian cause since his music relied heavily in its choice of content on the vernacu-lar, namely, his Irish heritage of reels and jigs on the one hand, the styles of Eastern music that he explored in his ethnic studies on the other. The dissonance of his tone clusters could upset serious listeners who were tra-ditionalists, but others could find it fun—a kind of circus stunt. His music was not considered forbidding in the way that the music of the "austere" Copland was. Dissonance was by no means the only thing that alienated people from modern music.

In the early debates, often highly agitated ones that took place at the left-ist arts groups—the John Reed Club and the Rebel Arts Group for the arts in general, and for music the Pierre Degeyter Club (named after the com-poser of "L'Internationale")—Cowell, obviously drawing on his own ex-perience of putting dissonant tone clusters under folktunes, advocated dissonant accompaniments for the worker songs. The words, he argued, dealt optimistically with the future when increased freedom and happiness would be the worker's reward, and they should be couched in music of the future. (The leftist jury of composers that awarded the prize to Copland's picket-line song was also obviously thinking in more avant-garde musical terms than the situation demanded.)

On the linguistic level there was the strong but ill-conceived tendency to equate the word "progressive" in politics and the word "progressive" in art so that it applied in the most literal sense rather in the sense that a more progressive society may demand a more derivative, backward-looking art that is accessible to the masses. In Germany, for example, some painters operating under the slogan *Neue Sachlichkeit* (New Objectivity) shortly after the October Revolution made claims of having "distorted reality to point up social despair and a revolutionary political message."[11] Judith Tick in her book on Ruth Crawford Seeger writes of the composer's passionate activism as well as that of her composer husband Charles Seeger around 1930. It seems that in a setting of some *ricercari* in her usual complex idiom, as Tick relates it, "By creating such profound opposition between voice and piano—at one point Charles Seeger claimed they need only be-gin and end together—Crawford embodied class conflict into the music itself."[12]

The debates at the politically radical arts groups were not all confined to sophistry such as this. There was, among other things, the legitimate issue of whether it was required to "write down" to what nowadays we call the "dumbed down" audience, or whether the goal was to elevate that audience intellectually and in its tastes. But things were to change. As the thirties advanced it was no longer to be a matter of argument. For worker songs the model was to be simple traditional folklike accompaniments and for orchestral music, though it was not officially spelled out, composers were to keep someone like Tchaikovsky in mind despite his personal bourgeois leanings.

Even Dmitri Shostakovich found himself in trouble. After playing for two years to enthusiastic sold-out houses, in January 1936 his opera *Lady Macbeth of Mtsensk* was the subject of a scurrilous attack in *Pravda*, the official organ of the Soviet government. Shostakovich was scolded for his "formalism," the severest censure that any composer could get in the USSR and one that could mean almost anything: in this case, probably his dissonance (indeed "cacophony"), "musical chaos," "bourgeois" vulgarity (the salacious plot, including fornication), and so on and on. It was also the year of the Moscow trials in which the government claimed there was a conspiracy involving some fifty leading officials, and it consequently bore down more than ever on the personal freedom of the citizenry. It took about two years for the ban on Shostakovich's music to be lifted and for him to come back into favor, but he never recovered from the sense of intimidation, of being a hunted man, that came from the direction of authority watching over his shoulder.

When Shostakovich came to America in 1959 as a member of a contingent of Soviet composers (under the watchful eye of Soviet music's hatchetman Tikhon Khrennikov, who had the assignment of making sure that none of the composers got out of line) Boston was a stop on their tour in November, and some of us had the opportunity to question the celebrated musician at a reception given by Richard Burgin (the BSO concertmaster I mentioned at the very beginning of this essay, who, by the way, thought it would be too bourgeois to have domestic help for the affair and consequently gave his housekeeper a day off and hired no other assistance, not realizing that successful Soviet composers lived in grand style). The subject of serialism arose, and looking like a caged animal (he never smiled) Shostakovich said he did not want his hands tied. He was standing with his back to the piano, and as if to illustrate his claim, he put his hands on the keyboard in back of him without playing. Could he also have been thinking of how the bureaucracy tied his hands?

I would not want to leave the impression that the Soviet crisis was uniquely responsible for the movement of American composers toward a simpler mode of expression. The notion of simplifying communication in the fine arts was very much in the air, and more than one development contributed to it—not least of all the WPA that Roosevelt instituted to relieve the staggering unemployment of the Great Depression. The original engineers of the project were thinking primarily of giving jobs to needy, unemployed blue-collar workers, and it was quite a surprise when artists of all persuasions qualified for relief and got on the WPA rolls to pursue undertakings they had always pursued, except that the WPA sponsorship provided sustenance and audiences. The most visible naturally (no pun intended) were the products of the painters who dedicated their talents to murals in public buildings—post offices in particular. This was not an occasion for esoterica or abstraction and they developed a fairly recognizable and simplistic style that has since become known as "WPA Art."

For composers there were WPA orchestras and demands for music for modern dancers and the WPA theater. In 1934 I was asked by the curator of the East Fifty-eighth Street branch of the New York Public Library (the Music Library in those days, where I practically took up residence, reading scores and music books, and listening to recordings) if I would be interested in heading a WPA project that had the objective of publishing a catalog of American music for the dance. I said that I certainly would be but there was the problem of qualifying for relief before I could get on the WPA. My father and his second wife lived above their means in a small apartment in a modest hotel on West Seventy-second Street in Manhattan. They felt I was not entitled at twenty-one to support and they could not afford it anyway. The most they could do besides providing some meals was to allow me to sleep on a daybed in the foyer. I relate this piece of intelligence as an example of what was involved in getting on the WPA. The point is the inspector who would visit me to determine if I were eligible for relief would never agree if he or she found me in those days living in a hotel building with an elevator. My explanation of the actual circumstances would be of no avail. So I moved to a rooming-house—one of those brownstones in the West Seventies and Eighties that had once been posh single-family homes.

I never did get on relief. It took a long time and before the waiting period was up I received a fellowship to a newly formed Professional division of the Longy School of Music in Cambridge. Evidently there were other ways of participating in WPA activities, for example as honorary guest if you were famous and did not depend on the pittance WPA paid. For how else would we have had the scion of the huge British pill conglomerate Sir

Thomas Beecham conducting the WPA Orchestra in New York? The Federal Music Project of the WPA is remembered by those who shared its benefits as a very vibrant and rich affair and not limited in the way that one expects anything administered by the government to be. For example a chorus is usually made up largely of amateurs. But with WPA sponsorship one could have a chorus of two hundred, which I recall hearing in Boston, made up entirely of professionals because there were many singers out of work who ended up on the rolls of the WPA, and there was almost no solo work for them. A chorus of that sort can be quite thrilling.

There were also special projects like the Composers Forum Laboratory established by an enterprising individual named Ashley Pettis. The idea was to have, normally, two composers whose music is played and who are present to answer questions from the audience during the entire second half of the evening. Pettis was skillful as moderator, with a poker face, never taking sides, and staving off foolish or indecent questions. He continued when there was no longer a WPA ("Laboratory" was dropped from the name), moving the project to San Francisco for two seasons at the start of World War II. Returning to New York, he resumed the forums under the auspices of the New York Public Library and Columbia University. In 1951, however, Pettis became a Roman Catholic priest, and though "Composers Forum" survives as a name, and there are replicas of the organization across the country, New York no longer has the regular series as it existed originally. Either the novelty has worn off, or there is too much competition from the plethora of new music groups and collectives that have sprung up and from concerts that have the composer on hand to participate in a panel (often with financial aid from an organization called Meet the Composer).

One of the notable consequences of the WPA projects in music was the emergence of symphony orchestras all over the country as a way of engaging the large number of unemployed instrumentalists. And on the podium you were likely to find not the formerly unemployed musicians but, as I have already mentioned, such eminent figures as Beecham, who, it is to be assumed, must have donated his services. This was not an isolated case because the WPA in New York also regaled us with the great Otto Klemperer, and Chicago had a fairly well established conductor by the name of Izler Solomon. It should be pointed out that the number of orchestras in America had been growing before the WPA helped the trend along. As Virgil Thomson once observed, "The 1930s witnessed an unprecedented expansion of the symphony orchestra into virtually every small town. . . . And they played American music, because Americans naturally enjoy American music until they have been taught not to."[13] There is a degree of wish ful-fillment in this observation, but it is true that there was a proliferation of music based on American subject matter because, among other things, composers felt an obligation to the government that was supporting them. (They assumed it was expected of them.) I am not sure how much real de-mand there was for American music of national content, but it is certainly true that the press played the unsavory role of fanning whatever discontent with this music that there was. Of no little importance in this matter was the fact that American subjects contributed to accessibility since listeners naturally felt at home with content drawn from their own backyard.

World War II naturally solved the unemployment problem by provid-ing work in the army and arms industry, and it was decided that the entire WPA project was no longer needed. The arts program, however, had grown into a major enterprise in the lives of the American people, and it seemed a pity to dismantle it. But any hope that it would be salvaged was shattered by the change in the political climate. The powerful right-wingers of the time were all too cognizant of the circumstance that the WPA, especially its arts program, was a product of the liberal thirties. One is reminded of the political right's hostility in recent years toward the National Endowment for the Arts, except that now the conflict, though politically motivated, has revolved around the question of alleged indecency more than around poli-tics itself.

2 Nationalism

It was a happy coincidence that the cultivation of a music with American character should be a major concern of American composers in the decade of the WPA for since about the mid-twenties they had been advocating that it was time for American music to "come of age"—a catch-phrase that I recall encountering rather frequently when I came onto the scene around 1930. One of the first achievements necessary to reach that goal, some of us were pretty well convinced, was to establish an identity so that the music would be recognizable as American in the way that French music was recognizable as French and German music as German. A music based on the national scene was also precisely what a country that supported it would expect. But there was mighty little of it before about 1920. Charles Ives had been writing distinctly American music since before the turn of the century but he had done so in oblivion. There had also been isolated instances like Copland's jazz concerto or Thomson's *Symphony on a Hymn Tune* of 1928, which was not performed until 1945 with the composer conducting the New York Philharmonic.[1]

The quest for a national character is not to be confused with breast-beating patriotism, "my country right or wrong," which is something many of us involved in the tendency would vehemently disavow. So it is unfortunate that the rubric "Americanism" fits it so well and is the one commonly used since that locution carries an aura of discrimination against the foreign-born among us, and it has been exploited, as Edmund Wilson once pointed out, "to serve some very bad causes, and is now a word to avoid." I have never felt comfortable with the slogan "Americanism," with its undercurrent of flag-waving, and so Wilson's admonition will be acceded to here and we shall find a very good alternative in "national character" or "nationalism."[2]

One composer for whom this apologia seems quite unnecessary was Roy Harris, who was politically reactionary and boasted of it. In terms of what his reputation is today it is hard to believe that Harris around the time of his Third Symphony (1939) was one of the two best-known American composers, the other, of course, having been Copland. Harris made a big point of claiming Beethoven as a model at the same time that he insisted on the American style and content of his music. He offered as collateral his birthright to American sources for his inspiration, having been born on Lincoln's birthday and in Lincoln County on the Oklahoma Panhandle.[3] He once told me how important it was for him to feel at one with the American soil, and he confided in me that as a youth he would go out naked in uninhabited areas in the wildest storms to relish that feeling and to consolidate his identification with the western earth. (After age five he lived in California.)

The employment of folksong is, of course, no guarantee that a national character will be embodied in the music. Dvořák, Ravel, and many others have felt free to borrow from the folksong literature of countries other than their own, frankly in the spirit of a tourist, so to speak, without forfeiting their own national identity. What is required if a truly national character is to be achieved is that the entire texture be impregnated with what we recognize as indigenous to the compiled material. This was not the case among composers around 1900 — composers who took as an example Dvořák's "New World" Symphony and compiled American folk tunes in a European symphonic setting. Joseph Horowitz, a specialist in American music of that era, has recently taken issue with this view of the failure of those composers to mold a valid American idiom and has deplored our neglect of them, blaming Bernstein and Thomson as well as historians of American music for a delinquency in this affair.[4] It's true that Americans have short memories and that there were a few, very few, composers active around 1900 and in the earliest decades of the twentieth century who deserve more attention now—though what native composers get the attention they deserve? I remember, however, during my Harvard days (the thirties) the composer Arthur Foote, for one, was quite a presence on the Boston scene; he and his contemporaries were performed, including George Whitefield Chadwick who died in 1931. So we had opportunity to judge their music and many of us were impressed neither by its national character nor by the aesthetic quality of much of it.

Most of the time Harris did not literally quote folk sources (though there are examples such as the variety of kitsch of 1941 for band, *When Johnny Comes Marching Home*). What he did, rather, was skillfully fash-

Ex. 2. Roy Harris, Third Symphony (opening)

ion melodic lines with the contours of American hymns as well as folk and patriotic songs. These certainly helped to yield an American character, but made curious bedfellows with the European symphonic aspects of the music. The quite impressive long unison line of the cello section at the opening of the Harris Third Symphony is almost all a folkish pentatonic, the few B-flats and Cs being the exceptions (Ex. 2). In other instances of his music such writing was likely to be embedded in a fabric of orchestral counterpoint (with the inevitable fugue and its Baroque evocation), as well as an ample orchestral sonority and a fairly ample, agreeable harmonic palette. All this combined to place him somewhat in the European tradition, in particular the tradition of the vaunted post-Romantic symphonists Sibelius and Shostakovich. Indeed, if one were to ponder why Harris's star has set within the circle of more discriminating listeners, a likely reason suggesting itself is that this tradition has somehow lost its cachet, to the extent that it ever had any. Why conductors, however, have stopped programming Harris is difficult to comprehend especially in view of his music's capacity to highlight the best qualities of any orchestra as well as the consideration that the public's preference is for Romantic music. Could it be because he never again attained the heights of his Third Symphony? Whatever the reason, it is regrettable because among other things his music surprisingly retains an American profile and would certainly be an adornment to today's programs.

Of all the numerous claims that have been made as to what constitutes the essential nature of American music surely the most penetrating is the one

Ex. 3. Aaron Copland, Variations for piano (opening)

made by Harris, which is odd since he was known more as a physical and inspirational type than an intellectual one, and he was not on easy terms with words, as many of his peers were. "Our sense of rhythm," he observed, "is less symmetrical than the European rhythmic sense. European musicians are trained to think of rhythm in its largest common denominator, while we are born with a feeling for its smallest units."[5] I remember discussing his theory with him, and we decided together that it was not only the smallest rhythmic unit that occupied the American composer but indeed the *single note,* as if we were forging a tradition from the very source, starting at the beginning of time—ironically as someone so different as Wagner did with the prolonged low E-flat in *Rheingold* from which the entire Tetralogy gradually emerges. Anyone who is old enough and had the good fortune of having been in a position to watch Copland at the piano, playing his variations when he could still cut it, would have been able to deduce from his approach to the keyboard what is being implied here. In executing the opening four virtually unison notes of the theme (Ex. 3), for each note in its turn the right arm would be raised far above the keyboard and descend hammer-like with great deliberation as if the sonority imparted by the isolated pitch were a matter of the utmost moment. (Thomson used to complain that Copland's touch was too hard.) It is odd that Harris's hypothesis in regard to what defines the American sense of rhythm did not seem to have much of an effect on his own music, to the extent at least that I could judge.

If a certain manner of exploitation of rhythmic devices is to be taken as a distinguishing feature of American music, it is inevitable for us to assume that it must have a great deal to do with jazz, pop, and rock. Today those genres are just as much a part of the ambience in which a British youngster grows up as they are a part of that in which an American youngster does. But it was not always so. There was a time when just the American environment was saturated with jazz or ragtime rhythm wherever you went, and it left its imprint, as it does now, on every boy and girl whether they were fans or groupies or not. And if they grew up as composers this experience was bound to manifest itself, taking a form in their music quite different from what Europeans like Milhaud and Stravinsky did with the genres in the twenties. For those composers used jazz as they might use any other folk music, preserving their own national identity while borrowing from another.

For the American composer the paradox is that the rhythmic complexities of jazz are likely to assume a guise in which their origin is no longer discernible, and the impression we have when we hear it is not one of jazz at all. The tricky rhythms of jazz, when rhythm is a matter of deep concern to one, can go through so many metamorphoses as to not inconceivably end up with Elliott Carter's metrical modulation. Carter wrote a very insightful article on this subject, first published in the *Score and I. M. A. Magazine* back in 1955. It resurfaced in the recent collection of his writings and like all of his pronouncements it is well worth attention.[6] Of special interest in terms of the present discussion is what he had to say about Roger Sessions and by implication himself. During the years when striving deliberately for an American style was all the rage, Carter and Sessions were openly hostile to the idea. They believed American composers are American because of who they are. Both of them were respected for a certain degree of weightiness and seriousness in music without any of the fashionable local color. It is a revelation to have attention drawn to the rhythmic intricacies that establish the American parentage of these two predominantly abstract masters. I think Walter Piston might be added to their number to make it a triumvirate, though Carter would probably find him wanting the complexity of Sessions's music and his own. This would not, I am sure, affect his admiration for Piston.

It is ironic that it should have been a Brooklynite with none of the credentials of someone born on the western plains or in New England, a composer of Jewish parentage and exposed to all the cosmopolitan experiences of New York, who developed an idiom that encompasses a wide swath of the American landscape. As has already been indicated, jazz, pop, and rock would be an important part of an American youth's background, especially one who dwelt in New York. The offbeat rhythms of the snappy number, the major third changing to minor were devices Copland absorbed and they always showed their traces in his musical language. But in 1924 when he returned from Paris where he had studied with Nadia Boulanger, the teacher of so many successful American composers who followed his example by going to her, he started, along with some of his peers, to "search," as he later told us, for what he called a "useable past," a locution that had evidently been suggested to him by Van Wyck Brooks, the dean of American literary critics during the first half of the twentieth century.[7] But Copland found that his American elders, composers like George Whitefield Chadwick, John Knowles Paine, Horatio Parker, and even Edward MacDowell, provided no suitable example. Failing to find one, he turned to jazz, since it was, as he later admitted, "an easy way to be American in musical terms." But after about three years he was disabused of its possibilities for serious music since it severely limited the range of emotion the music could encompass. ("All American music could not be confined to two dominant jazz moods—the blues and the snappy number.")[8] It was almost a decade before Copland realized that diverse American traditions were available to him even though he had not grown up as part of them.

A curious and amusing sidelight to this development is that the nearest the composer of *Billy the Kid* and *Rodeo* ever came to a cow was when the car he was driving ran into a heifer (or rather, the heifer ran into the car, probably attracted by the bright lights) outside of Tanglewood on a dark night. It happened I was in the car behind his. We were going to Copland's studio after a concert at the Berkshire Music Center for refreshments and our usual post mortem on the event we had just attended. Copland was talking animatedly and when he talked he drove slowly, so one could scarcely say he was being reckless. Like good citizens we called the cops, and they interrogated him (and the rest of us) as if he had committed some heinous crime. The local Berkshire inhabitants at that time (the midforties) were still resentful of Tanglewood for having intruded on their peaceful existence, so the Pittsfield papers made a big affair out of the delinquency of the head of the Berkshire Music Center. (The charge was "endangering lives and property. . . .")

By the mid-forties Copland had not only absorbed elements of the American west into his musical language, but also New England hymnody and Shaker music among other sources. All of them along with jazz, his first love, yielded an amalgam that for quite a number of years we recognized on the one hand as Copland and on the other as American music; though just as it would be difficult to say what French or German music is, it is difficult to say precisely what it is we recognize as American. Yet we have no doubt of the style's origin in Copland when we encounter it reflected in numberless film scores and much TV background music that clearly lean on him heavily as a model. Perhaps it is too close for us to have a proper perspective on it, and for this reason I think it is revealing to observe what sympathetic observers of another nationality have to say. The most perceptive in this matter is perhaps the English critic Wilfrid Mellers, who spent a considerable amount of time familiarizing himself with American music. The attribute that he found particularly characteristic is a certain immobility, and he believed that the *Andante* of the Piano Sonata was its "quintessential expression." And further, "its life is suspended above empty harmonies."[9] To back up his claim he indulges in some fantasy about the United States: the suggestion of timelessness "is not unconnected with America's geographic immensity." Elsewhere he refers to a "feeling of vastness, enormous airiness, and emptiness of space."[10] And Mellers is not the only one to react in this fashion. Another English critic, Peter Evans, discussing Copland's setting of Dickinson's poems, referred to him as "always the master of the timeless moment. . . ."[11]

Normally I tend to be skeptical of images of this variety that music can evoke by virtue of the unspecific nature of its emotional content. But I could not help thinking of these two British music critics when I encountered the same theme in an old essay of Alfred Kazin's with the title "The Stillness of Light in August," in which he refers to a "curious effect of immobility in Faulkner's characters as they run (as if they were held up in the air by wires)."[12] I was convinced that here there must be some shared American experience. Faulkner's characters are from the south and Copland's cowboy tunes are from the west. But though one may legitimately ask whether in a country as vast and diversified as ours there is a pervasive American character, some traits could be nationwide.

What Copland proposed was not widely adopted by the most serious composers as their American manner, its fate being rather its widespread exploitation by so many hack, commercial composers of the day. But what he accomplished did help establish a recognizable American profile somewhere and of some kind, and it contributed to some affirmation that American music had indeed "come of age." There was also, as I said above, the WPA, which, though not the determining factor in the quest for an American character, encouraged it. Since the demise of the project there has been less evidence of the quest but this cannot be placed altogether at the door of the WPA's dissolution since there was a change in the international art climate, as we shall see later.

In any discourse on the American character in music the name of Charles Ives will figure prominently. Ives was very much involved in the American scene in a way that urban composers would not be. Yet like Carter and Sessions he did not believe in deliberately cultivating an American style since if one were an American it would take care of itself, provided, as he put it somewhere, "the Yankee can reflect the fervency with which his gospels were sung." His own credentials as a purveyor of American tradition were as strong as they come. He was much attached to his native New England, and of no little consequence was the fact that his father had been a member of a Civil War band. According to the psychoanalyst Stuart Feder, Ives was uncommonly identified with his father.[13]

It is no surprise that Ives's music is larded with folksong including hymns, patriotic anthems, marches, and the like. The second movement of the Fourth Symphony is teeming with examples, a veritable blockbuster, with "Columbia the Gem of the Ocean" holding forth among many tunes most of us do not know. And yet as I have become more familiar with the music I have been troubled by the sense that the infrastructure is essentially a traditional European one which has been fractured—in the orchestral works, symphonic European. What makes the music sound so modernistic and dissonant is the way elements not too original are pulled out of shape, and if one takes a close-up of the music, as I like to do, the extraordinary atmosphere, the drama, the inspiration dissolve, and one becomes aware of a certain sheer disorder.

The earliest musicians to recognize Ives (according to Henry Cowell, his chief advocate, I may include myself among them)[14] were ecstatic and looked beyond his deficiencies. We excused him for his less than exemplary technique, his habit of not bothering to edit, polish, and otherwise put the final touches on a work because he knew it would not be played anyway. Also, there was the unfortunate circumstance that he had not enjoyed the opportunity of profiting from the feedback from critics, peers, and audi-

ences that a composer derives from a public performance, and, in his isolation, had been deprived of the opportunity to exchange ideas with fellow
composers. He was nearing sixty when he finally received some public recognition within modern music circles, but there seems to be disagreement
as to the precise event that led to this reversal of his status.

Cowell, who should receive most of the credit for the discovery of Ives
and his promotion, declared that the recognition dated from the first public concert in which his music was played, presented by an avant-garde New
York organization called Pro Musica in 1927. This concert, Cowell recalled
almost three decades later, "was a milestone in the career of Ives's music because the two most influential American critics made a real attempt to
understand the music." The critics Cowell referred to were Olin Downes
of the *New York Times* and Lawrence Gilman of the *New York Herald Tribune.* Cowell described the attendance as "a sophisticated musical audience" and even though most of those present rejected the music violently,
it was a notable occasion since it witnessed Ives's "coming out."[15]

Copland had another idea of the decisive moment when he later took a
backward look—a moment in which he himself played a decisive part. He
fastened his attention on an event that took place five years later. It seems
there existed, modeled after the French "Six," a Young Composers Group
that Copland, as stated above, had brought together for the purpose of
meeting fairly regularly to exchange ideas. I was a member of the group
but my position was ambiguous since I was not composing at the time. As
a critic I was welcomed among them to do the kind of public relations that
Paul Collaer had done for the Six. My fellow members were Henry Brant,
Israel Citkowitz, Lehman Engel, Vivian Fine, Irwin Heilner, Bernard Herrmann, Jerome Moross, Elie Siegmeister and, for a while at the beginning,
the expatriate Paul Bowles who was living at that time in Paris—a circumstance much resented since we were very pro-American.[16]

We decided all together to join Cowell in discovering and promoting
Ives. Our enthusiasm for Ives, especially that of Herrmann, later of Hollywood fame for his scores for *Citizen Kane* and Alfred Hitchcock films, was
such that Copland could not refuse us when we approached him to include
a work of Ives on a program of a prestigious festival of contemporary
American music he was planning for the artist colony Yaddo in Saratoga
Springs, New York. He even agreed to play the piano part himself in a
group of songs that would represent Ives. The audience, made up mostly of
avant-garde composers, rose to the challenge of the music, especially the
song "Charlie Rutledge" with its tone-cluster accompaniment and spoken
vocal line.

In his recollections Copland remarked, "this was the first time a group of professional musicians were paying serious attention to Ives. It was a turning point in the recognition of his music. Arthur Berger was prophetic when he wrote in his review for the *Daily Mirror:* 'History is being made in our midst.'"[17] It is perfectly plausible that Copland was unaware of the 1927 concert or deliberately ignored it since the schism maintained between the more avant-garde composers and his (our) crowd was such that Cowell and his far-out experimentalists inhabited an entirely different world from ours. We were regarded as a bit Francophile and elite, which were precisely the locutions the extreme radicals (Cowell, Varèse, Ruggles, etc., who wrote "ultramodern" music) were likely to apply to the League of Composers, the concert-giving organization "our crowd" had established in 1923 before I was part of it.

The last place one would look for a review of the Yaddo event is a Hearst scandal sheet, a tabloid like the old *New York Daily Mirror,* but I was a youthful stringer for that paper, and I wrote up the festival, making the statement that Copland quoted: "History is being made in our midst." It was also quoted by Cowell in his book on Ives.[18] Another of my earliest writings about Ives appeared in 1934. It was something more substantial than a music review for a tabloid paper; it was an article on the songs of Ives for a new music publication.[19] While I was a graduate student in music at Harvard University I was editing a publication called the *Musical Mercury,* published by Edwin F. Kalmus for the purpose of advertising the miniature scores that he had started publishing on a grand scale.[20] (He had worked in the copyright office and had learned that many valuable foreign twentieth-century scores were not protected.) Each issue had a score in the center usually unrelated to the content. I took advantage of my access to a musical readership (limited though it was) to write about the 114 songs which Ives had published at his own expense in a bound volume. In my article, along with expressing certain reservations that I already had in those days, I wrote, "those who would call Ives the father of indigenous music would seem justified." The title seems to have endured, except we say less pretentiously "American" music, without the implications "indigenous" might have in our multicultural society. But I am no longer sure it is apposite. One expects a father to beget offspring, but young composers for a long time did not emulate Ives as they have, for example, emulated Copland. That may very well change. The young new Romanticists are likely to be attracted more to the Ives approach than to that of Copland. Anyone using

Ives as a model, however, would do well to separate out what is crude in his music from what deliberately flouts academic correctness. It is sometimes difficult to differentiate between the deliberately irrational nature of his works and the instances of compositional weakness. One can only marvel at how, notwithstanding, he imbued his creative output with something personal and, essentially, elusive to the grasp of others.

The education Ives could get at Yale when he attended—or anywhere else in America—was, I assume, probably academic and mired in nineteenth-century Romanticism.[21] It had not changed much by the 1920s when young composers reacted against it by initiating a pilgrimage to Nadia Boulanger in France. Everything we know about Ives indicates that it would be preposterous to envision him joining such a pilgrimage even if he were of the generation that made it. As I have said, though he did not believe in being deliberately American in music by artificially contriving devices to make you sound American, he did believe your music's being American was a virtue and that it will be as American as you are. But he would still have been fearful something European might rub off on him if he had gone abroad to study. Boulanger, while well aware of *la grande ligne,* was adamant about the musician (creator or performer) having control over the tiniest detail. (I recall from my own studies with her just before World War II the shower of invectives she poured upon me when I illustrated on the piano a point in our discussion with a passage from Wagner and got the wrong inversion of one chord—which did not seem to matter since it was not germane to the point I wanted to make. But I was subjected to a volley of abuse that I never forgot whenever I illustrated a point again.) Such attention to detail might have helped Ives clean up the surface of his music. On the other hand, it might have ruined him as we now know him. His music is the product of the spontaneous outpouring of highly charged emotions at the expense of elegance of detail. Herein lies my ambivalence when it comes to making a final evaluation of Ives. However, he is certainly, I must admit, a figure who looms on the American music scene and who provides an experience we do not get elsewhere. This should be enough to stamp the mark of immortality on his brow.

As a member of the Young Composers Group and a critic who wrote about Ives's music, I was welcome to visit Ives as most of my cohorts did. That I did not do so, something I now regret, could be attributed to my concern over his reputation for getting very agitated if he were crossed in a discussion; owing to his ill health he would have to retire at once and go upstairs to bed. I was an argumentative young man and I was afraid my leftist politics would clash with his political orientation; also I might let slip a remark that revealed my reservations with regard to his music. The other members of the Young Composers Group were just as argumentative but this failed to discourage them. (I still have a frayed penny postcard from Copland inviting me to one of our get-togethers with "no polemics" scrawled on it in pencil. I have already mentioned the political differences. The aesthetic differences were just as severe. Only someone of his equanimity and tolerance could keep us from virtually lapsing into physical violence or falling apart as a group altogether.)

Let me return to the matter of the quotation of folksong in composers like Ives before going on to other things. One of the main problems for some exacting listeners is the price a composer pays for leaning heavily on compiled folksong, which will obviously be a singable, memorable linear component. But this kind of writing tends to give up its secret more easily than other, more dense writing. Much as I admire Stravinsky, as well as the inspiration and workmanship of his *Petrushka,* I tend not to be enthusiastic at the prospect of a rehearing of the work since I have it so thoroughly internalized by now. The same is true of my attitude toward certain folkish works of Bartók or Copland, both of whom I consider highly admirable composers.

It cannot be stressed too much that *ideally* works of the fine arts are not consumer products.[22] We might start to consume them but we never consume them completely as we do ordinary consumer products because we can, and we want to, return to them again and again to discover new dimensions within them, things we had missed before. If this were more generally understood we might not have the inclination toward crossover-concerts which have the often insurmountable problem of requiring us to shift gears in our listening, since they inevitably include compositions that juxtapose serious and pop music without properly synthesizing them, and we listen very differently to music we consume than we do to other music. (Note: It is not a question of one type of music being *better* than another.)

I am talking about prototypes, a matter of emphasis, since in real life the categories may not always be clean-cut at the borderline. Thus there are, to be sure, the inspired pop songs that endure—songs by Cole Porter, Rodgers and Hart, George Gershwin, or the Beatles. (I wonder how much nostalgia has to do with their durability.) Also, one might start out to write a catchy tune with the sole idea of having a hit and making money and still come out with a minor masterpiece. Inspiration is not something we know how to turn on and off, and it may show up in unexpected places. And I certainly would not deny that pop music (jazz, rock, etc.) has fed serious mu-

sic with many fine ideas (and vice versa) and that there have been successful crossovers such as Darius Milhaud's *Création du Monde* (Creation of
the World), Stravinsky's *Ebony Concerto*, and Milton Babbitt's *All Set*. I
should not, however, welcome an entire trend dedicated to this genre. Besides the objection I stated above (or perhaps a part of it), the emotional
scope is too limited.

Where commercial pop music is concerned, the idea of immediacy is in
both its conception and the aim for quick success. We remark on the pro-
ductivity of Mozart tossing off work after work in an instant because it is
in contrast to the practice of most serious composers who relish the composing process enough to dwell on it. They would no doubt expect that re-
ciprocally their listeners dwell on it too—perhaps listening at first several
times before they grasp a given work. (I doubt whether the current mar-
keters of pop songs anticipate such an audience response for their wares.)
Copland and Stravinsky were once comparing notes on their composing
practices, and they agreed that there was one thing they certainly had in
common: the slow pace that they preferred to maintain in the activity. Copland mentioned that it was not unlikely for him to do just one big work a
year. "Yes," said Stravinsky, adjusting the collar of his jacket in that familiar gesture to make it sit better around the neck, "I like to feel comfortable
with it." On another occasion Copland was asked why he did not use opus
numbers. He responded by saying he did not think it necessary because,
since he wrote about one work a year, putting the year of composition on
the score should be sufficient to indicate the place and order in which the
work stood in his oeuvre.

When we consider the amount of time serious composers spend on a
work it seems sacrilege to grant it the short life we usually grant a pop
song. We need new pop songs all the time because the older ones are
quickly consumed. That this is not the case with serious music makes for a
fundamental difference. When Philip Glass was preparing a live performance of a soundtrack he had created fifteen years earlier for a movie that
was being revived, he thought it might sound dated. But instead he was
quite impressed that, at least to his own way of thinking, it retained its
freshness all through what he considered a long time for any work. As I in-
terpret his reaction, he was perfectly aware of having crossed the line into
the field of pop (and also was evidently satisfied with himself for having
done so) where such things as going in and out of style in a brief period are
an issue and where his music would be expected to go out of style in the
same way as a popular song does. There are some works, like the three I

mentioned above, that do succeed in making the synthesis, thereby remaining works of serious music. They are, however, quite rare.

Obviously, there are elements other than those provided by folk music that define the American character, elements along the lines of the immobility that I have mentioned. But it is not too clear what they are. Bernard Holland of the *Times*, writing about what I consider the utterly Francophile music of Ned Rorem, observed, in a left-handed fashion, "If it is a duty to identify Mr. Rorem as an American composer, one can point to certain characteristics. First is the strain of puritanism in his spare, harsh lines and textures and next to it the paradox of openhearted melody in generous, long-breathing tunes." (I have little doubt that if these two characteristics came to sparring with each other for supremacy, the "openhearted" melody would win out in Rorem's highly sensuous and expressive music.) Holland goes on to cite evidence of Protestant American part-singing and even some bop chords. But I do not find it particularly convincing.[23]

There are, to be sure, some things, more concrete things, that serious American music has contributed to the whole world, though it would be hard to identify them as American unless you knew their genealogy. I am thinking, for example, of Cowell's tone clusters. I am not aware that he ever copyrighted them but Bartók, in gentlemanly fashion, is said to have written to Cowell for permission before using them himself. In addition to tone clusters, in the same area there is the John Cage prepared piano—prepared with nuts, bolts, screws, and bits of rubber. Cage, of course, with his theories of "non-music" acquired a reputation in Europe and Asia wider than any other American composer, with the possible exception of George Gershwin, has ever achieved. Finally there is minimalism, popularized by Philip Glass but early on practiced more effectively by Steve Reich, and perhaps also Terry Riley and La Monte Young. And as everyone knows when it is a matter of music it is not by its "serious" products that America is known abroad but by its jazz, rock, and so on. This, however, spoils the reception of serious music since we have been typecast as dispensers of a form of entertainment music, and music more profound is not expected of us. However that may be, the matter of music having an American cast no longer has priority, as I have already indicated, because we have entered an international stage and feel quite content with it. If achieving an American character assisted us in believing American music had "come of age," then our efforts have been quite sufficiently rewarded by the few manifestations I have mentioned. Mission accomplished. We need not push it any longer. Let it take its own course.

3   Is Music in Decline?

The prophets of doom who see every innovation in music as a decline or even a harbinger of the death of the art have a long history. Nicholas Slonimsky regaled us with numerous examples of their scurrilous attacks in his book *A Lexicon of Musical Invective: Critical Assaults on Composers since Beethoven's Time*.[1] In the past century there has been a particular orientation that may be traced back many decades to British critics like Ernest Newman, who established a tradition that has strongly colored the opinions of some of the most influential American critics. What characterizes this tradition is a nostalgia for nineteenth-century Romanticism and a consequent rejection of the most significant twentieth-century music in one indiscriminate bolus. An attitude of this nature on the part of a music critic can very well end up with a determination that it would have been better if no music had been written in the twentieth century rather than the kind that has been. Critics with such a view would have no use for W. H. Auden's sober admonishment that the critic "first and foremost . . . must be so fond of works of art that he would rather there were imperfect ones than none at all. . . ."[2]

According to Samuel Lipman in *Music after Modernism* the mainstream performers refrain from playing twentieth-century music since they place their careers in jeopardy if they do: "A performer's career can no longer be advanced, but rather only harmed, by any association with new music."[3] The chief *New York Times* critic emeritus Harold Schonberg almost a quarter of a century ago insisted that "the big names of yesteryear" had had sufficient exposure ("every orchestra played its share"), and that the public, having had "a chance to immerse itself, had decided against the music."[4] I wonder how the public had a chance to "immerse" itself if performers with their eyes on the box office did not play the music. That

Schonberg was blatantly inaccurate about the amount of exposure the new music has had was ironically pointed up by an article on the same Sunday music page as the one from which I just quoted. A plea for a new orchestra to play music by American composers (what ultimately became the American Composers Orchestra) states straight out, "orchestras don't play contemporary music; when they do they play it badly." Composers would have had no difficulty deciding where greater credibility lies—with Schonberg or the complainant. There is no end to the evidence against the scurrilous piece of misinformation that Schonberg was purveying.

That was all yesterday. Today, according to Paul Griffiths of the *Times*, a percipient observer of avant-garde musical trends, "Things are changing. Several times already this season the New York Philharmonic has filled Avery Fisher Hall for programs consisting entirely or mostly of new music. . . ."[5] Perhaps there is cause for optimism. But I cannot help thinking that part of the "improvement" is due to the more accessible music being written and another part to the fact that the big men of modern music have finally become icons. What of those who have had much to offer but never made it as big as your Stravinsky or Copland, names like Leon Kirchner, Irving Fine, Harold Shapero, or Don Martino, to pick at random from my own circle without much calculation? Also, it occurs to me that in regard to the bounty of "new" music in New York in which Griffiths takes such pleasure, as he should, it may be legitimate to ask now that we have arrived at the twenty-first century whether some of the music included in his survey, music which dates from the first half of the twentieth century, properly belongs under the banner of the "contemporary." Isn't it time for it to be considered part of the historical repertory? Isn't it time that when these works are played the presenters cease to pride themselves on engaging in some altruistic act and satisfy themselves with the knowledge they are doing no more than what they should be doing?

The avatars of the decline theory employ immediate appeal as a criterion. Those of us who reject such a criterion of artistic excellence are usually accused of believing the contrary, namely, good art always goes unrecognized in its time. Some people do believe this. At mid-century at the most avant-garde concerts some composers were known to have rigged boos and catcalls at premieres of their own music or those of their fellow avant-gardists. At the Donnaueschingen Music Days for Contemporary Tone-Art, the program organizers would be sure each year to include at least one work that would make a sensation—that is, at least one work that was so far out as to be sure to elicit catcalling from the audience. Once things got this far, near-rioting would inevitably follow. The smart avant-garde listeners by the mid-fifties seemed already at this early date to have had their fill of that sort of thing and were simply bored, so that they were not even going to take the trouble to protest.

It may not be accurate to say that a masterpiece is inevitably overlooked in its own day, but from time to time it is. Newman, in *A Musical Critic's Holiday,* went into various convolutions to deny this is ever true. His contention was that when works sound defective on first hearing they really are, and that a masterpiece will always be recognized at once. Moreover, if works are inaccessible when new they will always be so. To illustrate his claim he took the glorious slow introduction of Mozart's "Dissonance" Quartet, K. 465, and urged his readers to accept the preposterous conclusion that it is really a "rather dubious piece of writing" that "does not quite come off." [6] By this means he was attempting to exonerate Mozart's pedantic contemporary Giuseppe Sarti who, Newman insisted, was speaking for the audience of his day when he wrote that the quartet was the product of a mere "clavier player with a depraved (unsound, *goaste* in the Italian) ear." [7] In particular the celebrated striking false relation between A-flat and A-natural in the second measure, quite shocking for its time, was singled out as a monstrosity, whereas many of us feel it is a most inspirational touch.

Among all the naysayers the American critic Henry Pleasants was, perhaps, the most extreme, announcing that not only was serious music in decline during the first part of the century but that the whole tradition came to an end shortly after World War I. (His contention was that serious music had abdicated its place in the mainstream to pop music, which would henceforth reign supreme.) [8] By far the most outspoken and articulate adherent of the claim that the hallowed old tradition had fallen into a state of desuetude was himself a composer: Constant Lambert of Britain, whose eloquent tirade bears the snappy title *Music Ho! A Study of Music in Decline.* Published in 1934 when the adulation of Sibelius was gathering momentum for the big success the Finnish composer was to enjoy in the following decade, the book ends up, after castigating almost every composer of the time, with the declaration, "Of all contemporary music that of Sibelius seems to point forward most surely to the future." [9]

Sibelius—along with Shostakovich, who was similarly celebrated for the perpetuation of the nineteenth-century Romantic symphonic approach —has lost ground since about the sixties. But the pro-Romantic propaganda seems to have had at least some effect, producing a handful of young composers who have rallied around George Rochberg and David Del Tredici, both of them reformed serialists, which gives their conversion a certain cachet distinguishing them from the ordinary conservative, even though their past allegiance does not particularly intrude upon what we actually hear of their later music in direct perception. The main outcome, whether they sought it deliberately or not, was the ready-made acceptance of their music as they rode the wave of public preference for Romantic works of all kinds.[10]

However that may be, the new Romanticists were soon overshadowed by the minimalists, and the minimalists in turn seem to be losing ground among the young to what I find to be a nondescript manner either because I fail to comprehend it owing to the generation gap or because it needs time to be seen in proper perspective. There was talk of something even newer dubbed "New Age" music, but I am not aware that it has much identity except that the consolidation of pop and serious is somehow involved and perhaps also multiculturalism. I sometimes fear I am becoming a naysayer myself when I contemplate the very latest developments. But there is far too much good music being written today by composers who are underground, and far too much great music written since the twenties to justify just writing it off.

The contentions of the naysayers are based, in America in particular, not on standards of quality applied to the major works composed in our century, but on a certain statistical assessment of audience preference. It is not difficult to comprehend your average listener's preference for Romantic music: the prevalence of program music with a story to engage one and help to get one's bearings while listening, the familiarity of the conventional and conservative idiom with which one has grown up, the strong, overt feelings that come at the listener so that minimum effort is required to get intimately involved with what is being presented. Perhaps too, for those who half-listen, Romantic music, with its hill-and-dale progress, charting a path from one climax to the next, is the ideal vehicle for what George Santayana once referred to as that "drowsy revery relieved by nervous thrills."[11] Audiences have made side trips from time to time, notable among them the honeymoon with Vivaldi, whose motoric continuity makes a contemporary listener, nurtured on the steady beat and eight-to-the-bar of jazz and pop, feel at home. But there is always the return to the territory of choice and I do not think we can change that. Certainly no one should try, no one should turn audiences against Romantic music if they like it that much. Just leave a little space for something else.

What I think would help matters is a greater awareness that there is not a monolithic audience. As a matter of fact there is even a public that not only is uninterested in the standard repertory that the mass concert audience holds to be so sacred but actively despises it. Montreal's Metro, for instance, was invaded not so long ago by youths described as "punks" who loitered, chain-puffed cigarettes under "No Smoking" signs, and otherwise made themselves obstreperous; and it was found that piping the familiar opera and symphonic repertory into the underground stations drove the intruders away. Also, among the variety of audiences not the least significant is the huge one for jazz and pop, which threatens to snuff out the audience for serious music entirely. I do not know how much we can take into account idiosyncratic tastes, but they do exist. I once knew an excellent cook who told me she was bored when she repeated any recipe. Also, it was reported, though it may be apocryphal or exaggerated, that Liszt was also bored when he had to play any piece a second time. How different audiences can be, moreover, was driven home to me in 1960 when my string quartet, my most serially organized work—music we in America still considered "modern"—was relegated to the category of "old-fashioned" twelve-tone music when it was played at the festival of the International Society for Contemporary Music in Cologne, in June 1960. Composers like Luigi Nono and the Cage adherents became the figures of the moment.

Unfortunately, however, young composers cannot choose their audience or their particular performers, conductors, or concert organizations. It is mainly the listeners at the events of the major symphonies and opera companies—the conferrers of big reputation on any young person who happens to win the lottery as the token composer these organizations require to maintain their prestige—who are in a position to terrify the novice, to ensnare him or her in a situation in which there is a conflict of joy and agony: joy on the part of the creator in finally hearing what the symbols committed to paper sound like, agony from the hostile audience reaction, and perhaps also annoyances of one's own making, the almost inevitable miscalculations in scoring that are discovered when a neophyte's work is exposed for the first time to public scrutiny.

Composers can find a friendlier and more receptive environment for chamber music and solo works in the collectives established by themselves and their peers or at the recitals of performers who make the dissemination of contemporary music a point of honor. But it is a bit much to have one's first orchestral (also operatic) efforts tried out under world-class auspices. In the big concert halls it is as if composers are in foreign and hostile territory. Having won what often amounts to a lottery—to get in the door, to be accepted into the elite ranks of composers played by a major sym-phony—they realize that they are in the wrong place and their music at best is merely tolerated. Their first performance will very likely be the last, a token, something the orchestra has to do from time to time as a duty. You may wonder, then, why young composers submit themselves to the indig-nity. The main reason is not, as one may be inclined to think, that without such performances it is almost impossible to acquire much of a reputa-tion—though that is not at all an inconsequential consideration. The main reason is, rather, that even if a composer can interest a community or uni-versity orchestra in performing a work, and that is not without its difficul-ties, those organizations cannot always do justice to complex new music—though university and conservatory orchestras are getting better. (As a matter of record, the topflight orchestras also at times find complex new works beyond them given their limited rehearsal schedules and, as I have already indicated, they have had to turn down difficult music under con-sideration or actually postpone works already in rehearsal, blaming the composer, of course, for inefficiency.)

When I was at Harvard in the late thirties I recall walking, probably along the Charles, with Delmore Schwartz and passing on to him the news that a mutual friend, the composer David Diamond, was to have a work played by the Philharmonic. This was quite an event, an event of a kind that al-most never happened in our circle, and in those days it had the glamorous fillip of a coast-to-coast live radio broadcast on Sunday afternoon direct from Carnegie Hall. Delmore's response was to express proper pleasure for our friend but also to voice some envy that poets did not have the same op-portunities as composers to display the hard-earned results of their creative efforts under the bright lights of a huge public arena. All the poets had were the readings in intimate venues and publication in the little maga-zines. (Having a single poem in a big commercial magazine was the near-est thing to it, but not at all the same.) For my part I could only feel envi-ous of him and his fellow poets who could pursue their interests without having to answer to the unholy demands of that glamorous world.

Unfortunately it is difficult for composers to go underground (though some do) and simply disdain the public enterprises of the world in which they live just because they (or most of them) depend on certain facilities that world offers. Once there they must suffer the trials of having their achievements, very likely immature ones, as well as their mistakes exhibited before a huge tribunal consisting of people most of whom know much less about music than composers do but who have no qualms in passing judgments that are grist for the mill of the scriveners who toll the bell proclaiming music's demise.

Almost any member of the audience about to buy a secondhand car would surely have an expert examine it before putting money down. But where music is concerned listeners consider themselves expert enough. I wonder how much that circumstance is due to an overproduction of music of all kinds that leads to its devaluation since people hear (notice I do not say "listen to") so much music wherever they go. At a fine restaurant, gentle Baroque or Classical music (Wagner would be bad for the digestion and mercifully modern music too) goes with the candles on the table to establish a proper atmosphere; snippets of traditional masterpieces occasionally insinuate themselves into TV commercials (frustrating when they are suddenly cut off should you find yourself listening), and TV features, even when presenting disasters, seem incapable of doing so without background music. Curiously enough, nobody seems to mind when tense situations in the movies are accompanied by atonal music. (Some time ago for the TV series *Dr. Marcus Welby* the Hollywood composer Leonard Rosenman wrote quite admirable music in a style similar to that of Berg.) But it's something else when they have to listen to it.

As a result of all this ubiquity of music the audiences have a sense of being on such an intimate basis with it that they fancy themselves mavens. Admittedly, today's audience is better informed than the multitude in Mozart's day when serious music was the prerogative of the aristocracy, even though the emerging middle class was making demands to be provided with the opportunity of savoring the fine arts—a development that led to the establishment of public concerts. But our mass audience is so new and different, so much vaster, that there is really no basis for comparison. Even educated musicians would not always feel themselves prepared to pass final judgment on a complex new work after a first hearing. But the hoi polloi that fill concert hall seats have no qualms in doing so.

Joseph Wood Krutch, who was an astute authority on mass culture, once cited the old question, "Is the Good always the friend of the Best or is it sometimes and somehow its enemy?" and he asked, "Is Excellence more likely to win out to Mediocrity than it is to mere Ignorance or Nullity?"[12] Current audiences may be better informed than their counterparts of former times, but that does not make them experts. They may know something but it is not enough. The prophets of doom maintain that we are guilty of distorting historical fact and that what we are claiming amounts to this: any new work that seems repulsive now will one day reveal its beauty. The accusation is egregious and mistaken. We make no such claim. We do claim, however, that sometimes a complex new work needs time and attention before it can be truly appreciated, understood, and enjoyed. When Charles Munch was conducting the Boston Symphony Orchestra around 1960 he was bent on promoting the French composer Henri Dutilleux, who had not, and still has not, established himself in the United States. Whenever a Dutilleux work was unfavorably received by audience and press he would program it again. Munch also stands out in memory for another good deed relevant to this discussion. It seems that at the time he took over the post in Boston he was appalled to discover that if he wanted to locate a review of serious music in the *Boston Globe*, he had to look for "Amusements" in the index on page one. Munch told me he thought it peculiar. A symphony concert was not entertainment or amusement. I happened to be in a position to mention Munch's grievance to the editor of the *Globe* and the matter was promptly rectified. Either the intervention of a celebrated maestro or the difference in *Globe* management between then and now may have been responsible for the fast results. I was not so fortunate when I wrote to the ombudsman more recently to complain that the paper made no distinction between a review of serious music and one of pop, since the boldface caption above the review to classify each type simply read "music" in both cases. However, my complaint has never been acknowledged. The *Times* does make the distinction. But it has not been altogether innocent in this matter since for a long time the day's concerts were listed with theater, dance performances, and the like under the heading "Entertainment Events," a useful little module (a welcome one if it had a different heading). Also, in the Sunday arts section lately one finds articles on pop mixed in with articles on classical music. I strongly suspect it reflects the growing sentiment, one I view with considerable skepticism, that serious and pop inhabit a single domain. What disturbs me, from my vantage point as a fogy, I suppose, is that young people will grow up without a sense of the distinction between the two domains.

The public expects entertainment, and the *Globe* is reflecting that fact. Replicating the tactics of Cage without being aware of it, presenters have tried all sorts of gimmicks to liven up a concert, if only to have a performer go through some innocuous routine, like the singer who donned a trench coat and with a few props sang Schubert's *Die Winterreise* (Winter Journey); or another performer who started playing offstage and made a very leisurely approach to the performance area. (Such gimmicks are not entirely without precedent. Wanda Landowska when she gave a concert attempted to establish the atmosphere of a living room with her old-fashioned floor lamp and its tasseled shade.) More and more concerts, when new music is played, are preceded by a panel in which the composer confronts performers and auditors. The convention of having composers rise from their seats or possibly ascend the platform to bow after some performer or group has played their music is cherished as a long-established form of elementary theater. There have been instances where the widow or widower has gone up to bow after a performance of the late spouse's music, and other instances where the decision to play a work has been reversed when it is learned the composer cannot be present (similar to the convention for conferring an honorary degree).

The importance of a composer appearing in person to the presenters of concerts was driven home to me when I had a performance of my Septet, a Koussevitzky Foundation commission, by the superb Contemporary Chamber Players under Arthur Weisberg. It was part of a concert in memory of the celebrated Boston conductor at the Library of Congress which houses the foundation. It was not a premiere, but because of the special nature of the occasion the sponsors wanted me to be present. So, accompanied by my wife Ellen, I made the trip from Boston to Washington, where friends of close relatives had offered to put us up. They insisted we stay for dinner and when I protested that serving dinner before a concert puts a strain on the hosts to finish up in time, they assured me there would be no problem and the library was not far; a taxi would come and get us there in no time at all. (They themselves were not intending to go.) But they had not anticipated that taxis would be practically unavailable at the hour when theater-goers are on the march. They decided they would drive us over themselves but what they also had not anticipated was that there were terrible tie-ups owing to construction of a subway. My piece was first and it was some fifteen minutes long, just about the length of time we were late. As I walked down the long hallway to the area of the concert hall I noticed someone madly gesticulating. He evidently recognized me. He grabbed me unceremoniously and together we ran backstage where he pushed me onto the platform. I was just in time to bow and go through the ritual: shake the conductor's hand, then the concertmaster's (kiss them if they happen to be women) and finally, wave to the players—though not necessarily in that order. The sponsors were much relieved and happy, and they seemed to give no thought at all to my annoyance at having missed the performance and having made the long trip to Washington for nothing. Fortunately it was not the world premiere.

There can, of course, be occasions when the audience could not care less that a composer is in the hall to bow. Charles Munch gave the first Boston performances of my *Ideas of Order* in January 1964, a little over a decade after the New York Philharmonic had premiered it in Carnegie Hall. Nowadays when composers appear for a bow at Boston's Symphony Hall they use a door right front from a box on the first tier. In those days composers had to use the middle aisle that the main (so-called orchestra) floor still has only in the front part of the house. They had to walk down that aisle and reach the platform without mounting it, thus being in a position to shake the hands of the conductor and concertmaster who both leant over so they could be reached. The Friday afternoon concert, second in the series of three or four weekly concerts, was characteristically attended by a Boston Brahmin audience that came and left in their chauffeur-driven limousines and were notorious for sitting on their hands except perhaps to contribute a small ovation to a world-class player, an aged one in particular.

When my piece ended and some pro forma applause commenced, the conductor Charles Munch summoned me to approach the foot of the platform. But to my embarrassment before I reached it the applause had stopped. I wondered whether I should find a seat somewhere and disappear from the audience's line of vision. I went through with the pantomime, however, and was rewarded with some polite response.

It is pretty hopeless under current conditions, when even news has to be, in that unfortunate epithet, "infotainment," to expect your average listeners to put down their cash without expecting to get immediate kicks, far from exhibiting the desired willingness to be patient for that higher pleasure that ultimate apprehension brings. The symphony and the opera have been pretty much co-opted by the mass media. The "fifty pieces" that Thomson has reminded us constitute the essential literature played over and over again have become mass media items—so familiar by now that they are practically transparent and present no challenge to the listener or the players. Symphony-goers who pride themselves on their indulgence in "high culture" are likely to listen to Beethoven in the same abstracted way they listen to pop (Santayana's "drowsy revery" again). It strikes the ear not very differently from pop music on the radio somewhere in the background. The difference between Beethoven and mass culture is leveled off. We should disabuse ourselves of the notion that Carnegie Hall and Lincoln Center are citadels of high culture.

Now and then an enterprising and courageous individual comes along who is in a position to do something about this bleak aspect of the American concert scene. Serge Koussevitzky's espousal of the American composer during his long tenure as Boston Symphony Orchestra conductor (1924–49) is legendary even though he did not conduct the most difficult and complex American composers. One of the things that made him such a precious asset for American composers is that he made Boston his home, and when he spent summers in the Berkshires it was merely an extension of Boston. In this way he kept in touch with what was going on creatively in American music. Dimitri Mitropoulos did likewise in New York when he took over the reins of the Philharmonic just at the time that Koussevitzky retired from the BSO. But Mitropoulos lacked Koussevitzky's personal forcefulness in the realm of musical politics not only when it came to facing criticism for playing new music but when it was simply a matter of keeping his job beyond his first decade. (See the discussion of both conductors in chapter 17.)

Leopold Stokowski, an icon like Koussevitzky, during his tenure as music director of the Philadelphia Orchestra was able to get away with reprimanding listeners who were hostile to the avant-garde music he presented. In 1929 in particular, that peripheral year of prosperity, he had no qualms about turning to the audience and urging those dissenting to music such as Schoenberg's to turn in their subscriptions so that others who were waiting to obtain them could sit in their seats—there being no difficulty at that still flourishing time in filling the house to capacity. More recently the Philharmonic has provided us with Pierre Boulez, who did new music but not much of it American, and Leonard Bernstein, for whom contemporary American music was like the proverbial mother's milk but who, before long, preferred to display his conducting prowess in the symphonies of Gustav Mahler. Bernstein waged a virulent campaign against twelve-tone music. In one of his excellent TV programs, part of a series that was generally quite well done and a remarkable source of music education for the young, he practically departed from reason and gave a very bad example to his youthful listeners by saying before a performance of *Pierrot Lunaire*, "You better open that window in advance. *Pierrot* always makes me sick and needing to open the window." (As almost everyone knows, for the college trade he had a more elaborate, dignified, quasi-scientific approach to discrediting atonality in his Charles Eliot Norton lectures at Harvard in 1992. More of that later.)

One of the chief grievances American composers have against conductors, as I have said, is that many of them never become part of the American scene in the way that Koussevitzky was a Bostonian and Mitropoulos a New Yorker. Most of them do their stint and go back to their homes across the sea. They never give themselves any chance to know what local composers are up to. I was recently struck by the fact that this is an old complaint when I was reminded by the Americanist Judith Tick that in 1933 I was secretary of an organization called the Composers Protective Society, the main thrust of which was to issue a manifesto with a long list of grievances signed by some forty distinguished composers. (A letter in the *Times*, 4 June 1933, refers to it.) The grievances sounded very much like those we hear today, especially one that bemoaned "the familiar practice of conductors and virtuosi making up their season's repertory while abroad during the summer months." As the son of a loved and loving Polish mother I do not think I can be accused of chauvinism, but when Carnegie Hall recently invited Maurizio Pollini, Pierre Boulez, and Daniel Barenboim to oversee a survey of twentieth-century music I wondered why the foreign element was so strong among them. Not long ago we used to think of this as an old problem and that American performance had come into its own. I fear the European dependence is still rampant. (I wonder how much the prize for his String Quartet in an international Brussels contest was responsible for drawing attention to Elliott Carter before he had anything like his current fame in his homeland.)

The neglect of the American composer by the major symphonies was somewhat alleviated by the Louisville Orchestra's commissioning project, established by the mayor of Louisville in 1948 and subsidized much of the time by the Rockefeller Foundation. It was not an entirely professional orchestra, but by immersing itself in contemporary performance practice, working extra hard under its highly efficient conductor Robert Whitney, and scheduling far above the average number of rehearsals, the group made a valuable contribution as a noncommercial venture—not least of all with its LP recordings of many of the works presented in concert—until it became necessary for it to pay its own way, and that was the end of the new music project. (When I look back at a project like that one I tend to think things were better then, but I get a different impression if I view the whole picture.) Lately Michael Tilson Thomas has been stirring things up in San

Francisco. His programs are nicely interlarded with new music, some of it American, and he has planned programs intelligently, even succeeding in attracting young people, who elsewhere seem to have abandoned the serious music scene. (A colored photograph in the *Times* arts section, 22 June 1999, showed two percussionists in a contemporary work bare from the waist up, a piece of theater probably prescribed by the composer as come-on at the level of a men's wear advertisement for Ralph Lauren clothes. But I guess this is what's meant by injecting life into the proceedings.) The sad thing is the plain fact that the West Coast is a bit far from many important centers of American cultural life for some of us on the East Coast to benefit from Thomas's adventuresomeness. I suppose mention should be made of André Previn, David Zinman, and Leonard Slatkin, who have paid laudable attention to new American music, but it has been nothing like the heyday of Koussevitzky.

Mitropoulos, as I have said, carried on the Koussevitzky tradition in New York when he assumed the conductorship of the Philharmonic in 1949 and brightened up New York concert life. The orchestra's sponsorship of new music had been previously pretty dismal. This fact is brought home to us by an article in the *New York Herald Tribune* on the Philharmonic programs for the season of 1945–46 that attempted to show that there had been a "considerable" advance over the season exactly ten years earlier in the representation of American composers (slightly over 20 percent). When the tally is made of how many "American" works were included in the season's repertory it looks good. But if one examines the statistics closely it turns out to be a pretty poor showing. The intent was to praise the Philharmonic for its enterprising efforts on behalf of American music. The question to ask, however, is "what American music?" For there are the chestnuts, there is pop music, and there are the old works the presence of which on the programs is not particularly remarkable. The Philharmonic season included no less than five works of Gershwin, works of Jerome Kern, Richard Rodgers, and Sousa, Copland's *Lincoln Portrait* again rather than one of his challenging works (*Appalachian Spring* was also played but it counted as a fresh choice since it was new at the time), American classics by John Alden Carpenter and Charles Martin Loeffler, and one or two other works that are debatable.

There is something in the nature of a Catch-22 in a state of affairs in which on the one hand it seems perfectly logical to assume that people have not developed a taste for new music because they do not have the opportunity to hear it enough and on the other hand it is maintained that people have every opportunity to hear contemporary music but reject it because they dislike it. Certainly in much of the time that I witnessed the scene there was almost no opportunity for the concert-going public at large to hear the new music enough—American music in particular.

To assess the desolateness of the early landscape in this particular area it is necessary to bear in mind that in the thirties there was not the quantity of serious music that we now get on the radio from educational stations (even though lately there has been a marked curtailment). Moreover, the recording companies did not yet have the long-playing record which some years later would give them an incentive to seek out new names, since issuing and reissuing the same old "fifty pieces" would not be good business.

For a long time in the twenties and thirties, and even some of the forties, the important American composers were truly underground. Few people were aware that music of these composers could be heard at the concerts that Henry Cowell presented at the New School for Social Research in New York, usually with the composer present to discuss it and answer questions. An audience of fifteen at any of these events was considered practically a crowd. They were not advertised and the main metropolitan newspapers neither mentioned them or reviewed them. The list of composers presented included such names as Copland, Carl Ruggles, Ruth Crawford, Wallingford Riegger, Dane Rudhyar, and also, though he was too ill to attend and participate himself, Charles Ives.

Another oasis on this desolate landscape was the limited number of dance concerts of Martha Graham, whose enterprising and discriminating choice of composers for music accompanying her dance pieces endowed any of her programs with the character of an avant-garde concert of American music. Copland's seminal Piano Variations had some of its first hearings as the musical score for her solo *Dithyrambic* even before the composer had consigned it to manuscript paper in its final form. In much the same way later it was at the New York City Ballet that New Yorkers could hear the neoclassic masterpieces of Stravinsky as accompaniment to George Balanchine's splendid ballets—choreographic masterpieces which could scarcely be more successful in their synergistic grasp of whatever it was that Stravinsky aimed to convey. In the forties Stravinsky masterpieces could be heard almost nowhere else. The press on the whole was extremely hostile to this neoclassic phase of Stravinsky, blatantly favoring Sibelius and Shostakovich over it, although Virgil Thomson and, if I may be permitted, I myself, and for a brief period Paul Bowles before me, raised our lonely voices vehemently in favor of the aging neoclassic master from our perches at the *Tribune*. Also, Robert Craft, even before acceding to the position of Stravinsky's amanuensis, organized single-handed over a period of several years the only concerts in New York dedicated to the master's music of this orientation.

4 Rendezvous with Apollo: Form Is Feeling

What some of us who have been avid listeners of Stravinsky have always heard as being most significant in his works composed between approximately 1920 and 1955 are not his references to older music but rather the subtlety, ingenuity, and inventiveness of every aspect of composition. The subject is not the compiled Classical material, but what is done to it. (Specifics on this later.) I would not want to give the impression that I believe the Classical allusions vanish with this approach and are not apprehended as such—not only Classical, but Baroque, Renaissance, Romantic, and so on. In the final product their treatment by Stravinsky renders a result that occupies a position as far as possible from pastiche. The originality is palpable in the extreme. As Copland once observed, ". . . if you don't listen closely, there are times when you might mistake Mozart for Haydn, or Bach for Handel, or even Ravel for Debussy. I cannot ever remember being fooled by the music of Stravinsky."[1] It is odd that over the years so many listeners as well as the critics (the listeners coached by the critics?) focused above all on the music's references to Bach or any other old master as if that were the essential content. They found it altogether unnatural that the extremely avant-garde composer of the orgiastic *Le sacre du printemps* *(Rite of Spring)* completed in 1913 could have traveled in so few years to the chaste ambience of, for instance, *Apollon musagète* (1927), and they made it perfectly clear that they were unwilling to make the trip with him.

It is one of the unfortunate quirks of history that so great a part of Stravinsky's oeuvre should have been saddled with a label like "neoclassicism" that does it so much injustice. Schoenberg seems to have been the victim of a comparable injustice because of the locution "atonality" which he disapproved of, since it suggested "against tone," though it does not affect, imprison our hearing to the extent that "neoclassicism" does. A name somehow gives a thing legitimacy and, no small factor, it makes it easier to refer to it. The use of slogans to pinpoint the thrust of movements in the arts accelerated during the course of the twentieth century. As Wallace Stevens once put it, modern art "has a reason for everything. Even the lack of a reason becomes a reason. Picasso expresses surprise that people should ask what a picture means and says that pictures are not intended to have meanings. This explains everything."[2]

It does not look as if things are going to change in the foreseeable future as far as the labels for different trends are concerned, so we have to live with them because calling a movement something else when one designation is so deeply imprinted on the minds of so many people is, it seems to me, cumbersome. The best we can do is apply first aid and try to do some damage control. Meanwhile, if we find we have to have recourse to the term— and I should find it hard to avoid this particular one—my advice would be to use it in the broadest of senses. I recommend special vigilance where one believes one has espied a case of neoclassicism but on closer inspection it turns out to be an excursion to an old style in the spirit of a vacation trip from which one will soon return. I have in mind arrangements, among other things. For example, Busoni's and Schoenberg's arrangements of Bach do not make their perpetrators neoclassicists in any sense. Even Stravinsky's adaptation of Pergolesi in *Pulcinella* is not yet a neoclassic Stravinsky, as I have observed before on more than one occasion.[3] (I was interested to see that the Stravinsky authority Richard Taruskin felt the same way.)[4] Stravinsky's treatment of the borrowed Pergolesi tunes is not very different from his treatment of folk tunes in *Petrushka*, though I should be willing to admit that dealing with the Baroque composer's music may very well have fanned the flames of a desire to use works of the past as raw material instead of folksongs in the future.

Stravinsky in later life confided to Milton Babbitt how he felt about the recriminations leveled against him to the effect that he was unnaturally "returning to" the past (the Schoenberg work Stravinsky refers to is *Three Satires*, Op. 28, dated 1925, for chorus, in which some of Schoenberg's own words made fun of composers who were aiming at a "return to . . ."):

> Stravinsky told me how deeply disappointed and hurt he had been that Schoenberg had chosen (that was precisely his word: "chosen") to take the slogans of "back to Bach" and "neoclassicism" seriously, so seriously as to respond with an acerbic verbal satire, with music to match. For, to Stravinsky, "back to Bach," was just that, an alliteratively catchy

slogan which had no pertinence to professional activity or professional discourse. It was there, permitted to be concocted, like "neoclassicism," to be talked about by those who could not and should not talk about music, who didn't even bother to hear the music, but who, when they bandied about the catch words, were "talking about Stravinsky."⁵

To take Stravinsky literally in this reported conversation would oblige one to forswear both the evocation of the concept and the application of the rubric "neoclassicism" to his music and put it to rest as a sort of Madison Avenue slogan that had served its purpose. It must have been out of pique that Stravinsky disowned it in later life, and who can blame him when it distracted people from what is essential in his music? But as I said above, I think it best that we try to live with it. At one point it seems to have served Stravinsky. (See the manifesto *re* Classicism below.) It can still be useful in dealing with his music if one is circumspect and if one does not lose sight of the fact that Stravinsky does not identify himself with the sources that he draws upon in his music but keeps his distance or, as he sometimes used to say, uses them as the subject of his "criticism."

In this rare instance of his unburdening himself on the subject as part of a dialogue with Babbitt, however, Stravinsky seemed intent upon obliterating the whole concept from his past, and he was indeed free with facts to help him do so. For the blurred memory of an old man was playing tricks on him if what he remembered was the alliterative slogan hurled at him by the French musical public—a slogan he curiously remembered as being hurled at him by Frenchmen in English! We should be charitable and not take this little slip as something to make us lose sight of the essential burden of his confession which is not at all affected by it: namely, that at the point in his life when he recalled this affair he was thoroughly disabused of the concept neoclassicism and wanted to shift the blame to others for identifying him with it.

What I often find more disturbing than the recriminations leveled at Stravinsky for his backward look, his unnatural "return" to the past, are the frequent allegations that his music is devoid of feeling. These allegations have often materialized as a corollary to complaints about his retrogressive stance but they have then assumed major proportions. One would think that by now the matter was settled and that Stravinsky was no longer regarded as a paradigm of music without feeling. Only a few years ago, however, I came across a review in the *New York Times* that contained the following observation: "Using a mildly astringent language reminiscent of

Stravinsky but *with heart,* Mr. Perle presents . . ." (italics mine),[6] and to my surprise I found in conversation with fellow musicians that this view of Stravinsky is not altogether dormant.

Consistent with the Romantic thesis of music as self-expression (what John Dewey called, in its most unfortunate manifestations, a "spewing forth")[7] is the notion that composers in the music they write must not express any feelings but their own, as if emotions experienced by others cannot burn as intensely in their music as emotions they experience themselves. (If this were true, how would novelists be able to deal properly with characters that are hateful or in any way alien to themselves?) When music or a style is being appropriated, the feelings expressed originally are obviously the feelings of other people, and the argument is that they have somehow been wrung out in the process of being transmitted. In addition to this, mere mention of "Classical" is enough to prepare some of the listening public for basalt frigidity as the polar opposite of the hot intensity of Romanticism.

I wonder if it would not be a good idea to reserve the rubrics Classical and Romantic to apply to the artwork rather than to the artist, who may be different things at different times. I remember how surprised I was at a remark made to me some time in the forties by Paul Hindemith whom we all had pegged as a staunch neoclassicist. I was emerging from the old Metropolitan Opera House on Broadway at Thirty-ninth Street where I had been listening to *Siegfried* in order to review it for the *New York Herald Tribune.* (Hindemith remembered me from having met me a few years earlier in Cologne at an International Society for Contemporary Music festival which included my String Quartet among its offerings.) After greetings he told me, "that is an opera I would like to have written *myself.*" Since this chance encounter I have learned that he adored Wagner and that in the last scene of his opera *Mathis der Maler,* whether consciously or not, he quoted *Tristan.*

On the subject of feeling in Stravinsky's music, no one has been more culpable of contributing to confusion and misunderstanding than he himself by virtue of the notorious, thoroughly indiscreet statement that appeared back in 1935 in his autobiography (*Chroniques de ma vie,* in the original French)—a statement that would seem to corroborate the public's assessment of his attitude toward expression in music:

> Car je considère la musique, par son essence, impuissante à *exprimer* quoi que ce soit: un sentiment, une attitude, un état psychologique, un

phénomène de la nature, etc. . . . *L'expression* n'a jamais été la propriété immanente de la musique. [For I consider music by its essence power-less to express anything whatsoever: a sentiment, an attitude, a psycho-logical state, a phenomenon of nature. . . . Expression has never been an immanent property of music.] [Translation mine][8]

I was enormously relieved when he explained himself many years later—or as some may prefer to put it, reversed himself—in one of the books of conversation with Robert Craft:

That overpublicized bit about expression (or non-expression) was sim-ply a way of saying that music is suprapersonal and superreal and as such beyond verbal meanings and verbal descriptions. It was aimed against the notion that a piece of music is in reality a transcendental idea "expressed in terms of" music, with the *reductio ad absurdum* im-plication that exact sets of correlatives must exist between a composer's feelings and his notation. It was offhand and annoyingly incomplete, but even the stupidest critics could have seen that it did not deny musi-cal expressivity, but only the validity of a type of verbal statement about musical expressivity. I stand by the remark, incidentally, though today I would put it the other way around: music expresses itself.[9]

Stravinsky was obviously attempting to deal with the tricky phenome-non that music is essentially nonverbal, and he was warning listeners who are rendered uncomfortable by this phenomenon, listeners who will use words nonetheless, that they should beware of reifying them so that they appear to have more import than they can possibly have. The best part of his more recent statement is the warning against "exact correlatives . . . between a composer's feelings and notation." The phrase "beyond verbal meanings" has to do with the conviction that the music cannot be "repro-duced" in words or even an analytical diagram. (See the quotation from Arnold Isenberg in chapter 14.) But words and diagrams observing proper limits can be enormously helpful. Listeners who regard music as inviolate and ineffable are as commonplace as those who always see pictures and hear stories, and I would not want the reader to think I am endorsing ei-ther type. As to the first type their view quite justifies their listening in what Santayana called a "drowsy revery." They are not interested in tak-ing the music apart for better understanding. They welcome the prospect of merely being lulled by the billows of sound.

Stravinsky's original statement on the subject of expression had done the damage, and it is doubtful anything he would have said afterward could have been accepted as sufficient reparation. The conclusion that may be drawn from his disclaimer is that composers who may insist they are writ-

ing music that does not express either their own feelings or those of anyone else may yet be writing music that embodies feelings, since these,
whether there or not, cannot be fixed or localized verbally. If the words
used to characterize a musical emotion are unreliable, the words used to
contend that there is no emotion must be equally unreliable. We are indebted to Freud for the awareness of the way in which our unconscious
desires, implicit feelings, partly formulated beliefs manifest themselves
without our knowing it in the merest action of walking into a room, in
the presumably meaningless loops and curves of handwriting, in the apparently awkward movement of the hand (for those who still use old-
fashioned nonmechanical pens) that "fortuitously" shatters the inkstand
which, though we are not thinking of it at the moment, has displeased us
for some time.

Composers may evoke emotions without knowing what they are and
without being aware they are doing so. Tones themselves are, to start with,
emotionally toned. A high, loud sound has its aura of excitement, however
limited or diluted that may be under certain conditions. A high piercing
laugh does not represent glee by convention; there is an intrinsic relation,
what some psychologists have called a functional relation, between the
laugh and the quality of our exultation (a relationship of the kind that an
onomatopoeic word has to its object). At the same time, the scream's meaning is not specific. Indeed, embedded in laughter at a distance it may be mistaken for a sign of distress. A composer's choice of a high sound to complete
a formal pattern involves an accompanying, probably unconscious, approval of the feeling that comes in its wake. It is a feeling, moreover, that
is not a mere matter of association like the relation of most words to their
object. If the listener can resist assimilating the sound to anything obvious
in the outside world, its function and meaning will be precisely what they
are by virtue of its place within the music's structure.

It is true that Stravinsky and his orbit of composers reacted against the role
that emotion played in nineteenth-century Romanticism, but to label them
neoclassicists on this account is to assume a composer has no other choice
but to be either Classic or Romantic. There are, however, certain traits that
we associate with the one or the other, and a composer may exhibit them
without being altogether either Classical or Romantic. I have already mentioned self-expression as one objective of Romanticism and now I should
like to expand that to include expression of any kind when it is an objective
that takes priority over form. (The neoclassicist's preoccupation with form,

by the way, is another reason listeners are likely to assume a delinquency in feeling, as if the one excludes the other.) Quite apart from whether, in the result, there is more form than feeling—if it makes any sense to talk in this fashion—the paradigm of the Romantic composer has him or her, in the process of creation, starting with an emotion and subsequently looking for the notes to express it. (This may not be literally true but it is a good blueprint to keep in mind.) By contrast, the Classicist starts with the tones, and only then the emotion, according to the nature of music, comes in their wake. According to André Gide this would be a likely characterization of the way Chopin worked, so although the standard history books have him down as the paradigmatic Romantic by virtue of the nature of his music and the time in which he lived, the French novelist took him to be a Classicist.[10]

The reclassification of Chopin as a Classicist would no doubt be considered a means of downgrading him by many observers. The mere effusion of better and more feelings is supposed to be superior to perfection of constructive values. Anyone who took piano lessons in the twenties was not unlikely to have been saddled with the kitschy salon pieces of a British composer named Cyril Scott and perhaps exposed to his theories as well, which included the notion that "Beethoven with his pomp and splendor surpassed the tinkling dulcitude of Mozart." Tinkling dulcitude, indeed! A few of us are old enough to remember when Mozart was considered lightweight somewhat in the manner that Stravinsky is still considered by some listeners (and critics, as I mentioned) to have written music devoid of feeling.

This notion of the essential Stravinsky has many adherents, and it goes along with a common view of a reduced role of emotion in Classicism. The Romantic composer is credited by some observers with expressing not only more feelings but better ones—the loftiest, the most godlike sentiments: "le sérieux à tout prix" (seriousness at any price) in Darius Milhaud's choice phrase. Unhampered by the straitjacket of the requirements of form, composers were presumably free to express themselves. Indeed all composers, observed Ferruccio Busoni, "have drawn nearest the true nature of music in preparatory and intermediary passages (preludes and transitions) where they felt at liberty to disregard symmetrical proportions and unconsciously drew free breath." He went on to asseverate that the rest or *fermata* "most nearly approaches the essential nature of art." (Little did he know that someday one John Cage would put into action what were presumably his hyperbolic musings.)[11]

The Romanticists took the high points as a norm, and they could even find them in music of the Classical period—the almost Wagnerian statue scene in *Don Giovanni* or the aria "Er Sterbe" in *Fidelio*. Naturally, the preoccupation with such moods and the enormous creative gifts lavished on them contributed to surpassing skill in their expression. Music was said not to have feeling when it failed to express heightened emotions: amorous exaltation, intense longing (*Sehnsucht*), profoundest mourning, agitation, ecstasy and such. I suspect we tend to overlook in all of this that "coldness" is also a feeling. We say to someone "your hands *feel* cold," but when a piece of music is cold we say it lacks feeling.

Classical composers felt that emotion did not always have to be at great heights or depths to be vivid and meaningful. Moreover they realized the potentiality of form to embody and unify contrasting emotions. The composer's primary concern was to bring to bear the appropriate technical requirements for their proper expression—not as two different things, for they were aware of them as two aspects of the same thing. This is quite different from assuming the formal aspects are but a bridge to the feelings— a kind of Achilles heel one has to put up with. When the conscious mind is engaged mainly in arranging tones in suitable and striking configurations, the feelings that inform them are likely to spring from deep sources the subtle ramifications of which would be far too elusive to grasp in any other way. Yet, by the notes chosen, even under the strictest formal constraints, these deep, sequestered feelings become somehow accessible. Like the portrait painter who relies too much on his model, the composer in his desire to reproduce emotion faithfully may remain too wedded to a conscious level, leaving little room for chance (what Stravinsky called the *trouvaille*—literally "find" or "discovery") in handling the musical elements and for adventures into hitherto untapped recesses of the unconscious.

An effort, a struggle to conform to a stringent structural requirement may be apprehended as emotional tension. An excellent example is the dialectic play in Mozart which may have its origin in what may sound like a colorless and mechanical pursuit: the composer's determination to maintain the hegemony of the tonic against the forces that seek to undermine it. The problem can arise in functional tonality out of the phenomenon that in the major scale the chord on I (the tonic) is to IV (subdominant) as V (dominant) is to I because of the intervallic equivalence of the two tetrachords of the major scale (C to F and G to C). Thus, the tonic has the potentiality to sound like V of IV, thereby losing its priority. One way to avoid this is to use V of II (supertonic) to deny and then replace V of IV, and II itself to deny and replace IV (an expanded version of deceptive cadence). To understand this let us start by rearranging the notes of the major scale. In the conventional do-re-mi, etc., there are two intervals between the scale degrees: semitone and whole-tone. But let us place the notes so the adjacencies are defined by a fixed interval. Now if we consider the fifth and its inversion, the fourth, as the "same" interval for our purpose (each has notes of the same letter names but in a different inversion, and in a useful convention of Princeton terminology they constitute an "interval class") we find that it is the only interval encompassing all the notes of the scale in an arrangement in which the adjacencies are indeed defined by a fixed interval. Also, by virtue of certain intrinsic natural relations and the dictates of the tonal system, it is an interval class that provides the closest relationship available between any two pitches in functional tonality, which gives the succession of pitches a unique property. If C major is used as an example the series is B-E-A-D-G-C-F, and it should become apparent that if we continue moving in the same direction with the adjacencies always defined by the same interval (fifth-fourth), we find ourselves in different keys, the keys with flats. So F, as the "last note" of the "white-note" scale in this particular formation, is capable of being poised potentially to leave the collection; but D (root of the II chord) is a means of getting back into it because it is in the middle of the collection so ordered rather than at its end.

I shall use portions of the *Allegro*, following the slow introduction, of Mozart's "Dissonance" Quartet in C major, K. 465, to illustrate the exploitation of this property of the major scale, but there are many other examples in Classical literature.

As the *Allegro* begins (Ex. 4a) it is significant that Mozart's first change of harmony in the second bar over a C pedal is IV. In bar 28 a suggestion of (incomplete) V of IV occurs briefly as a passing-tone event, followed by the remediating V of II to prevent a resolution on IV. Starting in bar 35 for three bars, IV insists on being tonicized, only to be frustrated by the inevitable V of II. Note how V of IV makes two attempts (bars 36–37) to reach its goal before it is turned back. Note also the expressivity that comes in the wake of the reluctant return to C major in bars 38 and 39. Reluctant is also the epithet that can be more generally applied to the sense we get of being repeatedly turned back in the course of the movement from attaining the triumphant F major that seemed on the verge of being tonicized. The crucial element is V of II, and once the reentry is negotiated there is more than one way of proceeding. If you wish to compare the various occurrences, note that the one starting with bar 60, being in the second group, in conformance with the specifications of the *sonata allegro* formula, will

Ex. 4a. Mozart, "Dissonance" Quartet, K. 465, *Allegro* (opening of exposition)

naturally have II on A instead of D. The other occurrences are found at bars 87, 159, 168, 179, 207, and 227. At the beginning of the development (Ex. 4b) there is an amplified version (thirteen bars) in which there is intense conflict between V of F and V of VI of F (D or II of C). Observe the dissonant clash of C-sharp from the suggested D (harmonic) minor with C-natural from a potential F major in bars 113–14. The sense of conflict does not really abate with the V^7 on F. That does not occur until bar 119, and in a surprising way. Precisely how would carry us too far from the main thrust of this discussion.

The slow movement, *Andante*, entering in F major, satisfies all the unfulfilled drives toward the subdominant and accordingly conveys a sense of arrival, of peace (Ex. 5). It has been pointed out to me by a musicologist that there is nothing special about the slow movement of a sonata form of the Classical period being in the subdominant, since it was a convention and therefore one would expect it. I do not claim that Mozart created the structural device of a subdominant second movement as an element of surprise or special satisfaction, but rather, that once the convention was in place he seems to have taken advantage of the arrival of the conventional subdominant as the movement's tonic to make it meaningful by injecting a struggle to get to it. (It is an interesting example of the difference between the approach of the musicologist and that of the composer-theorist.)

When I consider the C-minor fugal exposition that opens the second part of Stravinsky's *Symphonie de psaulmes* (Symphony of Psalms) of 1930 I cannot help thinking that the arrival of C minor, in a very general way, has an impact that is roughly analogous to that of the arrival of F major in the Mozart *Andante*, as we shall see. It is the kind of analogy I should expect latter-day positivist theorists to regard as otiose. But if we are willing to allow some latitude in our thinking, and are willing to recognize similitude without always insisting on equivalence, we may find that it is Stravinsky's application of a similar structural device in purely modern terms that places him in a certain limited debt to Classical tradition much more meaningfully than his familiar practice of appropriating or alluding to the characteristic configurations of the eighteenth-century Classical composers. But let me have him explain it to you in his own words. The following appeared in a one-time British magazine *The Dominant* in 1927, a translation of a statement published earlier in France under the caption *"Avertissement"* (Warning):

Ex. 4b. Same, *Allegro* (opening of development)

Ex. 5. Same, *Andante Cantabile* (opening)

There is much talk nowadays of a reversion to Classicism, and works
believed to have been composed under the influence of so-called Classical models are labeled neoclassic. . . . I fear that the bulk of the public,
and also the critics, are content with recording superficial impressions
created by the use of certain materials which were current in so-called
Classical music. The use of such devices is insufficient to constitute the
real neoclassicism, for Classicism itself was characterized not in the
least by its technical processes, which, then as now, were themselves
subject to modification from period to period, but rather by its constructive values.[12]

What Stravinsky appears to have been telling us is that to be a neoclassic composer is not simply to parrot the eighteenth-century Classicists but
to apply structural principles in composing—that is, modern structural
principles that would serve some of the same purposes as the principles in
Classical music. The first of the three parts of *Psalms* employs strategies in
their own way analogous to those in the Mozart quartet in the matter of
delayed and frustrated resolutions within a context that may no longer be
legitimately defined as functionally tonal. Instead, the pitch relations, the
"tonal" areas, are moderated by an infusion of the octatonic scale that
Stravinsky favored, especially in his "Russian" works and in only some of
the neoclassic ones. The octatonic is a scale in which the adjacencies are
defined by two intervals in alternation: whole-tone and semitone. As a consequence, in contrast to the diatonic, which has seven forms (interval orderings) of the scale, there are only two forms: one starting with the
whole-tone and the other (relevant here to the first part of the *Psalms*)
starting with the semitone. In chapter 15, which treats the scale more fully,

Ex. 6. Referential octatonic scale, Stravinsky, *Symphony of Psalms*, part 1

both forms are discussed. But for our present purpose it is sufficient to consider just one of the two forms, a representation of which is given in Example 6. This scale on E is a referential octatonic scale used as a basis for important tonal relations in *Psalms*. In semitonal counting (loosely speaking, "going up" the chromatic scale), it may be represented thus: 0–1–3–4–6–7–9–10–12. If we take overlapping three-note groups (conjunct trichords: 0–1–3; 3–4–6; 6–7–9; 9–10–12), we highlight the inherent symmetry. Thus, in each trichord the interval number one accounts for the relation between the first and second member, and the interval number two accounts for the relation between the second and third member: for example, E-F-G; G-Ab-Bb etc. It will be recalled that the symmetry between the two tetrachords in the major scale was the enabling factor in the fascinating dialectic play of the relations in the Mozart. There we had only two symmetrical elements to contend with. Here we have four and the potential of the symmetry to challenge the tone center is accordingly greater.

If E is the tone center (has pitch priority) the first note of each conjunct trichord is capable of being its clone by virtue of its parallel position. Within the octatonic ordering of the pitch collection in *Psalms* Stravinsky exploits only two of the four available pitch priorities: E and G, and he is thus closer to Mozart than if he had exploited all four. In the loose analogy with the Mozart I wish to propose, the E stratum (to borrow Edward Cone's nomenclature)[13] corresponds to Mozart's tonic and tends to be Phrygian when it is not octatonic, while the G stratum, which is rather unruly, tends, without departing from the octatonic collection, to take the form of the dominant (V) of C. Whenever a resolution to C seems imminent, the E stratum interrupts it, somewhat in the way that the deceptive II in Mozart keeps us from resolving on IV. The irony is that the form of the octatonic scale used here has a C-sharp which is a direct contradiction to the C-natural toward which we are striving. So as long as the present form of octatonic scale is in operation (no "accidentals" or departure from the "key" being employed) there can be no resolution on C. The opening C of the oboe in the *fugato* of the second section is quite enough for us to experience a sense of a long-awaited resolution, somewhat the way, though more intensely, that we experienced the sensation of the F-major opening

Ex. 7a. Stravinsky, *Psalms*, part 1, revised 1948 (piano reduction by Soulima
Stravinsky) (opening)

of the Mozart *Andante:* an arrival, that is to say, yielding at last the goal
that had been repeatedly thwarted in the previous *Allegro* and also something the conditions for which had been proposed again and again without
materializing.

The main point is that the thwarted tendency toward C in Stravinsky is
achieved by very different means from the thwarted tendency toward F in
Mozart, but there is an underlying principle that they share. The main participants in the dialectical play as Stravinsky conceived it are briefly announced at the opening: an E-minor triad, transformed by virtue of spacing and doubling to sound like no E-minor triad ever heard before, suffices
to represent the E stratum. (The extraordinary spacing is not merely for
color but has the structural function of placing the secondary pitch priority G in relief.) This is followed immediately by octatonic woodwind figu-
rations hovering about a dominant seventh chord on G in first inversion
(Ex. 7a). The woodwind passage returns twice more, each time longer than
it was before and followed each time by the opening E chord that thwarts
it, bringing to my mind the scene in Gluck's *Orfeo* where Orpheus pleads
with the shades to admit him into the underworld and they respond repeatedly with a peremptory "No." Finally the E prevails and there is briefly
a Phrygian passage that gradually merges into the earlier figuration, orna-
menting the G seventh chord. Just before the entrance of the chorus we
seem ready for a resolution on C. The chorus, however, enters on E and we
find ourselves back in the earlier octatonic zone, the effect of not getting
the anticipated C provoking, as I experience it, something like the sensation
of losing one's step (Ex. 7b). A more compelling approach to C occurs over
eight bars from rehearsal Nos. 5 to 7. There is an extended dominant of C
in the chorus for four bars, followed by the incomplete V[7] over a C-pedal
in four flutes and an oboe which is quoted in Example 7c, the entire passage
providing an occasion for one of Stravinsky's most striking ironies. Here
within easy reach are the conditions for the establishment of the goal of

Ex. 7b. Same, part 1 (from second bar after No. 3)

Ex. 7c. Same, part 1, No. 6

C priority. But we will not achieve it as long as the dominant elements stubbornly persist and clash with C instead of resolving on it. The oboe's figuration that seems to be heading for a resolution on C dissolves instead into a return to E as at No. 4. This drama is reenacted in another form before No. 12 and in the last four measures, as I noted above, we finally get the unmitigated cadential V^7 (Ex. 8a) that resolves on the C of the fugal exposition (Ex. 8b).

With regard to what his critics and Stravinsky himself have had to say about the absence of feeling in his music, there can be no more eloquent disclaimer than parts 1 and 2 of *Psalms*. Thus, on some level—it was undoubtedly unconscious—Stravinsky felt there must be an element of affinity between the sense of pleading for C minor and individuals beseeching God to lend them his ear: "Exaudi orationem meam, Domini . . . " (Hear my prayer, Lord). And also, in part 2, something loosely parallel to the satisfaction of arrival at the thwarted C minor in the words "Expectans expectavi DOMINUM, et intendit mihi . . ." (Waiting for the *Lord,* he reached out to me). Notions like this sound naive—another reminder of how powerless words are for dealing with music. I beg the reader to take them in the broadest metaphorical sense. I have recourse to them occasionally simply to make a point. They would sound equally naive were we dealing with any of the other arts, even poetry where words are the medium. Wallace Stevens in one of his letters, after explaining some points in his poem "Sunday Morning," observed, "Now these ideas are not bad in a poem. But they are a frightful bore when converted as above."[14]

What often leads to the conclusion that emotions are absent where music ideally fulfills its structural *essence* is the difficulty of localizing them with respect to our normal connotative methods of thought, as I have attempted to do. Yet the emotions are nonetheless specific. If there can be so much ambiguity in poetry, where the verbal symbols so closely represent their objects (think of William Empson's *Seven Types of Ambiguity*)[15] we must expect music to allow for still broader interpretation. In much Romantic and Impressionist music there may be less room for disagreement over the emotion embodied in a given musical passage. But in more abstract works the whole unconscious is given free play. If the emotion seems ambiguous, seems to elude us when we try to encapsulate it, it is not because it is in itself ambiguous or elusive. The emotion expressed, as I have said, is perfectly specific. If we lean too heavily on verbal characterization

Ex. 8a. *Psalms*, part 1 concluded (final cadence)

Ex. 8b. Same, part 2, *fugato* (opening)

we may make the mistake of concluding that where emotions are least definable they are absent altogether. This is unfortunate since, as it has often been observed, if what a composer has to say could be easily said in words, there would be no point in trying to express it in tones. Emotion in music is least friendly to efforts at localizing and narrowly defining it. If it is argued that there is no basis for claiming the emotions are there, it is equally true, as I have said, that there is no basis for claiming that they are not there. They seem most evasive of definition when form and feeling are, as they should be, most thoroughly identified with each other. Once this identification is accepted it serves as a protection against the common error of claiming that intellectual factors merely provide a kind of receptacle into which the feelings are poured.

5 Reinventing the Past: Pastiche, Collage, or "Criticism"?

The seeds of simplification as a reaction against the growing density of Romantic and early modern music were beginning to sprout at the dawn of the twentieth century at about the same time that a new complexity was gathering momentum in the early music of Schoenberg and Stravinsky. Erik Satie's achievement of a pared-down texture that gave him the undeserved reputation of being trivial dated back as far as the eighteen-eighties, the time during which he wrote the familiar *Gymnopédies*. It was well in place when the two twentieth-century giants started out with what was regarded as their blasphemous modernism. Stravinsky's later neoclassicism, such as it was, may be regarded as part of a trend that originated with Satie—a second wave, perhaps—precipitated in Stravinsky's case as a reaction to his own complexity in the *Rite* and anticipated by the international character of *Histoire du soldat* (Soldier's Tale, 1918) with its dance numbers in the manner of a Baroque suite.

It was a similar incentive, the quest for a less rigorous alternative to the lucubrations postulated under the growing influence of serialism, that led much later to the formation of a group of young American composers as dedicated to Stravinsky in his then current mode as the young American serialists were to the twelve-tone Schoenberg. This took place just about at the start of World War II, its headquarters being Harvard University with which I still had contact since I was working on a dissertation that I never finished.[1] I would call myself a charter member of the group, but as in the case of the French Six, we never thought of ourselves as a formal group until we were called one. We had no name but we were variously referred to as "The New Boston Classical School," "The Harvard Neoclassicists," or simply, "New England School."[2]

The Harvard composers who were in at the beginning of the "school," if such it may be called, were Harold Shapero, Irving Fine, myself, and briefly Leonard Bernstein, who was soon wooed away by "bigger" things —the symphony orchestra, Broadway, and such. From Harvard the movement fanned out over the country and embraced a few additional converts: Alexei Haieff, Louise Talma, Leo Smit, and John Lessard in New York, and Ingolf Dahl in California. Also Claudio Spies, now of Princeton, had become one of us while he was at Harvard. Listing the principal names as a "Stravinsky school" at the end of our first decade, Copland included Lukas Foss, who was part of our peer group, but whose real mentor was Paul Hindemith, and who had not studied in Paris with Nadia Boulanger like the rest of us.[3] Almost no one in our fraternity, with the significant exception of Shapero, had recourse to Stravinsky for his "return to the past," or for an example of how to do so ourselves. For that, one would have done better to turn to Hindemith, who was not interested in allusion or appropriation, but who extracted a certain linearity from Bach and imposed his own brand of chromaticism upon a modal diatonicism. For our part, the allusions to the past were far from the main thing we listened to or emulated in Stravinsky, as I have already remarked. We found that his original ways of manipulating tones, timbres, and rhythms opened up entirely new vistas for our own development.

But this originality of middle-period Stravinsky was completely invisible to members of the press, whose typical response was to complain about the utter lack of personal style and integrity and to bemoan how the disparate sources on which he drew resulted in total incoherence. Yet the very same reviewers who complained about the lack of style in Stravinsky lost no time in castigating us, the young Harvard Stravinskians, for the slightest trace in our music of the influence of the master's middle manner. I have never had a more flattering review than the intentionally unflattering one written by a Boston newspaper man who observed in a parenthetical aside, "if Mr. Berger's name were not attached one might easily guess it to be one of that author's [Stravinsky's] smaller ballet scores."[4] How does one reconcile the claim that middle Stravinsky has no individuality with an observation I quoted above, made by a listener whose musical judgment must surely be respected? I refer to Copland's saying he had "never been fooled by the music of Stravinsky." And how could Stravinsky's influence as a neoclassicist be so palpable if he lacked any style of his own?

Neoclassicism in whatever field of the arts has long had a bad press, its products treated as hand-me-downs, not even as acceptable as something recycled. In an exchange on the subject of *The Picasso Papers* by Rosalind Krauss, Harvard University's Harry A. Cooper, Associate Curator of Modern Art of its art museums, recognized her book as "the first serious attempt to deal with Picasso's neoclassical work as something other than simple failure or welcome release."[5] On the other side of the matter we have Paul Henry Lang, in his once widely circulated history, *Music in Western Civilization*, dwelling on the contribution of Brahms in a thoroughly disparaging manner, singling out, for example, "his penchant for complications" and "the willful interference of the learned connoisseur of the past" in what might otherwise be inspired music. According to Lang, Brahms sensed the likelihood that with his music Classicism would reach the end of the line and the music he wrote consequently expressed his regret: for example, passages like the coda in the first movement of the Second Symphony which were "filled with the deepest sorrow, with the noblest resignation, for he knew that they rightfully belong to another world. The pessimistic tone becomes at times so acute that one actually hears the strains of funeral music. . . ."[6]

The breach between those of our persuasion (i.e., the Stravinsky camp) and the serialists has been exaggerated. It was and still is the kind of issue in which the press delights. Indeed, as recently as 3 August 1997 an article under the by-line of the late K. Robert Schwartz appeared in the *New York Times* with the headline, "In Contemporary Music, a House Still Divided," which dug up the old controversy and attempted to get more mileage out of it. The friction that did exist between the young Stravinskians and serialists was scarcely judicious, since we were all accomplices on trial before the public for the same offense and in unity there might have been some strength. The antagonism between the two groups was trivial compared to the public's antagonism toward both. Nevertheless, the serialists tended to be condescending. They considered themselves the intellectuals, and we were a bunch of opportunistic composers pandering to public taste.

It is still believed in some quarters that the neoclassic music's admittedly greater accessibility was what must have fueled the movement. On the contrary, what much of the public saw in middle-period Stravinsky was a gross mishandling of their favorite older masters. They would rather, for example, have had their Bach untouched. If audiences had had it in their power, I used to think, they would have followed the example of the Boston police who marched into Symphony Hall in 1944 and enjoined a performance of Stravinsky's arrangement of the "Star-Spangled Banner" which was about to be repeated under his baton at the second of the weekend concerts of the Boston Symphony Orchestra, offered in conformance with a wartime directive that the anthem be played at the start of every concert. It seems that according to a Massachusetts law any "tampering"

72 / Twentieth-Century American Composition

with the national anthem or any other national property was prohibited, and evidently when the "Star-Spangled Banner" had been played the day before (14 January 1944), the authorities had been informed. At that first performance the audience started to sing along according to the custom. But as reported in a special news item in the *New York Herald Tribune* the next day, "soon the odd, somewhat dissonant harmonies of the sixty-one-year-old composer became evident. Eyebrows lifted and voices faltered," and before long everyone gave up trying to sing along.[7] Stravinsky conducted the singing with his back to the orchestra, and in one of his conversations with Craft he seems to have had a different interpretation of the occasion. As he recalled it the audience did not sing along, but this did not prevent him from concluding that "no one seemed to notice that my arrangement was different from the standard offering."[8]

At one time, in order to counter cries of how unnatural it was to "turn back," I thought it important to demonstrate the logic of Stravinsky's abandonment of his "Russian" period style and to make it perfectly clear that the merit of a given work was not established by the degree to which it conformed to some foregone requirement of what historical progress should or must objectively be.[9] This was not difficult to do. We live at a time when interest in the music of the past far exceeds interest in music of the present. This interest has brought an enormous amount of old music to light in scholarly critical editions that make every effort to transmit it in authentic form, in contrast to nineteenth-century musicians (Busoni, for instance) who prided themselves on making Bach sound like Brahms.

There is no reason why an artist should be expected to develop logically, no reason at all why he should need a passport to enter any terrain that beckons him, no reason why he cannot change direction in midstream. But in the thirties the social dialecticians who cautioned us against Schoenberg's lucubrations also considered Stravinsky's new approach, as one leftist commentator put it, a sad casualty of the "prepotency of bourgeois forces"—a high-flown phrase that has stayed with me for over half a century though I do not know where I read or heard it. In donning the cloak of internationalism, Stravinsky, it was alleged, had deliberately detached himself from his native land as if he were embarrassed by its political situation, thereby cutting himself off from the sources that were at the root of his inspiration.

The assimilation of artistic to political ideologies in the thirties was not exclusively a phenomenon of Communism as it was in the case of the Seegers to which I referred in the first chapter. An American composer of French origin who called himself Dane Rudhyar to underline his dedication to Hindu theosophy was quite prophetic in 1927 when he foresaw the horrors of Fascism, "the great reactionary and hyper-nationalistic movement that was sweeping Europe," as augury of the closing tableau of European civilization. And he bemoaned the fact that composers, not Stravinsky alone but most of them, were assuming a stance that ought to be called "musical fascism." He saw Darius Milhaud as "perhaps the first," and also included along with Stravinsky such figures as Hindemith and Casella, and "even" Schoenberg. As a theosophist he was steeped in the ancient traditions of the East, and he thus advocated that if there was to be any "going back" it should be to primitive Eastern sources before art was tainted by European culture. He was probably one of the first of our now fashionable multiculturists. According to Rudhyar it would seem that almost no one was innocent.[10]

I find this idea of musical fascism as unconvincing as the motivations the Communists ascribed to Stravinsky. It is all out of a desperation to explain Stravinsky's direction on the part of those who find it absolutely beyond their comprehension. Suppose it were something as insignificant as Serge Diaghilev's request for a ballet score based on Pergolesi that kindled Stravinsky's interest in utilizing the music of the past in some way, much as Robert Craft is said, by introducing him to the literature of serialism, to be responsible for the composer's conversion to twelve-tone method. Would it render the evolution any less viable? Many motives have been suggested as having precipitated Stravinsky's neoclassicism and among them none are more ingenious than those proposed by that formidable scholar of his "Russian" period, Richard Taruskin, brilliant historian though he admittedly is, who has made a career out of deconstructing the neoclassic Stravinsky, thus giving further credence, as if any were needed, to the average listener's notion that the composer's progress was all downhill from the end of the "Russian" period.[11] Taruskin quotes the French critic Jacques Rivière who wrote of the *Rite* at the time of its premiere that it was in reality "absolutely pure . . . no veils and no poetic sweeteners; *not a trace of atmosphere . . . everything is crisp, intact, clear, and crude.*" And more, "Never have we heard a *music so magnificently limited.*"[12] This prompted Taruskin to observe, "One is tempted at this point to say that by hailing Stravinsky as an 'anti-Debussyste' and a Classicist in *The Rite*, Rivière in effect turned him into one."[13] On another front Taruskin argues, "So far from an investment in the 'German stem,' the *'retour à Bach'* was an attempt to hijack the Father [an allusion to the once fashionable literary thinker Harold Bloom], to wrest the old contrapuntist from his errant countrymen (who with their abnormal 'psychology' had betrayed his purity, his health-giving austerity, his dynamism, his detached and transcendent craft) and restore him to a properly elite station." And further, "Until old age—until he made peace with 'the German stem' Stravinsky paraded himself as 'Wagner's Antichrist.'"[14]

The French neo-Catholic philosopher Jacques Maritain in his seminal book on aesthetics *Art et Scolastique* (Art and Scholasticism) which he started to write in 1918 (a few years after the *Rite* came out) coupled Stravinsky with Wagner among composers whose music would "debauch the ear." But when he did the second edition Maritain evidently came around to Rivière's view and revoked his decision in a footnote that reads in part:

> Je m'accuse d'avoir ainsi parlé de Stravinsky. Je ne connaissais encore que le *Sacre du Printemps*, j'aurais dû voir déjà que Stravinsky tournait le dos à tout ce que nous choque dans Wagner. . . . son oeuvre admirablement disciplinée . . . répond le mieux à la stricte rigeur classique. . . .
> [I regret having thus spoken of Stravinsky. All I had heard was the *Rite of Spring*, and I should have perceived then that Stravinsky was turning his back on everything we find distasteful in Wagner. . . . his admirably disciplined work . . . best answers the strict classical "austerity. . . ."][15]

As I have already indicated, I am *not* convinced that Stravinsky's taking up residence in America is what determined his influence among young American composers, though they both happened around the same time and his presence may have helped. Yet it was altogether appropriate that the movement should have Harvard as its locus and should have had its beginnings just when Stravinsky delivered the prestigious Charles Eliot Norton lectures there (1939–40). Also Nadia Boulanger, who would have spawned the movement without any help from the master, came to Cambridge in 1938 as visiting faculty at the Longy School of Music and remained through most of the war years. (Stravinsky said she knew more about his music than he did.) A whole cluster of circumstances was favorable to the burgeoning of a Stravinsky school. Not least among them was the presence of Walter Piston as the senior composition teacher at Harvard with his neoclassic leanings, for example, and especially the powerful influence of humanism over the intellectual attitude of faculty and students of the entire university as a result of the long tenure of the distinguished proponent of the humanist movement Irving Babbitt. Babbitt's remonstrances against Romanticism echoed and reechoed through the corridors of that hallowed institution for many years after he had departed from it.

Stravinsky's allusions to the music of the past were not directed toward achieving results that would be modeled after the sources, since the interpolated material could be willfully distorted, like the human bodies in Picasso's cubist paintings, or cut into bits and pieces as if they were to be used for a collage. Scraps of newspaper in this process are not usually chosen for their verbal content. Painters do not expect them to be read. What is at issue is the shape and texture and how they relate to other shapes and textures on the same canvas. The listener whose attention is arrested at the point where a musical fragment evokes its past is like the viewer who spends his time reading the newsprint on the scrap of paper of the collage. To the extent that Stravinsky subsumed linear shapes, methods, and ideas from the general practice of the music of the Classical era he was doing something not altogether unlike what he had been doing when he compiled ready-made Russian folksong, though in the end the methods, aim, and result were very different. By the time he did the same thing with Classical music it was just as much in public domain as his folk sources. In a very real sense, moreover, as many listeners will agree, the Classical sources never really disguised the real Stravinsky: there was still a strong residue of his native rhythmic heritage that animated his later works. Michael Tilson Thomas has observed, "Even in his abstract music . . . there was an organic dance-rooted quality." Further, as a conductor "he made gestures and let out moans, grunts, and gasps—the kind of thing one could associate with peasant dance and song."[16]

The late pianist-composer Leo Smit observed, "When Stravinsky reworked older material, it became something so new that even the composer himself became confused at times over where the other left off and Stravinsky began."[17] Smit told me about an encounter with the master in the forties at one of the gatherings of musicians my late first wife Esther and I had at our apartment in New York when the subject came up of *Baiser de la fée* (The Fairy's Kiss), the ballet based on Tchaikovsky. He asked Stravinsky where in Tchaikovsky did he find the theme of the fortune-teller. Stravinsky replied that he wrote it himself, but years later Smit found it in a Tchaikovsky song, "Oh Pain, Oh Pleasure," the key having been changed from A major to A minor. (In one of the many conversations with Craft in a book published in 1962 Stravinsky admitted, "At this date I only vaguely remember which music is Tchaikovsky's and which mine.")[18]

In the matter of the "return to the past" among the members of the Harvard Stravinsky school there was, as I have indicated, one exception who took it seriously, and that was Harold Shapero, arguably the most talented of us all, whose talent was occluded for most listeners behind the grid of his unabashedly Classical allusion—allusion to Beethoven in particular. The problem of penetrating the grid to reach the undoubtedly personal aspect of his music suggests to my mind what was true in the opposite sense of the *Rite* in 1913 when it was new. In the first of his Norton lectures at Harvard (delivered in French), Stravinsky said:

> Dans le tumulte des opinions contradictoires, mon ami Maurice Ravel intervint presque seul pour mettre les choses au point. Il a su voir et il a dit que la nouveauté du *Sacre* ne résidait pas dans l'écriture, dans l'instrumentation, dans l'appareil technique de l'oeuvre, mais dans l'entité musicale. [In the tumult of contradictory opinions my friend Maurice Ravel intervened practically alone to set matters right. He was able to see, and he said, that the novelty of the *Rite* consisted, not in the "writing," not in the orchestration, not in the technical apparatus of the work, but in the musical entity.][19]

Hearers were so overwhelmed by what they considered revolutionary in the *Rite* that they failed to perceive, as we do now, that it was essentially a further stage in Impressionism. The values of traditional and modern are reversed in Shapero's case. To apprehend his individuality within the outward veneer of conservatism will take time, application, and a willing attitude, just as, contrariwise, the capacity to apprehend the traditional in the *Rite* did. I am reasonably sure the individuality is there since one can detect its influence when it shows up in a disciple like Leo Smit, or in Shapero's peers, Bernstein, Irving Fine, and perhaps myself as well.

Shapero's *Symphony for Classical Orchestra* completed in 1947 when he was twenty-seven was acclaimed by Stravinsky and Copland and promptly performed a year later under the baton of Bernstein, who recorded it for Columbia Records. But despite this illustrious beginning Shapero's composing activity tapered off in a manner that some of us have found puzzling. Could it have been the backlash that set in early on that discouraged him? A little over a year after Bernstein gave the symphony's premiere with the BSO, for instance, the League of Composers presented Shapero's lengthy Sonata in F minor at New York's Museum of Modern Art, and it created what I should not quite call a riot, but certainly a decided turmoil. (My review of the concert in the *New York Herald Tribune*, 8 March 1949, will be found in the appendix.) George Perle, the composer (twelve-tone at the time but more recently involved with an interesting system of his own) and the author of the invaluable introductory *Serial Composition and Atonality*,[20] stood up and shouted, "Viva Beethoven!" I wonder if the antagonism would have been as great if Shapero had made it better known how much he consciously strove to achieve Beethoven's *grande ligne?* Even as a "homage to a Classical composer" it would still be a triumph, with a beauty and sensitivity quite its own. The expectation, the mindset can have a great deal to do with how one hears music—the assurance that the composer is not trying to put something over is a positive element.

On the other hand, things can be pretty awkward when the mindset and the actual experience clash, as in the case of the former powerful *Times* critic Olin Downes, who was vehemently opposed to Stravinsky's internationalism even before it evolved into neoclassicism and who was positive he would hate any music cast in that mode. Thus, he had to go through some pretty ridiculous linguistic contortions when he found that a Stravinsky piece which in principle he should not have liked was actually to his taste, though his conviction of its allegedly unsavory backward-looking aesthetic should have dictated otherwise: "*Histoire du Soldat* appeared after he had ceased to be creative. . . . Perhaps some of the inertia of the creative will, the despair of sterility, contribute to the effectiveness of this score. Stravinsky of obviously waning powers achieves from his very decline something of a masterpiece."[21] (There is a certain irony in the circumstance that Downes's convoluted reasoning is not unlike what Lang—quoted earlier in this chapter—had to say about Brahms, since basically the two composers are so different from each other.) Downes was a master of the art of reversing his position without seeming to contradict himself. Another review that demonstrates his legerdemain in this matter dealt with *Apollon musagète* on the occasion of its world premiere in Washington, D.C., on 27 April 1928, when after constantly complaining about Stravinsky's unwarranted harking back to the past Downes now saw it, so we may gather from his *Times* review, as the "effort, the heroic effort, of an artist who turned away from the anarchies of the present and tried to retrace his steps . . . ," thus employing what was formerly his negative criterion as a positive one.

Shapero may have been a charter member of the young Harvard Stravinskians, but he never went in much for the interrupted line, the jagged shapes, the precipitous cutting, the dissonance, the hiccups and asymmetry of rhythm, the skeletal texture and other such devices of Stravinsky that appealed to the rest of us. These were what characterized the master's music of his so-called neoclassic period and distinguished him from others who have been designated "neoclassicists"—Hindemith and Prokofiev, for example—and these were the aspects of the master's music that were for us an incentive. It is not at all unlikely that if Shapero's symphony were composed today without the stigma of being neoclassic it would be accepted as a representative product of the new Romanticism. (Beethoven, let us not forget, was at the crossroads of two tendencies.) From this perspective it may be true, as John Rockwell claims, that "composers today are seek-ing various ways to escape the trap of a too rigid linearity. Starting as far back as the neoclassicism between the wars, composers began to plunder the past, to elevate long outmoded ideas to a fresh contemporaneity."[22] But the statement requires some qualification, since neoclassicism is a modernist movement in which a certain tension is provoked between the past and present, while the recent new Romanticism has been frankly a "going back." Within the ambience of postmodernism, new Romanticists have felt perfectly free to appropriate outrightly any given idiom of the past. According to the literary critic Denis Donoghue, modernism was "doom-laden," an "embattled state in which a degree of unity—of appre-hension if not of being—is possible," in contrast to postmodernism, which is "debonaire."[23]

It is idle to quibble about labels but I have some trouble calling the new Romanticists "neoromantic," since that locution was used by Virgil Thom-son for a movement that originated in France, particularly among painters, including Eugene Berman. The chief musical representative of the move-ment was Henri Sauguet, and Thomson singled out Irving Fine as its American representative. What distinguished neoromanticism was its evo-cation of *early* Romanticism, the intimacy and unpretentiousness of Schu-bert or Schumann before the genre was puffed up with the grandiosity of Wagner and Mahler.

The new Romanticists to whom Rockwell was referring included com-posers like George Rochberg and David Del Tredici. A contemporary Ro-manticist who does not "go back" to the past is Leon Kirchner. The whole atonal movement, despite its preference for condensation, ironically had some roots in Wagner and Mahler, evident in the Gargantuan *Gurrelieder* and the hyper-Romantic *Transfigured Night.* Kirchner's powerful and in-tensely felt music picks up the thread where Schoenberg and Berg left it be-fore they became engaged in a more rigorously organized approach to se-rialism. For Kirchner, despite some serial elements, it is almost as if strict serialism never existed, but it has not been his aim to return to the nine-teenth century. Nor was a return, in his case to the eighteenth century, the aim of Stravinsky and his satellites, as I have already said, when they had recourse to eighteenth-century models. The idea was, rather, to challenge, to have a struggle with the compiled elements. (At one point Stravinsky used to tell us it was his form of "criticism.") The new uses to which the compiled materials were put truly constituted their "reinvention."

In listening to this music, if one does not assume the role of tune detective, dispensing demerits upon every allegedly "illegal" allusion to other music, one must inevitably be aware of the ingenuity and invention that can be found to be there, its accessibility not at all occluded as it might be in, say, Webern or Xenakis by difficulty or strange modernist procedure, but clearly audible to the sympathetic and attentive listener. Coached by musicographers of all types (historians as well as critics) to believe that "looking back" is unnatural, audiences are only too happy to have an excuse to drop any music considered "unnatural"—especially if it is new music such as this—from their usual repertory, and to use their listening time instead to bask in the warmly familiar, unchallenging company of their customary "fifty pieces." True, a work like the *Rake* is not entirely neglected, but why should it not be a staple, like *Der Rosenkavalier*? And there are all those orchestral masterpieces of the thirties and forties we almost never hear and for my taste are still too infrequently played: *Jeu de cartes* (A Game of Cards), *Danses concertantes*, "Dumbarton Oaks" Concerto, the "Basle" Concerto, and the two symphonies. Also, *Perséphone* and *Oedipus Rex*, the two choral masterpieces.

The last time I saw Stravinsky it was on the West Coast, shortly before he died. I bemoaned with him the sad fact that we heard so little of his music of this epoch at concerts, or even in recordings on the air. He looked at me with a glint in his eyes that prepared me for one of his characteristic barbs, and said, "Only my *Scheherazade* they play." I think of this when composers of my generation—or I myself—complain that they don't play our music. We have scarce reason to complain when they don't even do justice to Stravinsky. Incidentally, I thought he coined the witticism on the spot until I found it in an entry to his diary for 15 December 1961. When proudly told somewhere in New Zealand that half a program of his works had once been given he thought to himself, "my *Scheherazade* no doubt." [24]

When I refer to the accessibility of Stravinsky's music of this middle period I have in mind a certain phenomenon that is characteristic of some great art through the ages (though it is not obligatory for any artist to conform to this prescription). As in Shakespeare or Mozart it is as if the music operates on two levels. The blood and thunder, the intrigues in Shakespeare, or

Ex. 9. Stravinsky Chords

the catchy tunes and rhythmic symmetry in Mozart are enough for some people, who may be quite unaware anything else is there to apprehend. But this is to overlook the subtleties on several parameters: for example, the way in which under Stravinsky's ministrations the ordinary traditional harmony textbook triads undergo an extraordinary metamorphosis, animated by new doublings, spacing, and chord superpositions (not to be confused with polytonality). I have already quoted the opening E-minor chord of *Symphony of Psalms* (Ex. 7a above), in which the most banal traditional textbook triad is transformed into something wondrous the likes of which we never heard before. (Most of the chords are not so obviously based on simple triads as this one is.) Being able to discriminate among these various sonorities and to be sensitive to their beauty is like what a connoisseur of fine wines is capable of doing. In Example 9 the reader will find some of Stravinsky's typical widely spaced and otherwise unusual chords. Often it is simply a metamorphosis resulting from the addition of one non-chord tone to the pitch content of a traditional triad. What makes all the difference is the unconventional spacing and doubling.

It may very well be that Debussy's concern for timbre had something to do with Stravinsky's choice of unusual spacing and doubling. But there seems to have been more to it than that. He once confided in me, when we

Ex. 10. Beethoven, "Diabelli" Variations, No. XXI

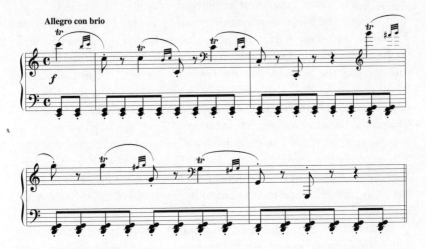

were discussing Shapero's wide chord and linear spacing which Stravinsky referred to as "l'écartemente" (separation), that he himself, like Shapero, had been inspired in the employment of this device by Beethoven. Stravinsky must have been referring to such instances as the opening of Number 21 of the "Diabelli" Variations, Op. 120 (Ex. 10). He worked at the piano and he was fortunate to have large hands capable of negotiating the stretches in widely spaced chords without rolling them. Stravinsky once showed me that he could easily play an octave with his second and fifth fingers, which made me understand how he was prompted to write the trill in the *Arietta* of the *Concerto for two solo pianos:* an A-flat with the thumb and, with the second and fifth fingers, the adjacent B-flat plus its octave above.

Being sensitive to the precise quality of the chords is only one of the requirements for hearing what is essential in neoclassic Stravinsky. There is the matter of the pitch organization which, because it is often diatonic and may have a pitch priority analogous to the traditional tonic, lends itself to relaxed listening in which one might fancy one hears tonality though the music is essentially nontonal. In my analysis of one of the parameters of *Psalms* I have drawn attention to the stratification that made it difficult to decide whether E or G had priority. A somewhat different bifurcation is encountered in the *Serenade in A,* where the title leads us to expect A as tone center, and A major or A minor as the basic key. But it turns out we have the pitch collection (notes or scale degrees) of F major in which the segment starting on A is Phrygian, and unlike myriad English and French modal works of the century, it exploits dialectically the symbiotic relation between the two pitch priorities (A and F). For example, the recurrent F-major triad has the A italicized somewhat in the way the G was italicized in the *Psalms* chord. The Symphony in C exploits the same major third relationship as the *Serenade* but the functions are reversed so that C, the lower note in the dyad, has ultimate priority. In the symphony, Phrygian E quite noticeably infiltrates the C-major domain. It may be quite unnecessary, but I repeat the warning that it is not a question of polytonality. It is a question, rather, of a single collection of pitches (or pitch classes, as our Princeton theorists would have us say) with two different interval orderings and two different tone centers or pitch priorities a major third apart that have a symbiotic relation to each other by virtue of their shared pitch collection.[25]

Once again we are up against the difficulties of verbalizing, for these are fairly simple operations to hear, but they may sound complicated, even— that forbidding epithet—"intellectual" when described. I shall investigate later the relationship between such formulations and the proper apprehension of music as heard (see chapter 13).

6   Serialism: Composer as Theorist

When I paid a visit to Arnold Schoenberg in 1941 at his Hollywood abode I found I had to approach the house through an ornate massive iron gate behind which, next to a small pool, two huge St. Bernards were barking menacingly at me and Esther who accompanied me. We were fearful (at least I was) of the dogs, so instead of opening the gate and walking in, we rang the bell, and when there was no answer we drove to the nearest gas station and phoned. Schoenberg said that because of the wet weather the bell wasn't working, but the dogs would not harm us and we should simply walk in past them. We followed the instructions and were ushered into a daintily furnished room, obviously a parlor for visitors that did not look lived in—no casually placed papers or magazines, no books that I recall. It was not an ambience in which I expected to find Schoenberg, who was anything but the "clean-cut" type, as the saying goes.

The meeting had been arranged by Darius Milhaud, a more recent refugee than Schoenberg from besieged Europe. Milhaud had been (with my consent as leading composition teacher) appointed visiting professor at Mills College during my second year on the faculty, and was then accorded tenure to replace me thereafter (his salary to be paid by a wealthy San Francisco family). We had become close friends and Milhaud was "désolé" that I was being terminated, so he thought Schoenberg might help get me hired at University of California–Los Angeles, where he was then a tenured professor. Schoenberg asked me whether I knew anyone on the board of trustees of his university since he thought that was the way one got a job in America. I didn't, so that was that, and we then talked about other things. I had a greeting to deliver from Milhaud: "Mille baisers pour petit Arnold" (a thousand kisses for little Arnold). Looking at the austere and sour expression on Schoenberg's face, I did not dare to bring to my lips such a light-hearted sentiment. We talked of the state of music and one remark he made in the course of the conversation astonished me and remains with me verbatim and vividly: "In ten years they will be teaching my twelve-tone composition [it is important to note that he did not say 'system'] in the American high schools." I have often wondered if Milton Babbitt had not, just a bit later in the decade, done his work of systematizing and attempting to explicate Schoenberg's compositional approach with recourse to set theory et al., whether the prophesy might have stood a chance, not a big chance, of turning out to be true. I was inclined to agree with Babbitt, on the other hand, when he maintained more recently, in an impromptu remark, that "Schoenberg's fantasy—that his twelve-tone system would one day win out and result in one musical language arising again—was preposterous."[1]

It was certainly no surprise that at the beginning Babbitt's theories met with a good deal of dissension, mostly from older musicians who had been born too early to have been brought up with the new math and were unfamiliar with or unreceptive to positivist philosophical thinking. A certain amount of density and complexity in its concepts was to be expected in the explication of a new musical language, especially in one that was so dependent on numerical relations. After all, serialism was undergoing birth pains similar to those that tonality, which it aimed to replace, must have undergone at the start of the eighteenth century. Readers of Jean-Philippe Rameau's *Traité d'Harmonie* (Treatise on Harmony) in 1722 when it was published must have had difficulty with its codification of the rules of harmony, a difficulty compounded by what its English translator Philip Gossett characterized as the "tortuous lines of thought" in its explication.[2] The Princeton school, which is how it has been known since Babbitt was a professor at the university, took upon itself a similar responsibility, and we expected it to be difficult, but we were not prepared for quite such an esoteric language—especially trying for those of us who were not at ease in science—that aimed at brushing away the cobwebs, the ambiguities, the metaphysical baggage of traditional musicography, not only in the treatment of serial music, but in that of any music at all. Ironically it introduced other impediments. The process of cleaning up the language did not make it clearer and friendlier for many of us, for, in the words of its pilot: ". . . there is but one kind of language, one kind of method for the verbal formulation of concepts and the verbal analysis of such formulations: 'scientific' language and 'scientific' method. . . . our concern is not whether music has been, is, can be, will be, or should be a science, whatever that may be assumed to mean, but simply that statements about music must conform to those verbal and methodological requirements which attend the possibility of meaningful discourse in any domain."[3] (Babbitt was addressing a learned audience of musicologists.)

New terms were to be expected, and so were concepts that would be difficult at first. But I am not sure many of us were ready for a situation in which language formation would become an end in itself. It seemed, moreover, to have been spawned by a desire at first to keep the discoveries private, and little attempt was made to define the proliferation of new terms for the outsider.

I argued with the true believers over why some perfectly ordinary terms had to be changed: for example, "simultaneity" for chord, or "set" for the original expressions "row" or "series" (still used abroad), even though I granted that set theory might be useful in dealing with operations performed on the row. The response I received was that some of it was ordinary language, and there should be no difficulty understanding the new terms. That was not to my satisfaction and when I raised the problem with my friend Noam Chomsky he suggested an analogy that was very revealing. I don't recall his exact words but I can paraphrase it. Suppose we came across the following sentence: The *letter-sequences* "boy" and "lad" may be said to be fairly synonymous and each "letter-sequence" has three letters in one syllable. We could figure out from the context what "letter-sequence" meant, but we would want a good reason why a new term for anything as commonplace as "word" is needed. A new term ("simultaneity") for chord seems hardly necessary though I admit it is an attractive concept. I did not find it convincing when I was told it was necessary simply because chords have evolved to a point where they are very different from the traditional textbook triadic type and a new term would pay tribute to that difference—if indeed my informant was a reliable spokesman of the movement. As I see it they are still chords, even if they are merely the convergence of contrapuntal lines and are not built in thirds like traditional triads and seventh and ninth chords.

Jean Piaget has established that the child is capable of "concrete operation" at the age of seven and by adolescence acquires a capacity of abstraction, recognizing that a fixed quantity of liquid, for example, does not change when it is poured into a differently shaped vessel.⁴ It is surprising that despite its capacity for abstraction on so many levels the Princeton school should have found the ordinary language locution "chord" inadequate to refer to the simple event of two or more pitches being struck simultaneously. True, "simultaneity" may be useful for those times when it is appropriate to draw attention to the fact that the convergence of pitches came about as a consequence of linear operations. But it seems to me we should be able to use the locution "chord" without summoning up the ghosts of tonally functional triadic harmony. Just as Piaget's quantity of liquid remains fixed through all changes of shape, so the chord can be a fixed element (namely a "chord") though its content, shape, structure may vary along a vast, unlimited continuum from simple triad to tone cluster. (The Piaget is a very loose analogy but I trust my point is evident.)

In the years when I was more deeply involved in Princeton thinking I myself, I should confess, sometimes felt that the old words did not convey my thought since I did not have confidence in the reader's ability to separate the signifier from implications it had accumulated over time. I was dealing with the diatonic modes in "Problems of Pitch Organization in Stravinsky," published in *Perspectives of New Music (PNM)* in 1963,⁵ and I was concerned over the baggage the modes had accumulated over the centuries as the mainstay in Greek and medieval music and especially the associations that clung to them as a result of their evocations of the gentle pastoral in some early modern music of Impressionist leaning. And so I called them simply "scales" and distinguished them from one another thus: "D-scale" (Dorian), "E-scale" (Phrygian), etc. As I look back it seems to have been quite unnecessary. (I should add that I'm aware it is nowhere on the grand scale of Princeton terminology but, as one who has complained as loudly as anyone about the new esoteric Princeton language, I feel I should report my complicity in the hope it may help me avoid the remonstration "you did it too.")

Some of us wrote twelve-tone music without observing the rules promulgated by what I once named the "New Theorists" of the Princeton school, with New Criticism of the American literary domain in the back of my mind—something Joseph Kerman was quick to pick up (see chapter 14). Such composers were considered not "strict" but, after all, Schoenberg had also written twelve-tone music without the benefit of the Princeton theorists. By the sixties composers at various stages of twelve-tone composition had proliferated, and it was clear that the title the neoclassic Stravinsky had held as chief influence over young American composers since about the middle thirties was being wrested from him even before his own surprising conversion when he threw in his lot with Schoenberg.

Serial composers were designated cerebral and academic even if they were outside the learned Princeton circle. This was because they had to be constantly vigilant to be sure that they were operating within the discipline of serialism. It was quite unlike what was required of tonal composers or the pre-serial composers of this century. Besides being brought up on tonal music, most composers had to spend two or more years studying its theory and practice, so the process of choosing notes, harmonies, rhythms, etc. *seemed* to be guided to a considerable extent by intuition, but was actually the product of long and rigorous drilling. As with riding a bicycle, you drew upon your previous instruction without having to commune with yourself in discursive terms to find out what to do next. Whether such a state will ever be attained in the relationship of most of us to serial composition is hard to say, though some people seem to have reached it already. But the processes that govern the composing methods need not insinuate themselves into the process of directly apprehending the heard result. It is nigh impossible to persuade listeners and critics that this is so—that is to say, that they do not need some special password they had never needed for the music written before.

At the same time the necessity of responding to the requirements of a discipline of such rigorous intellectual caliber as serialism has made theorists out of some composers in a way that has had no precedent in recent centuries (though it could have been found among medieval composers).[6] And this, in turn, was an advantage to composers who sought, for their very survival, some escape in the universities from the alternative of having to cope with the commercialism of the marketplace, such as it is. Stravinsky warned young composers to stay away from university teaching. He was concerned about the conformity that it bred. There is a danger that in the scholarly papers required from faculty by the university for advancement, professors of music will try too hard to conform to the standard of fellow faculty in science and philosophy, and drive music theory further than it already is into the mire of scientific obscurantism. There also is a question of the public image, the upholders (critics in particular) of the age-old complaint that new music is too "academic" now being able to point to the tangible evidence that can be adduced from a composer's lifestyle—claiming, namely, that composers are writing academic music because they are in fact academicians.

The theories that Babbitt has constructed, though difficult to follow, have done much to illuminate serial practice for some of us in the way Heinrich Schenker, very loosely speaking, illuminated tonality. I have felt, however, that those close to Babbitt could have done a better job explicating the language for those of us who were at a distance. Instead they were concerned with using the language to add their own scientific constructs. I have in mind such theorists as Ben Boretz, Godfrey Winham, Jim Randall, Michael Kassler, Philip Batstone, and John Rahn, the cream of the intellectuals. One had to understand the language to recognize that they all had different concepts to advance, but for some of us on the outside they seemed to be saying somewhat the same thing as Babbitt and one another. We should have welcomed the kind of simple explanations that were provided by Gerald Warfield in his cogent annotations for Babbitt's "Some Aspects of Twelve-tone Composition"—the seminal article originally published in *Score and I. M. A. Magazine* in 1955—when it was reprinted in *Twentieth Century Views of Music History* in 1972.[7] Unfortunately it was fifteen or twenty years late.

Even so elementary a matter as Babbitt's numbering the members of a twelve-tone row (which he called "set" after set theory) from zero to eleven was puzzling to some of us at first. For many of my generation our indoctrination into the rites of twelve-tonery had been the English translation of a French treatise by René Leibowitz and we numbered the twelve tones as the Europeans still do, from one to twelve.[8] Not everyone of my generation was brought up with instruction in the new math, with its set theory and concepts such as Mod. 12. Nor were we privileged with the intelligence that the numbering of the row zero to eleven had analytical advantages: for example, among other things, that under this convention the interval number of any member of the set plus the interval number of its inversion would be twelve. Ultimately, however, it made a good deal of sense to me, and was even a revelation, something some of us had never thought about. Namely, the numbering made it evident to me that we were counting intervals, not notes. When the first member of the row is sounded there is no interval (though I realize some perfectionist might insist there could be a unison).[9]

Very likely Babbitt never thought anyone would have trouble with a matter like this, which is how I thought when I did this sort of thing in a small way, updating the names for the modes. I bring it up because I have been someone who has complained loudly about the new terminology. To be truthful, therefore, I must admit that I joined the club well before Babbitt came upon the scene, as Edward T. Cone was to remind me in his 1965 essay "A Budding Grove." [10] This was a witty article that attempted to come to grips with the plethora of new terminology, and it surprised me with its listing of a term I had employed, "white-note," referring to diatonic writing with no or almost no added accidentals (no notes out of the collection or, as in traditional music, out of the key). We used the term in our group of Harvard Stravinskians around 1940 and we thought it was perfectly obvious what it meant. The Greek chroma is "color," therefore, the absence of *chromatic* alteration would result in a situation "without color"—ergo "white." Also the exemplary diatonic scale, C major, without chromatic alterations consists of the white keys. That Europeans used a numbering of the twelve tones of the row from one to twelve, which only seemed natural, and we, following the example of the Princeton theorists, found ourselves obliged to use a numbering from zero to eleven led to confusion at first for many of us. We soon, however, became accustomed to it and accepted it as still another instance of the general kind of diversity of local usages that confines some people in the world to the duodecimal system and others to the metric for measurements, etc.

When I took exception to Milton's advocacy of scientific language for music theory I had to remind myself of my admiration for Aristoxenos, the ancient Greek father of all Western theorists of harmony, who could call his contribution scientific, yet carefully distinguish it from the scientism of his contemporary Pythagoras and insist on the judgment of the ear. Where Babbitt's language was concerned, outside of terms borrowed from set theory it was not the scientific orientation that caused us most trouble but our conviction that the concepts were difficult enough without the additional burden of the occult language in which they were conveyed. There was much discussion of obscurantism in the early days of the Princeton theorists, though it failed to give rise to a sufficiently clear and explicit elucidation on a large scale. Even their mouthpiece *PNM* aired the dilemma many of us found ourselves in. There were three almost consecutive early contributions dealing with the matter. I have already mentioned one of them, Cone's glossary, an article that had a good-natured appendix in which the author amusingly discusses serial music in "ordinary language" and then in "up-to-date musical parlance." He lets Babbitt down gently, observing, rather too generously in my view, that the way Milton would refer back to his first use of a term was "a model of correct scholarly practice." In my experience I did not find this too often to be true, and where it was true it was not sufficient to clarify the terms.

Another article on the subject of terminology in *PNM* appeared in 1966, in which a composer of no mean intellectual attainment, Ernst Krenek, expressed himself angrily:

> . . . many terms currently in use belong to a vocabulary lying outside of the scope of usual musical terminology. For all we know, they belong to the jargon of the special branch of mathematics known as set-theory. The application of this language to musical matters can be understood only by individuals who are at home in both fields. This group is limited to those graduates of Princeton University who have attended the courses of Milton Babbitt, who is in the enviable position of being an eminent musician as well as a distinguished scientist.[11]

The first of the triad of pieces in *PNM* dealing with this subject was my own: "New Linguistic Modes and the New Theory" (1963), which I have used as the basis for chapter 14.[12]

Composers, as I have already remarked (and as it is very well known), spend a minimum of two years mastering tonal theory and often considerably more during their student days. It should not be surprising that they should also have to spend time studying twelve-tone method. In the early days of twelve-tonery they had to do so under very different conditions—not while they were getting a preparatory education, since the subject was not yet taught, but while they were already accepted as professionals in the music field. (It is still far from adequately covered in the schools.) Since so many were teachers they had to articulate in a language other than musical notation what their objectives were as composers, not only to be sure that they were properly functioning within the requirements of serial discipline themselves but also to convey to their students the principles and practical methods of placing tones in meaningful relationship.

Whether they present their theoretical notions superbly or inadequately, composer-theorists are liable to be viewed with suspicion, their creativity seriously placed in doubt in the eyes of those who believe that an absorption in directly apprehended qualities is upset beyond repair by any digression into discursive thinking or talking about those qualities, and above all by the type of analysis summarily dismissed as "technical" (implying that the most penetrating critico-structural investigation, largely by virtue of its illustrations in music notation and its charts, is on the same level as, say, a handbook on trumpet fingering). It is ironic that those who feel that taking a work apart is like pulverizing an object, so that it is no longer recognizable as such, should be wary of music examples as too technical, when in fact they return the analysis to the musical entity. To avariciously guard the creative experience as a very personal and intimately "intuitive," indivisible, and mysterious affair is the prerogative of some composers; and virtually to boast about their total lack of interest in the "technical" not only is their prerogative but, in the case of the generations that came upon the scene before all this self-consciousness and soul-searching began, may even be a justifiable necessity, since their most distressing compositional problems have probably by now been worked through to their satisfaction, and to a point where doubt may be inhibiting. Theodore Chanler, a much underrated twentieth-century composer, mainly of songs—and not incidentally a person of considerable intellectual attainment—nicely presents the case of the mature composer who would rather not confront his inspirations to see and understand what it is he has done: "The trouble with musical analysis, which assigns a function to each part of a whole, is that artists have perverse mentalities: once they know the reason for a thing it ceases to interest them. A good deal of the urge towards rational analysis is nothing but a wistfulness towards science, sanity, exactitude, and brass tacks."[13] It is a view I have heard expressed by other composers, including Stravinsky, especially since the advent of the computer and its possibilities as an analytical tool. Unlike Schoenberg, who dropped more than a few hints that led his annotators to the achievement of a thorough knowledge of his organizational methods, Stravinsky was reticent in such matters, seemed to discourage those he would regard as interlopers, and actually exerted a restraining influence upon those who would presume to penetrate his armor.

The opposition to musical analysis since about the mid-twentieth century has been motivated, I believe, by the resentment against its being guided by scientific principles. But there is more than one kind of analysis, more than one kind of theory. Rational human beings (I believe they include composers) are genetically inclined to verbalize experience. (The capacity for language, as Chomsky argues, is innate.) They do so not only for practical purposes, but to ask, often gratuitously, "how," "why," and "what." For the "intuitive" composers to insist there is but one type of composer, the nonanalytic type, is like the most prescriptive reactionary insisting that there is but one way to write music: the traditional way. The skeptical attitude toward the composer-theorist is an aspect of a general antagonism toward music analysis and theory. The artwork is inviolable and anyone who takes it apart to show how it is made commits what is tantamount to a criminal, or rather, perhaps, a sacrilegious, act. Indeed, where the artwork is concerned there is something of a religious component. The masterpiece is to be taken on faith. We dare not question. It is the same sanctimoniousness that prompts many musicians to interdict performances of one or two movements of a three- or four-movement sonata or symphony though this was common practice in the nineteenth century when many of these works were created.

7 Rapprochement or Friendly Takeover?

In the fifties the two leading camps in the world of contemporary composition, the followers of Schoenberg and those of Stravinsky, who had inhabited opposite sides of the barricades for well nigh half a century, finally made peace. The eventuality was sometimes referred to as a "rapprochement," but for some composers, Stravinsky among them, it was actually more like a friendly takeover on the part of the serialists. Or perhaps it would be fairer to say that for Stravinsky and the others it started as a rapprochement (for example, in a work like *Agon*, completed 1957, in which twelve-tone canons remarkably coexist without any clash at all alongside a great deal of dissonant diatonic writing) and culminated in 1959 as a friendly takeover. One could view works like *Movements for Piano and Orchestra*, given the affinity of its idiom to that of the Second Viennese School, especially of Anton Webern, as exemplifying such a process—notwithstanding, at the same time, Stravinsky's unmistakable signature particularly in rhythm. For other composers it never got beyond the stage of rapprochement (Copland, for example). Though the point at which Stravinsky finally abandoned diatonism seemed sudden and ever so surprising, he was no stranger to nondodecaphonic serialism which he had practiced at least since *Symphony of Psalms* but with ideas usually consisting of fewer than twelve tones. Significant examples are the Interlude in *Orpheus* (1947), pp. 45–46 of the orchestra score, and the *Concerto per due pianoforti soli* (1935), from the middle of p. 10. So it was not a case of a sudden volte-face on Stravinsky's part. Yet it seemed like one, since, though it was understood he would adopt the systematic processes of serialism, it was a surprise to some that the result as manifested in *Movements* would be so close in manner to the traditional serialists.

Around the time of his conversion Stravinsky engaged in a bit of deconstruction of recent history that echoed what Boulez had been touting since his celebrated testimony "Schoenberg is dead." Stravinsky made a point of claiming that Schoenberg had a neoclassic phase in the mid-twenties and furthermore that "'neoclassic' now begins to apply to all of the between-the-wars composers. . . . The music of Schoenberg, Berg, and Webern in the twenties was considered extremely iconoclastic at that time but the composers now appear to have used musical form as I did, 'historically.' My use of it was overt, however, and theirs elaborately disguised."[1] Stravinsky warms up to his task of deconstructing history by looking back and placing Schoenberg at that time side by side with himself. "Your so-called period of formulation came only in the late 1920s, with the establishment of so-called 'neoclassicism'—Schoenberg's, Hindemith's, and my own."[2] The idea that Schoenberg had used sonata form and the dances of the Baroque suite was thought to define him as a neoclassicist. Stravinsky boasted of what "Schoenberg and I" had done in this area, and indeed his *Serenade in A* and Schoenberg's Suite Op. 25, piano works composed at almost precisely the same time in the middle twenties, to my way of thinking seem to occupy somewhat the same musical space in the oeuvre of each of them.

All of this fits in with the claim of Boulez, as quoted in an interview, that Schoenberg and Stravinsky "both went wrong by the late twenties, when they tried to adapt their post-tonal harmonic languages to neoclassical forms."[3] Now it seems to me there is a serious misconception here—a confusion between the superficial textbook formula of, say, sonata, fugue, or minuet, and the essential structure of an individual's concrete creative musical production in using these formulae. The choice of one or another conventional form, especially without the functional tonal procedures so essential to them, is a bit like choosing a jacket. The person donning it scarcely changes at all, and what is essential to him or her is not in the jacket but in the nature of the individual wearing it. What I'm trying to say is that sometimes the Classicism was quite superficial and the music that flowed from Schoenberg's pen was essentially modern. Too much is made of the use of the traditional forms which are really surface phenomena to be found in a textbook. The relation to the original music composed under the same titles in the Classical or Baroque eras is either one of name only, or at most an attribute on the outermost plane.

It makes for a neat historical picture to assume that Schoenberg's death in 1951 should have served as the symbolic occasion for Stravinsky's conversion since it could be taken to be a consecration of Schoenberg's contribution as a historical fact, a milestone. And for Stravinsky it would thus be one more historical source upon which to draw, just as he had drawn in the past on the Renaissance, Classicism, and Romanticism. Schoenberg's advocates, not surprisingly, bemoaned the fact that Stravinsky had not made the move before his illustrious contemporary passed away so that the latter could have had the satisfaction of so magnanimous a compliment. But it should not be forgotten how much the clarity, economy, and transparency of serial writing itself served as the catalyst bringing about Stravinsky's move. For those attributes could be defined as Classical attributes.

It may very well be that Schoenberg's death was not what provided the impetus for Stravinsky's surprising reversal since he never gave us any reason to believe it was so, though it was scarcely the kind of information he would be inclined to divulge. There were other probable causes and there are those who cannot be dissuaded from the firm conviction that Robert Craft, as his amanuensis and adviser, took advantage of his position to indoctrinate Stravinsky into the wonders of serialism and prod him into advancing to what at that time seemed a more contemporary position. In the sixth and last of his books of conversation with Stravinsky, Craft glosses over the matter with a show of wit: "Clearly I am thought of as a plenipotentiary (rather than as a famulus, which is more often the case, or satellite, or jester), as well as a gray eminence who 'operates' I.S. and is responsible for shanghaiing him into the '12-tone system' (as if anyone could even lead *that* horse to water, if it didn't want to go, let alone make it drink)."[4]

Very likely there was no single reason. It could have been a tide change, and one of the things that could have brought that about is a certain metamorphosis that twelve-tone composition had undergone since the thirties and early forties when it had been thoroughly imbued with the national character of its origin. It had exuded, in the view of some hostile observers, what was construed to be the airless aroma of dimly illuminated Viennese attics and seemed adapted only to the expression of the gloomiest sentiments. In the course of the forties it began to liberate itself from these associations and developed into an international technique suitable for anyone anywhere and adaptable to a variety of national characters, as well as a variety of moods. We had Luigi Dallapiccola in Italy, Pierre Boulez in France, Milton Babbitt in the United States, and in Britain, not quite a twelve-tone composer, Peter Maxwell Davies who used magic squares in a somewhat serialist fashion. At the same time the limited expressive range that had adhered to atonality and serialism since their inception was noticeably relieved by an influx of feelings of all varieties, to such an extent that Dallapiccola was heard declaring, "now it will be possible to write an *opera buffa* in the twelve-tone system!" The change was very much in the air and it was not any single individual who seemed to have been responsible for its development and proliferation.

Of no little significance in this regard was the circumstance that Aaron Copland, whose accession to serialism was every bit as surprising as Stravinsky's, should have undergone somewhat the same development as his fellow composer and at the same time, but just falling short of crossing the line into an *echt* serialist camp. Around 1930, notwithstanding his palpable individuality, his debt to the Russian master had been generally acknowledged and he was dubbed "Brooklyn Stravinsky." But by 1950 he was very much on his own and in complete command of his destiny. I am quite sure that his development at that time had nothing to do with Stravinsky's. Copland's profile, as I have said, fits the description of rapprochement more than Stravinsky's. Copland had also dealt with short nondodecaphonic serial elements in the thirties, notably in his Piano Variations. But when he became a twelve-tone composer he never quite let go of his diatonic, tonal indoctrination. Even in those works written around 1960, when he came closest to serialism, for example in the Piano Fantasy (1957) and *Connotations* for orchestra (1962), there was still a residue of the "good old" major and minor triads. He never went as far as Stravinsky did in the direction of chromatic serialism. To those of his followers who felt he had let them down, he explained, "As I see it, twelve-tonism is nothing more than an angle of vision. Like fugal treatment, it is a stimulus that enlivens musical thinking. . . . it is a method, not a style."[5] Discussing the work on one occasion, he said that his aim was to combine "elements able to be associated with twelve-tone music and with music tonally conceived." As for the row he employed in the Fantasy (ten rather than twelve tones: E♭-B♭-F-D♭-B-F♯-A-G-D-C), "a good case," he told me, "could be made for the view that the over-all tonal orientation is that of E major."

Curiously enough, about a year after Schoenberg died, an interviewer for the *New York Herald Tribune* confronted Stravinsky with the question ". . . there has been much talk recently about the possibility of your embracing twelve-tone atonal principles?" And Stravinsky replied: "Talk is talk and cheap. Certain twelve-tone things I like, certain I don't. For instance, I have tremendous respect for the discipline imposed upon the twelve-tone man. It is a discipline that you find nowhere else. . . . Twelve-tone composers have to use the twelve tones. I can use five, eleven, six—anything I like. I am not obliged to use more. I do as I wish in the scale or mode I prefer. I am also able to work in series, like the atonalists, if I want to. But what is more important is that I do not have to. You see?"[6] His objections evidently dissipated themselves in less than a decade.

I cannot vouch for the fact that my fellow composers among the Harvard Stravinskians, who still maintained their identity as a group in the fifties, joined the ranks of the serialists without being provoked by Stravinsky's example: Louise Talma, Irving Fine, and Ingolf Dahl, for instance, could quite conceivably have been following the master's example. In my own case I do not think it was Stravinsky who, for the most part, was responsible for my change of direction or, more precisely, my return to an earlier stage of my development. My first compositions that were not exercises in Classical style for credit in my college courses were twelve-tone or what I thought around 1930 was twelve-tone—compositions I wrote immediately after being stunned by my first hearing of any Schoenberg. Later, in my diatonic music I preserved a certain fragmentation and the angularity and wide skips characteristic of Webern (though these characteristics, it should be noted, are not of the essence of serialism), to the extent that Babbitt was motivated to give credence to the locution "diatonic Webern" which was being used with increasing frequency in the fifties to characterize my music of that period.[7]

When I did return to serialism, notably in my String Quartet (1958), far from being accused of emulating Stravinsky in this development, I was once embarrassed by the suggestion that I might have influenced him! *Chamber Music for Thirteen Players* was a work I wrote in 1956 close to my arrival at serialism, and tongue-in-cheek I described it as "neoclassic twelve-tone." Reviewing this work in the *New York Times*, Eric Salzman wrote, "This is just the sort of thing that Stravinsky has done recently only Berger did it first. Come to think of it, the work was first performed at a concert series in Los Angeles which Stravinsky often attends. Wonder if he was there?"[8] Knowing how sensitive Stravinsky was to criticism I was terrified that he might see the review. My concern intensified when I heard the story that was circulating by word of mouth about Stravinsky being summoned before the pope during the period in which he was rehearsing the *Rake* in Rome. The specific time proposed was right after a rehearsal, and Stravinsky told the pope he would like some time to wash and clean up. "Come as you are," said the pope. In the course of their conversation the pope asked him what bothered him most of all things. "I'm ashamed to admit it," he answered, "but I cannot bear adverse criticism," at which the pope gently put his hand on Stravinsky's knee and said it was just the same with him. I have no reason to believe Stravinsky ever saw or heard about Salzman's remark. He was, after all, far away in California and not a daily reader of the New York papers.

I had been reverting gradually at that period to my incipient serialism of the early thirties. The British composer Peggy Glanville-Hicks wrote about me as follows in 1953: "Twenty years ago it was said of the Atonalists and Neo-Classicists that 'never the twain would meet.' Nowadays, particularly in America, one sees blends of various kinds taking place between atonal contrapuntal and neo-classic vertical or harmonic composition, and Arthur Berger is one of the most successful, most delicate results of the hybridisation." [9] Notice that she avoids the epithets "serial" and "twelve-tone." The experts may be able to identify a strict twelve-tone serial work. But for most listeners what is heard is a certain style that strictly serial works share with a variety of atonal practices. Counting notes to determine if all twelve are there and participate in a constant rollover is a naive and unreliable approach. Discussing his *Composition for Four Instruments* Babbitt observed, "Not incidentally, I was not aware—either during its composition or well after it—that the twelve pitch class series underlying the work never appears as a totality in any explicit representation. As a referential norm, it is pervasively and persistently influential, acting at constantly varying distances from the work's surface." [10]

An exchange in *Partisan Review* in 1948, when that periodical was in its heyday, between a spokesman for Schoenberg (René Leibowitz) and a spokesman for Stravinsky (Nicolas Nabokov) left the impression of a desperation on the part of the Stravinskians in their last-minute struggle to survive. It was patently an augury of their defeat. Leibowitz, whose pro-Schoenberg forces were on the rise, could be sufficiently confident of success in this matter to indulge in some humor, and he remarked on the irony of the two antagonists having settled down close to each other in Southern California and having both come "as far as a European can 'go west.' It is strange that two men so different in every respect should have chosen this place to live and work in. For even though they are both living in a city that is dominated by the motion picture industry, neither one has anything to do with motion pictures." [11] For Nabokov serialism had the "earmarks of a Messianic cult," and far from being innovative it was the last stage in a harmonic development that could be traced back to 1600, whereas Stravinsky, on the other hand, had proclaimed a new domain that would start a new cycle—the domain of rhythm. [12]

8   Postmodern Music

This essay is based on an article that appeared in the Boston Review *in April 1987 under the title "Is There a Postmodern Music?" as part of a series on postmodernism. It may be of interest to recall some of the questions raised in the earlier days of the movement though they are less pressing now.*

Musicologists, critics, and even the public are usually so eager to codify, categorize, and label that it is quite surprising the slogan "postmodern" has accumulated so little mileage among them.[1] The attraction of a label for any movement in the arts is the function it serves to encapsulate its reason for being. As Wallace Stevens observed in remarks quoted earlier, modern art "has a reason for everything. Even the lack of a reason becomes a reason." Where postmodern music is concerned, just what was subsumed under the rubric was not altogether clear to many of us at first and may not be clear even now. We could only infer from its sporadic occurrences what manner of creative effort it was likely to embrace within its domain. As I looked into the matter I recognized that the concept was more prevalent within the area of music than I had thought it was. Any aspirations on anyone's part, however, that it might replace the essential twentieth-century tradition, it is fortunate to relate, were promptly shattered. That tradition, it has been seen, was by the middle of the century what is generally referred to as "serialism," "atonality," or "twelve-tone composition." For some time listeners had regarded serialism as a "modern" tendency— modern in the sense of being advanced, problematic, and of today—or indeed, of tomorrow: "music of the future" in Wagner's notorious formulation. But suddenly we were confronted with something like an oxymoron. The directive came down from the manipulators of propaganda in the field of composition that "modernism" was old-fashioned. To their confusion listeners were now informed by the daily press that there was a branch of the fraternity of composers known as "the Northeastern academic serial establishment." Serialism was no longer the "new music" they had thought it was, but rather some staid pursuit better suited to the classroom than the concert hall, in short, "old-fashioned modernism."

Now it is perfectly true that one may legitimately ask how long can a work like Schoenberg's *Five Orchestra Pieces*, Op. 16 of 1908, remain "modern" in the sense of contemporary. Many listeners still find it challenging and "dissonant," and those are the attributes that they consider as defining "new" music or what they are accustomed to call "modern," blissfully ignoring the requirement that it be contemporary. The Museum of Modern Art in New York was chagrined when it had to face the fact that according to a stipulation in her will the paintings of van Gogh and Seurat, bequeathed to it by Abby Aldrich Rockefeller, who died in 1948, had to be surrendered to other museums at the close of the twentieth century since she felt that they could no longer be classifiable as "modern."

Another semantic problem arises with the assimilation of "modern," a concept notorious for its aggressive innovation, to "academic." Since in the twentieth century "academic" long signified composers who had persisted in pursuing the well-worn paths of nineteenth-century Romanticism, which posed no problems to either composer or listener, it is paradoxical to find the label applied to composers who do pose a challenge, whose work was (and still is) less accessible to average listeners than most music they hear. The serialists were not called "academic" simply because academe was now their haven (though this helped). By throwing in epithets like "austere" and "arid," critics left no doubt that they were giving their impression of the music and pointing up serialism's reputation for being cerebral and systematic as well as without feeling.

When he was still a *New York Times* music reviewer, before he assumed the influential post of editor of the Sunday arts section, John Rockwell used the phrases "uptown" and "downtown." Serialism was "uptown," referring to the New York area where the squares hung out with their old-fashioned concert halls and Lincoln Center. "Downtown" was where the action was—the SoHo lofts and art galleries. The sentiment downtown was that after almost a century of pulling its weight Schoenberg's legacy should be declared moribund. You did not find the avatars of "the Northeastern serial establishment" there. While the denizens of SoHo were likely to deplore the fact that serialism dominated the college music curriculum, they no doubt found it natural that it should take the place once occupied by Romanticism as an academic discipline since serialism was declared to be seriously dated in the concert hall.

The music we once called "modern" was now regarded as "academic" but the fragmentation and rhythmic asymmetries, the absence of catchy tunes and tone centers, the relative novelty of this putative "academic" music offered none of the comforting familiarity of the earlier academics, the Romanticists—composers like Daniel Gregory Mason or Howard Hanson. But if the old academics were scarcely played anymore, you still could find this comforting familiarity, curiously enough, in the much-touted scions of a "new" faith, the so-called post-Romanticists: George Rochberg and David Del Tredici. The question arises why these latter-day Romanticists should have been considered to be representatives of "new" music when they were not very different from the early twentieth-century academic Romanticists or even from those Romanticists who had been around for decades as part of a well-established line of moderates—composers like William Schuman, David Diamond, and Ned Rorem. In the cases of Rochberg and Del Tredici their rejection of their earlier serialism was the kind of act that some may have considered courageous and that gave their conversion its cachet. It would certainly be taken into account, as we shall see, by believers in postmodernism, for whom it would enhance the reception of the music even though it had nothing to do with the direct listening experience. Bernard Holland, until recently chief music critic of the *New York Times*, suggested a telling metaphor for the new Romanticists when he wrote that Rochberg's music "does remind us of the frontiersman who, having fought his way arduously through badlands and hostile Indians to the promised West, abruptly decides to settle in Philadelphia."[2]

Postmodernism must be what Rockwell had in mind when he declared, "Rochberg eagerly embraced the suddenly fashionable notion that modernism had failed."[3] Serialism was the "modern" that these composers had left behind. It is interesting that what postmodern art critics said (and still say) about Abstract Expressionism (the abstract side of it) sometimes sounds like what music critics have been saying about serialism though the two are very different—to wit, registering complaints about formalist practices that are considered modern by their practitioners but, so the argument goes, are no longer modern in the sense of contemporary.

An important aspect of postmodern aesthetics has been the goal of creating art that is accessible—accessibility is still the rallying cry in general today.

It is a goal so obsessively pursued that one would think it were a substantive aesthetic virtue. Of no little consequence as an impetus for programming Romantic music is the circumstance that the majority of the accumulated keyboard music dates from the nineteenth century, since it was essentially not until then that the modern piano was developed. So it is natural for pianists in assembling their programs to lean heavily on nineteenth-century Romantic music. The fact that concert-goers have so much opportunity to hear this music and become familiar with it obviously determines in large part its accessibility.

Another important concern of postmodernists in all the arts is not to have their return to nineteenth-century Romanticism or their tendency to arrogate to themselves the finished works of others confused with neoclassicism. They do not at all approve of the tension that arises in neoclassicism, as I have already remarked—the tension, that is to say, resulting from the way in which the present interacts with the past. Postmodern literary critics find this tension unacceptable in T. S. Eliot, and postmodern composers have had the same feeling when they encounter it in Stravinsky. This attitude may be detected in the pains to which the writer of liner notes for a Del Tredici LP went to tell us that the composer's "new tonal writing has been achieved with an enlivening spontaneity, rather than as the result of an agonized 'rapprochement with the past.'" [4] As the literary critic Denis Donoghue puts it, for postmodernism "the past is not a terrible burden to sustain but a box of images to be resorted to for pleasure." [5] Quotation among postmodern artists, far from provoking a struggle with the source, is likely to be altogether complacent, even literal—sometimes carried out to an extent that would normally be designated plagiarism, as in the instance of the artist Sherrie Levine displaying her reproductions of photographs of Walker Evans, signed by herself as her own works.

The degree to which post-Romanticism shares the orientation of the postmodernists is verified among other things by a concern with accessibility and a fascination with cloning nineteenth-century composers. It is also worthy of note that though Cage was active before the slogan gained currency in the field of music, postmodernists have claimed him. As an example of postmodern usage, Donoghue observes, Cage's "music is as hospitable to street noises as to silence or Mozart." [6] (It is not literally true but it gives a general idea of the aspect of Cage that is considered postmodern.) In many ways Cage's contribution to twentieth-century culture is more significant for the other arts than for music. Its conceptual nature has its counterpart in the visual arts through the medium of so-called conceptual art—what one reads or is told about a painting is more important than what one sees. This is certainly a tenet of postmodernism. An offshoot movement of the Cage legacy known as Fluxus was quite explicit with regard to this conceptual aspect. Fluxus was actually designated "postmodern" by its founders, and is described by one Peter Frank as having been dedicated to an "offbeat" music which, "while demonstrably descended from the visual and musical traditions, depends neither on visual nor on musical standards. It does not even have to be viewed or performed; to know it is to experience it, and often *just to know of it* is to experience it" (italics mine).[7]

The aesthetic boggles the mind (I'm sure it is supposed to). I am, it is true, an old fossil. But this is not what I was brought up to believe art by its essence is. All art is *presentative.* Music presents auditory relations to an attentive, unanaesthetized listener (which leaves out those in a drug-induced stupor) within a given period of time. Though we get the gist of a lecture reported by a reliable auditor, a report of a musical performance yields nothing at all of the heard quality of the aesthetic experience, though it may describe its style and advance an opinion as to its worth. There is a touch of pedantry in art works that depend for their effect on what we are told about them. Take Cage's notorious *4'33"* (the silent piece of 1952 originally for piano). How do you know a piece is in progress if you are not informed such is the case? It is important to have a well-known and admired pianist sitting before the keyboard so that the disappointment of not hearing any sound emanating from the instrument is all the greater. I remember on one occasion when the piece was performed some laughter and noisy conversation passed between myself and a neighbor, as a result of which we were shushed by conscientious auditors. Afterwards when I apologized to John he told me it was exactly the kind of random event he hoped for—blithely unperturbed by contradicting himself, since at other times he had insisted that his purpose was to provide a brief period of silence for people in this noisy world.

I met Cage many years before any of us heard of postmodernism. It was 1937. Esther was driving our new Ford convertible (I almost never drove) with the top down, and we had just entered the campus of Mills College in Oakland, California, where I would teach for two years though this was my first visit. Two young men stopped us to greet us since they seemed to know, perhaps from photographs, who I was. They were John Cage and Lou Harrison, auxiliary faculty members whose role was to supply musical accompaniment for the activities and classes of the Martha Graham–school dance professor Marian van Tuyl. The California sky was crystal clear but Harrison said, in a dark monotone that suggested some Eastern guru before they were the rage, "It's going to rain." I asked, how did he know, it certainly didn't look it. In the same monotone, and in words that were really guru-like, he said, "The drums never lie."

Cage had something else on his mind. He asked my wife, "Do you have a wash-boiler? I lost ours." Now a wash-boiler even in those days was an obsolete affair that no one used any longer or could even identify. It was a large, handsome, oval-shaped, copper pot over two feet long and standing about a foot and a half high. Clothes were boiled in it to thoroughly clean them. Later when I attended a dance concert of the Mills students I found out what Cage and Harrison did with it. They would fill it with water, hit a gong with a mallet, and immerse the gong so that the sound would slide down in pitch in the manner of a siren in reverse. My impression at the time was that they came up with the far-out ideas together. It would seem that Cage was the one with the missionary zeal and posture to become a celebrity on the basis of them.

No, indeed, musicians in general have not taken to the expression "postmodern." On the basis of a small unscientific random poll, I found they guessed it must refer to the Cage variety of music, since it seemed reasonable to their way of thinking that what lies beyond current modernism should be still more modern.[8] On the other hand, they were surprised to hear that an ostensible conservative like Del Tredici might be considered a postmodernist. They had not enjoyed the benefits of being enlightened by sophisticated postmodern reasoning such as that we heard from the distinguished architectural critic Charles Jencks under the rubric "dual coating"—namely, "the mixture of meanings, popular and elite, which could be read by different groups of people, on different levels."[9] It is an interesting notion that merits some thought, but music, being deployed in time, presents problems since the two levels can scarcely be independent when conveyed simultaneously. A simple line sounding as a counterpoint to a complex one will be overpowered and absorbed by the latter.

To apply "dual coating" to a musical situation, let us suppose listeners find themselves seduced, since Del Tredici is such a fine musician, by the loveliness of his evening-long *Child Alice* (1977–81) when they start to listen. But his superb musicality and sensitivity are not enough to prevent the lingering pastiche of familiar Romantic sources from becoming tiresome as they wait for the "elite" (in Jencks's sense) moments at which the composer enters the scene with his own inspirations to redeem what has already transpired—those few and far-between moments where there is any intervention of the composer's admittedly attractive musical personality. Rochberg has attempted at times to segregate his post-Romantic and "modern" music so that they inhabit different movements of the same work. This minimizes the chances for their interaction, but it could be an advantage (if I may be so bold as to suggest) if it were to be made perfectly acceptable for us to leave the hall (for a cigarette break, we might have said at one time) during the musically derivative movements that did not address what Jencks would regard as our own higher "level" of listening.

Another post-Romanticist who probably has the qualifications to be labeled a postmodernist is Frederic Rzewski, an American composer who is better known in Europe than in the United States. He has been somewhat more successful in dealing with the two "levels." In *The People United Will Never Be Defeated* for solo piano (1957), the variation form provides the condition for the proximity of the two levels and the politically radical Chilean tune affords a sure means of unifying them. But even so, his forceful musicianship and brilliant keyboard writing do not compensate for the feeling we may have that he is unconvincingly apportioning out his favors—now a variation for the elite, now one for the workers. Marc Blitzstein, author-composer of *The Cradle Will Rock*, warned us in 1936 that the mass audience will have to learn how to listen intelligently and expressed the hope that a more efficient means of training for that audience would someday be developed. (The same sentiment inspired that gem of a song by Bertolt Brecht and Hanns Eisler, "In Praise of Learning," with the opening words, "We must be ready to take over" so we will be better educated to do the job right when we hold the reins of government and power.) Postmodernists in general would do well to heed Blitzstein's warning, since aiming at the lowest common denominator has not proved to be the most propitious way to reach the public.

Choice of idiom, I must admit, is really the composer's affair. It is his privilege, if he so desires, to raid the nineteenth century for his language and impose upon himself the near impossible task of achieving freshness in a medium so used up. Artists must have a grip on themselves to prevent them from an automatic response to the dictates of their ingrained technique. Nothing exposes them to the danger of being controlled by it rather than controlling it as much as working with materials that are too familiar and that constantly present their own well-worn solutions. Still, we would hope that artists would not be guided in their choice of direction either by the marketplace or by any notion of historic inevitability. If they still in all sincerity choose nineteenth-century Romanticism, then we, a minority though we may very well be, are free to exercise the option of deciding that we have no need of additional examples of such music—there being much more of it in storage than anyone can absorb in a lifetime. But the public relations machine is sure to dun us with testimonials to the composer's noble intentions in taking such a course, in his being disaffected with decadent current techniques. And if I have any understanding of postmodernism, conceptual factors such as the determination of a previously serial composer to forswear the iniquities of modernism, though the fact is not directly embodied in the sensory relations—that is, in what is heard—will be treated as in some way, though I'm not sure how, enhancing the aesthetic experience.

Mapping this mode of appreciation on to *Child Alice*, for example, we would have to contemplate Del Tredici's disavowal of his early twelve-tone practice and his disarming admission that he slipped back into tonality because it seemed appropriate for Lewis Carroll. Or perhaps there is a message in the music's obsessiveness—Del Tredici being even more repetitious than almost any Romanticist as a caricature of one of the least endearing aspects of Romanticism.

I cannot help feeling I am back in the classroom, fighting the tyranny of teachers who insist that we cannot appreciate a work without knowing the influences upon it, its date, the origin of its form, the temper of the times in which it was written, and details of the composer's life and loves. Program notes that provide things like this to think about may relieve the boredom of listeners who have difficulty keeping their minds on the music; but if anything exudes the stale odor of the academy it is surely this type of information gathering. It is ironic that this discussion started out by questioning the use of the epithet "academic" for the serialists only to find that it applies more appropriately to the latter-day Romanticists to the extent that they are postmodern. If listening is to be so conceptual, so dependent on what is not directly presented to unanaesthetized attention, it will be so different in essence from what we have traditionally assumed listening to be that it would seem to constitute a new branch of the arts almost as different from music as dance is. Though I hesitate to foretell the future, I cannot help suspecting that, far from posing a threat to modernism within the evolution of the essential music, postmodernism will be something we look back upon as a fringe movement—in the realm of music at least, since Jencks makes it sound so apposite to architecture. Change need not be linear. There is every reason to believe that postmodernism will not become part of music's mainstream and will not, in the longer view of things, replace the grand old twentieth-century music tradition which is, even at this late day, still alive and healthy, and which, if properly nurtured, may yet have some surprises in store for us.

Thus, contrary to the claims that we may be at the end of an era and the start of a new one, possibly a postmodern one, it seems to me we are witnessing composers consolidating the gains of one of the most radical shifts in music's evolution—the shift away from tonality. For anything comparable we must reach back to 1600 when monody emerged to take the place of polyphony. It required a century and a half before the implications of that revolution began to be realized in the time of Mozart and Haydn. Monteverdi was the central figure in that reform—very loosely, what Schoenberg was to us. By 1650, after Monteverdi's death, the scene was quiet. It was a period of waiting for some significant developments of the experiments of 1600. Several fine composers kept monody alive, while others clung to the old polyphony, ultimately producing a giant who was so out of style that he was barely noticed until the nineteenth century. Need I provide his name? Hardly, but I will anyway: J. S. Bach.

The point is that after Monteverdi, composers nurtured the new monody for over a century until it was ready to flower in the wondrous manifestations of the Classical era. This is how we should be nurturing the trends that some disdainfully call "modernist." The practitioners of serialism and those working in techniques that developed out of it make up a flourishing group in their own bailiwick, where they have established a strong creative environment—precisely what is needed for important new work to develop. New ideas cannot grow in a void. Even composers who seek a more accessible language would do well to fashion it out of the extant tradition instead of wiping the slate clean and, in the manner of some post-Romanticists, pretending that the twentieth century had never existed.

The lull that must have existed around 1700 was of a kind that could very well have brought in its wake an impatience on the part of those who were not content to use the present to consolidate their gains. We have certainly had composers like that in our century. For them music must advance loudly and naughtily, upsetting one dogma after another. For example, in the years from just before World War I to the Wall Street crash we had atonality, neoprimitivism, expressionism, postimpressionism, polytonality, micro-tone experiments, Italian Futurism, Dadaism, surrealism, *Gebrauchsmusik*, neoclassicism, the *Groupe des Six*, etc. Later, writings on music were haunted by evocations of that bad boy era, some rejoicing that things were back to normal, others lamenting the absence of the sensational until John Cage came along in the forties to turn things so completely upside down. Some rejoiced and were ready to declare it the end of an era and the beginning of a new one. But to the great relief of many of us Cage admitted that what he was talking about was "nonmusic" and "nonart." Though he had a great influence over the essential musical tradition we can rejoice in the knowledge that he left it intact. But he certainly left his mark one way or the other. I met the Polish composer Witold Lutoslawski in Cologne in 1938 when my String Quartet was played at the festival of the International Society for Contemporary Music. We spent pleasant hours exchanging ideas. He used improvisation in his music but it was remarkably controlled and I did not think of him at all in the Cage tradition. And yet he told me how important he considered Cage was as an influence and example in that he had destroyed music in order that composers could start all over again with a clean slate.

II

WRITING ABOUT MUSIC

9   Virgil Thomson and the Press

A short poem by T. S. Eliot with the title "The Boston Evening Transcript" starts as follows:

> The readers of the Boston Evening Transcript
> Sway in the wind like a field of ripe corn.[1]

The *Boston Evening Transcript* was a grand and sedate old conservative paper addressed to the Boston brahmin but read by a somewhat wider audience, and it was for that paper that I reviewed music events while I was a graduate student at Harvard in the thirties to supplement the stipend from my fellowship. With its very small type, its simple, sober layout, and its minimal and very discreet advertising, the *Transcript* resembled nothing so much as the *Times* of London of that era. Among other things it devoted a great deal of space to obituaries and stories dealing with estates and other matters related to the wealthy deceased. It was a good paper addressed to a readership of developed intellect. No copyreader fussed around with my reviews and attempted to display superior knowledge. My copy, which could be quite demanding of a reader's musical knowledge, went directly to the compositor and was published as written—something one could not depend on in those days where other papers were concerned.

When the paper folded in 1941 its typical readers, casting about for a replacement, found that only the *Christian Science Monitor*, published in Boston, was and looked refined enough to qualify. (Both the typography and some of the content of the *Boston Globe* and *Boston Herald* were considered vulgar.) But when they started to subscribe to the *Monitor* they found one serious hitch: the policy of the Christian Science Church precluded publication of obituaries along the elaborate lines of those in the *Transcript*.

Perhaps my most glamorous assignment during my entire tenure on the *Transcript* was a festival of the arts in Hartford in 1936 presented by the Wadsworth Atheneum in collaboration with an organization that had the provocative calling, Friends and Enemies of Modern Music.[2] Virgil Thomson, on one of his visits from Paris where he dwelt much of the time, was in complete charge of the music. A high point for me, even surpassing a concert performance of Stravinsky's *Noces* (Wedding) of 1923, was Erik Satie's *Socrate* (1919) with decor by Alexander Calder (including a huge mobile that effectively turned black at the moment when Socrates dies). The festival was altogether a brilliant affair, attended by New York high society, and culminating in a masked ball for which costumes were designed and often created on the spot by celebrated avant-garde visual artists of the caliber of Calder.

Thomson's representation on the programs was modest: *Sonata da Chiesa* (literally, "church sonata"), a chamber work of 1926 scored for an eccentric combination that was shocking then, though it would not be now: E-flat clarinet, trumpet in D, viola, Horn, and trombone. In a review that occupied several columns in the *Transcript* I wrote briefly about his work, saying I found in it "a monotony which makes the music extremely trying." On the Satie I wrote enthusiastically and at considerable length. In a handwritten letter dated 22 March (Thomson never typed and consequently had to have a special compositor who could read his handwriting when he later became critic of the *New York Herald Tribune*) he discussed aspects of my review and vouchsafed a gentlemanly response to my rough treatment of his piece, saying, "it has been over and over again bitterly attacked" and "has a way of cropping up every few years and getting both varied and vigorous reactions out of people"—the implication being, as I read it, that I might have another go at it and might like it better. He went on to compliment me "for being really intelligent about Satie (which is something so rare, even in France, that you'd be surprised)."

When the late novelist and composer Paul Bowles decided to leave the *Tribune* to return to Paris (and ultimately to literature and a life in Tangier) Thomson, then the paper's first-desk music critic, thought of me as a replacement, and I suspect it may have had something to do with my appreciation of Satie, which had altogether extenuated any nastiness about his own music in my review. This was in 1946, by which time I was comfortably ensconced in a reviewing position on the *New York Sun*. Thomson succeeded in spiriting me away from that job.

For anyone who knew Thomson in the thirties the likelihood that he himself would ever become a regular member of the music reviewing staff of a metropolitan newspaper was altogether unthinkable. In his existence as a freelancer he could take off for Paris at any time to occupy his apartment on the picturesque but noisy Quai Voltaire with its unobstructed view of the cathedral of Notre Dame. In the days when World War II was fast approaching, perhaps as late as 1939, I recall meeting him at a concert in Paris at which Béla Bartók played his *Sonata for two pianos and percussion* with his wife Ditta. During the intermission Thomson emerged from the hall yawning and looking bored. "Composers really only like to listen to their own music," he told me. At about the same time his book *The State of Music* appeared with the following devastating opinion of journalists:

> Journalists are plentiful everywhere and entertaining too, full of jokes and stories. Only their jokes are not very funny and their stories are inexact. Their information is always incomplete, because nobody ever tells them the truth about anything. Their philosophy of life and art and their technique of expression are incurably, dogmatically superficial. Their private lives are full of banal melodrama. They are, to a man, either dyspeptic or alcoholic or both. They must be avoided in bands, because they bring out the worst in one another. Singly they are fun but rather indigestible.[3]

Many readers may be surprised to learn that when Thomson revised *The State of Music* for the 1962 edition, despite having been himself in the interim a journalist and thus a member of the newspaper fraternity he had satirized, he did not delete this paragraph. But those readers did not know the cavalier and defiant Virgil Thomson. He did soften the last sentence: "Singly they are warm and companionable, make devoted friends." Most revisions, however, were for cosmetic reasons; for example: "Though they think themselves pundits all their philosophy of life and their techniques of expression are incurably, dogmatically superficial."[4]

It was this provocative aspect of Thomson that appealed to Geoffrey Parsons of the *Tribune*, who was a connoisseur of the arts and interested in their coverage though he was officially in charge of the editorial page. It was his idea that the *Tribune* hire Thomson. He acceded to the *Tribune's* first desk, succeeding the learned and highly respected Lawrence Gilman, in 1940 on a reluctant return from war-torn Paris, which he had found to be great fun. Parsons was enormously impressed by Thomson's lively contentiousness in *The State of Music*, and intrigued by the prospect of a feisty voice to succeed the dignified and scholarly Gilman. He thought it time someone stirred things up. But he had to watch Thomson closely during the first two years, steering him in the right direction.

Of course, of no little consequence in Thomson's choice of me as an associate critic was the fact that I was a composer. Having composers as critics was one of the innovations he brought to the New York scene from his experience of years of living in Paris. In our country composer-critics are frowned upon. It is assumed the critic's own tendency as a composer will create a bias. But almost all critics are biased one way or another without being composers. It was up to me to try to become aware of my biases and to prepare the reader for them.

Composer-critics place themselves in a difficult position. A review of someone who has played or will play one's music is a case of conflict of interest. If the review is unfavorable the performer will never play the composer-critic's music again. Newspaper editors curiously object to the expertise of the composer-critic. But this is just one more instance of the notion that a music critic should not deliver an expert opinion but rather simply pass on the superficial impression of the average listener (something that would not be tolerated in the case of the bridge columnist). Quite apart from his or her biases the composer-critic can differentiate between the genuine creator and the imposter and can recognize technique or the lack of it in any idiom. In an ideal world composer-critics would specialize in reviewing composition, and other critics would do performance. In addition to Bowles and then myself, who were regular staff members, Thomson used a number of composers as stringers, including Peggy Glanville-Hicks, John Cage, Elliott Carter, Lou Harrison, and David Diamond.

My recollection of working for Thomson does not tally at all with Ned Rorem's as offered up in one of his books of memoirs. Rorem was Thomson's personal assistant for a while, helping him fulfill his obligations in his various affairs as composer, author, lecturer, etc., and he had this to say: "When I arrived each day at ten, he would have performed his ablutions, and now, in clean orange pajamas from Lanvin, propped up and surrounded by an ocean of pillows, with a sharpened pencil and a big yellow pad (he never learned to typewrite), he conducted the musical life of Manhattan from his bed. . . . he would spend the morning hours on the bedside phone, mostly on business for the paper: making assignments to his staff of critics . . . or telling them his reactions to their reviews from last night."[5]

In my introduction it will be recalled I quoted Rorem's contention that our memory of the past is inevitably "embellished" by what we have experienced since. I remember the past quite differently in this matter. The dealing out of assignments was the task of the music editor (Francis D. Perkins at that time) who kept our various specializations in mind, so that if there were a choice I would get contemporary music. I remember only one occasion when Thomson called me down and "reacted" to my review, and he was quite justified. This was in connection with what I wrote about the stormy concert I mentioned above when Harold Shapero's massive and impressive piano sonata was played.[6] I was so excited over the Shapero and antagonized by the rowdy dissidents that I bent backwards and downplayed other works on the program, in particular the Duo for violin and piano by Leon Kirchner, who had recently descended on New York and had impressed some musicians whose judgment I held in high esteem. I had occasion to revise my opinion of the Kirchner in a review I wrote soon afterwards, and though my tastes do not normally extend to the high degree of intensity and Romanticism (a twentieth-century kind, as I said earlier) of his music I have come to admire it for its forceful musicianship and to respond to its emotional power.

Though I'm not altogether certain, I believe my main incentive for wanting to be a music critic was the opportunity it would give me to advance the cause of contemporary music—American music in particular. And working for Virgil Thomson was an ideal way to fulfill that objective. As a composer himself he was, not surprisingly, much concerned about the way composers were treated in the press. One thing that could advance a composer's reputation, he was convinced, was to have his or her picture in a metropolitan newspaper. "People remember the picture," he would say, "not what is written." He would not have approved of the current practice at the *New York Times;* despite the fact that the paper is much more lavish with photos than it formerly was in the fields of both music and dance, it is very sparing about picturing a given composer (short of a celebrity) who is the subject of a favorable review. Generally, the composer's only chance of appearing in a picture in such instances is if he or she happens to be a player or conductor in the music under discussion.

This is something quite foreign to the conventions Thomson had established for the pages of the *Tribune.* For example, one of his early reviews (1942) dealt with a concert of the prestigious contemporary music society, the League of Composers at the New York Public Library (Forty-second Street branch), the program comprising works by young American composers.[7] The music was almost all of high quality, if I may be permitted to say so, since it included my fairly new woodwind quartet, and I was delighted that Thomson wrote, referring to my music, "in the opinion of this listener, it was the most distinguished piece of musical work on the program." (Remember, this was before I joined his staff.) And yet the picture accompanying the review was of another composer on the program! But Thomson, with unusual openness about the inside workings of the paper, explained in his review: "My use of Mr. [Richard Franco] Goldman's photograph to illustrate this review does not mean, however, that I consider his work the most important played. It is due rather to the impossibility over a weekend of obtaining any photograph other than one already in the files of this newspaper." That Thomson would go out of his way to discuss the matter of the picture is obviously an indication of how important it was for him. I wonder what they thought upstairs of his sharing such inside information with his readers. (He felt no obligation to conform to newspaper code. His handling of the League concert as a major event, moreover, though it was quite an offbeat occasion in those days when critics, especially first desk critics, normally confined themselves to the standard concerts in the customary midtown venues, was another challenge to tradition. The *Times* did not cover it at all.)

It was not altogether characteristic of Thomson to use the star system as he did in the case of my woodwind quartet on that occasion. High up on his list of advice to budding critics was the warning that their estimate of how good or bad a work is was not the most important thing in a review. The reader wanted to know mainly what the work was like. Coleridge put this notion nicely when he wrote, "He who tells me that there are defects in a new work, tells me nothing which I should not have taken for granted without his information. But he who points out and elucidates the beauties of an original work does indeed give me interesting information, such as experience would not have authorized me in anticipating." [8]

It is not that Thomson considered a sober assessment unimportant. He simply did not think it should be the whole story or a major part of it. With regard to the assessment itself he had definite ideas. Among other things he disapproved of tallying good and bad points as if the reviewer were correcting an exam, and he had no patience for what he called the "swinging door" review: a negative first part and a glowing second part (or vice versa). The reader wonders whether anyone that bad could be that good, and begins to suspect that the favorable comments have been forced to provide the artist and reviewer with some quotable sentences. Ideally, the good and bad should be placed in context: "Despite faults," which may be listed, "there were many fine points," also to be listed. Even the best performers falter at some point during their concerts, probably in the warm-up period, especially if they are singers. What is required is that the reader get an idea of the bottom line.

The critic's main obligation, reporting what the performance or the music is *like*, is more difficult. The locution "what it is like" can be taken two ways and critics too often take the easy way. They use the word "like" in the sense of "it is *like* Webern" or "it is *like* Stravinsky," thus not only avoiding the necessity of describing the composer's manner but leaving the impression that the composer has trespassed on other people's territory. Thomson used to insist that many notions which we ascribe to individuals and which we trace as influences from one musical personality to another with the acumen of musicologists are in the air, in the wind—properties accessible to all, in the public domain. The critic should make the distinction between servile imitation and legitimate indebtedness to a seminal composer whose endowment has determined the direction of music's evolution. Music as an art did not issue directly from nature (despite birdsong) in the way that painting and literature did; it exists by virtue of composers who have forged a tradition.

Out of the sounds of nature it is possible to develop a Western tradition of an art of noises (nonpitched percussion), distinct from what we know as music, such as was found in Asia and Africa. The beginning of such a development was to be observed in mid-century in the nonmusic venture of Cage and his entourage. Quite appropriately, this fringe "music" has been accorded the name-tag "Sound Art."[9] The rubric intelligently recognizes that it is not new in the sense of being a new stage in a long tradition, like serialism, for instance, but is new in the sense of being altogether a new art, based on sound but not specifically pitch, which is only one kind of sound.

Classical music, on the other hand, exists by virtue of its tradition, and while it may be influenced by the new art of sound, it is not essentially altered by it. In his first book of interviews with Robert Craft, in answer to the question, "While composing do you ever think of any audience?" Stravinsky responded, "When I compose something, I cannot conceive that it should fail to be recognized for what it is, and understood. I use the language of music, and my statement in my grammar will be clear to the musician who has followed music up to where my contemporaries and I have brought it."[10]

Surely one of the most burdensome aspects of reviewing on the New York beat during most of the forties as I recall it was the obligation of meeting the midnight deadline. The *Sun* was an evening paper so one might assume the reviewer had a lot of time and could write the review at leisure early the next morning, or at least finish it then. But it had to be in at night, and since the paper had its headquarters way downtown in the City Hall district, to save the time I would spend on travel someone would come to my door before midnight to collect my copy. (I lived not far below Times Square.) What exacerbated the situation was the fact that concerts started later in those days than they do now. Some listed eight forty-five as the starting time and it could be almost nine o'clock before the performer emerged from the dressing room. (This had the advantage of allowing one to have a more civilized dinner hour.) From time to time we would close a review with an apology to the effect that our deadline prevented us from remaining to the end of a concert.

The only time I had any comment on my writing from "upstairs" while I was reviewing in New York, it came in the form of a communication from the managing editor of the *Tribune* advising me not to include observations of this kind in my reviews, evidently, as I assumed, because it would compromise the newspaper's reputation for coverage. A few reviews had been published a day later than they should have been, but always with a note on the day they were to appear informing the reader of the postponement. As I look back at the files I kept of my reviews, incomplete though they may be, I observe a note of this kind published as an actual news item on the day after the stormy concert I mentioned earlier at which the Shapero piano work was played. I must have had trouble sparring with my conscience, since, while I genuinely admired the Shapero, he was after all a friend and fellow composer in the New England Stravinsky circle, and I was not altogether unaware that there was a conflict of interest.

I recall one concert in 1951 that thoroughly mocked the deadline and required us to publish the review a day later. It took place in what was formerly the McMillan Theater of Columbia University (now the Miller Theater) and consisted of works of Cage.[11] The program included an important premiere, his *Imaginary Landscape No. 4* for twelve radios operated by twenty-four "musicians" with the composer conducting. The work did not come on until about midnight. In those days most radio stations signed off at that hour, so the players who studiously followed Cage's specifications received silence except, since it was during the Korean War, for an occasional "Korea" being mentioned by one of the few stations remaining on the air. (Could that have been what inspired the notorious silence piece for piano composed the following year?) Broadus Erle was concertmaster, an outstanding violinist from the admirable New Music Quartet. (Who needed such a fabulous violinist just to turn dials? But that was an essential part of the whole affair—still another feature to promote wide-eyed disbelief.) He later confided to me that he completely ignored Cage's specifications and kept relieving the prevailing silence by returning to a broadcast of a Mozart violin concerto. With an important premiere so late in the program it was impossible to apologize for leaving early, so I had to miss the deadline, and the fate of the review was to be published a day late.

Concert reviews in Paris had long been consigned to delayed appearance, often as much as a week later. Consequently when the practice was adopted in this country (in the fifties after I left the field of concert-reviewing) it was Thomson who was naturally its most ardent advocate. Now if they wanted to, or if they had to under unusual conditions, critics could choose not to be pressed by the deadline. (In my day the deadline required us to finish up in an hour from the time—about eleven o'clock—we reached the office.)[12] Critics did continue to review some concerts for publication the next day if they were especially newsworthy—the opening of the Metropolitan Opera season, for example—or if they were the weekly presentations of the New York Philharmonic, which took seriously the responsibility of getting its subscribers out at a reasonable hour. As a matter of fact when curtain-time was moved up to eight o'clock, which is what it is today, one reason cited was the concern of concert-goers over the growing number of muggings reported and their desire not to be on the city streets too late.

Up to the time I left the paper we were still writing reviews at night on the old schedule, and the paper would decide when to publish them. The deadline was still there, but the pressure was lifted since missing it was no big deal; the review could be published two or more days later. Writing the same night was the prerogative of the reviewer who wanted to have the event fresh in mind or to avoid having it hang over as a distraction. (Bernard Holland of the *Times* told me that he prefers to sleep on it and do his review the next morning unless it's a special newsy occasion. I would be afraid that if I left a review to the next morning I would spend a sleepless night formulating it in my mind.) Handing it in at night did not mean it would necessarily be published any sooner, and the critic was not usually told when it would appear. The prospect of meeting the deadline on the chance that the story might be published the next day has become less and less attractive as the deadline has moved earlier and earlier—on the *Globe*, for example, from half past midnight a quarter of a century ago to half past eleven at the time of this writing.

Thomson's most cogent reform at the *Tribune* revolved around the question of what governs the choice of concerts to be reviewed. What does a concert require to qualify for a review? "Real estate has nothing to do with musical excellence," Thomson insisted. Up to his time normally concerts were reviewed if they took place at one of the three or four bona fide concert halls: Carnegie (including its small venue then known as Carnegie Recital Hall), Town Hall, and the formerly much used Times Hall, with a few exceptions like the Ninety-second Street YMHA. The new policy was especially favorable to the contemporary music groups that operated on a shoestring and at best could command space in an art gallery which was unlikely to be in the central district normally covered. The other papers naturally had to follow the *Tribune*'s example.

Another thing Thomson did to liven up the music scene was to take an active part in the new and short-lived Music Critics Circle of New York, which was probably modeled after the drama critics' group. The Music Critics Circle, which was created very soon after his accession to the *Tribune*'s first desk, gave prizes to contemporary works performed during the season. I remember the critics being very conscientious about familiarizing themselves with the works nominated and, since they would have been recorded at the concert, about listening to them at Town Hall where the recordings and reproduction equipment were kept. (We did not in those days necessarily have our own or adequate hi-fi equipment in our homes.)

The Thomson regime, it seems to me, put considerable pressure on performers to do new music. In the mid-forties there was an unusual meeting between the critics and the moguls of concert management to discuss why programs contained the same music over and over again and how they could be rendered more interesting. The managers made the point that world-class artists prepared a program for the entire season and it had not only to suit the taste of sophisticated listeners in cosmopolitan areas but also, in sixty to a hundred appearances, appeal to backward audiences in the provinces who would absolutely not stand for any departure from the familiar fare and would be incapable of dealing with difficult, inaccessible music.[13] I raised the point that there were many accessible works that were rarely played and that could vary the programs, works by Thomson (who was not present), Copland, Satie, and so on. In response to our complaint one of the most powerful managers in the business—it could have been Arthur Judson or Ward French, I don't recall—declared without hesitation that perhaps he had fallen behind since he did not know the pieces I referred to, as if it were perfectly natural for the management rather than the artists themselves to determine what a proper program should be. Management saw nothing amiss in holding programs down to the level of their own limited experience and taste.

Thomson got away with a good many things in his fourteen years as

Tribune critic including a gay sex scandal. One of his peccadilloes was doz-ing during concerts. When I was reviewing for the *Sun* we quite often were at the same concert, and I could observe him in this condition and occa-sionally hear a snore or two. What amazed everyone was the fact that when he came out in the intermission his remarks indicated that he hadn't missed a thing. When I moved over to the *Tribune* Thomson and I would go out to dinner together from time to time before covering our respective assign-ments. Once Thomson cautioned me against having coffee (the decaf vogue had not started yet) and to be sure to have enough wine so that I would be able to sleep at the concert. There were times when I wished I could sleep but I lacked the talent—though I recall falling asleep at the Metropolitan during one ear-shattering passage in a Wagner opera, drowned in the sound and luxuriating in the red plush interior of the old opera house.

10   Music on My Beat

With apologies to Howard Taubman, the title of whose 1943 book I bor-
rowed for the heading of this chapter.

My career as a journalist had modest beginnings on two school papers, one
at Townsend Harris High School (New York), the other at the College of
the City of New York with which the high school was affiliated. I left CCNY
after two years since it had no music program and music was the field I had
decided to major in. I enrolled at New York University—the School of Education since it was the Depression and I wanted some assurance I would
get a job, even if it were nothing more than one in a public high school for
which the degree qualified its recipients.

While I was at NYU a distant cousin, Gustav Davidson, a book reviewer
for that Hearst tabloid, that scandal sheet, the *New York Daily Mirror*,
asked me if I wanted to pick up some extra change to help pay for my tu-
ition by doing ghostwriting for him. He wished to add concert reviewing
to his book reviewing but was aware he knew too little about music to do it
without help. However, though I would have to occasionally ghostwrite reviews, it was not all that straightforward. It seems that he himself ghost-
wrote a column for the managing editor, Emile Gauvreau, called "Now and
Then," consisting of modules each a few sentences long commenting on
current affairs: culture, politics, and such. The deal was that I was also to
ghostwrite that column for my cousin (the presumed ghostwriter) without
the alleged author knowing I was doing so. I was rather radical in the political domain in those days so I slipped in some leftist material. I somehow
tend to think that the nominal writer of the column never read it, nor did

the presumed ghostwriter or anyone else on the editorial staff. It was after all a very conservative paper, but no one said a word about my somewhat radical comments.

After not too long my cousin tired of being known as the music critic. It evidently was not as glamorous a role as he expected it would be. He now seemed to have no objection to my initialing the reviews I wrote, and after a while he allowed me to sign the more important ones. Finally he dropped the whole activity into my lap. This had rather dire consequences from the newspaper's vantage point, for my interest in contemporary music was such that when Rubinstein or Rachmaninov played in Carnegie Hall to sold-out houses and advertised in the paper, I, without any qualms that I should do otherwise, would make my way downtown to the New School for Social Research and review the little seances I have described above. It turned out that the leading avant-garde composers of New York (and consequently of America) started to buy the low-down sheet I was writing for just to read my reviews of the new music events since none of the other papers covered such concerts. But the honeymoon did not last long. Julian Seaman, music critic of the old *New York World,* found himself out of a job when his paper merged with another New York paper, the *Telegram,* in 1931. He succeeded in being hired to join the re-write desk at the *Mirror* and pointed out to the editors, who seemed not to have paid much attention to anything as insignificant as their music coverage, how I was delinquent in my duty to the readers in not covering the concerts that would really interest them and moreover that advertised. I was promptly fired and replaced by him.

Music criticism did not last long on the *Mirror* even after Seaman became its critic, but there were so many reviews in the other papers every day that it scarcely mattered. In the forties when I was reviewing Classical music events in New York (first on the *Sun,* then on the *Tribune*) a recitalist or any presenter of concerts could look for reviews in about a half dozen morning and evening newspapers as well as, during their brief tenure, *PM* and the *Compass,* and, surprisingly often, the *Brooklyn Daily Eagle.* (This did not include the tabloids which, except for the brief episode in the thirties that I have mentioned, did not review serious music.) One could not be certain of finding reviews every day in all of the papers one opened—papers like the *New York Journal American* did not have the staff for that—but one could depend on the standard-bearers: *Times, Tribune,* and *Sun.*

The *Times* today, as virtually the only survivor among these newspapers, in its lonely eminence obviously exerts enormous influence since nobody can soften the blow by adducing a more favorable daily review in another paper in the event of a *Times* panning. And yet there is sometimes a question how much the concert review contributes to an artist's success as distinguished, for example, from the theater review. The outstanding pianist William Kapell, who met a tragic early death in a plane crash, was so depressed at the unfavorable reviews that he was receiving after making a great impression with his debut, that one day he burst into the office of Arthur Judson, the big mogul of the concert management industry, and practically in tears shouted that he was ruined, what was he to do now? Judson quite calmly told Willy he had nothing to worry about since he was solidly booked for sixty concerts the next season, quite a number of them solo appearances with the top orchestras in the world.

The relation of favorable reviews to the box office warrants rigorous study—by a sociologist, perhaps. It is not as obvious as the influence of a critic's advocacy of this aesthetic rather than that one in the area of composition: Olin Downes on Sibelius and Shostakovich, Harold Schonberg on the new Romanticism, or John Rockwell on minimalism. Most of us in the critical fraternity have given rave reviews to debut recitalists only to be disappointed a year later when they played to empty houses.[1] Or perhaps I should say a review does not have much weight without a high-priced publicity agent to do something with it. Also, having a picture along with the review is a big plus. When I was reviewing the event that launched Leonard Bernstein's spectacular career in 1943, his last-minute replacement for Bruno Walter, the ailing maestro of the New York Philharmonic, I returned to the offices of the *Sun* to find a double-column picture of the young assistant conductor which came from Associated Press.[2] The fact that the concert was one of the orchestra's weekly coast-to-coast broadcasts on a major network, now long gone and lamented, endowed the occasion with more than the usual merely local interest. (The reason I was at the newspaper office, instead of having a messenger pick up my copy at home to save me the trip downtown, was that it was a Sunday afternoon, so there was plenty of time before the midnight deadline.) My review was to be commendatory but after all Walter had prepared the orchestra, so I did not consider the showing exactly sensational, since Bernstein was the medium for Walter's interpretation. Still, with the big photograph there it would come across as such whatever I wrote. The picture is what the reader remembers, as Thomson reminded us.

To return to the case of Willy Kapell, the unfavorable reviews festered in his head and like so many others in the arts (Tennessee Williams in theater, for example) he took up the position of enemy of the press. In one nasty encounter he almost came to blows with a colleague of mine on the *Tribune* by the name of Jay Harrison. Following a New York Philharmonic program a wealthy couple of my acquaintance gave an after-concert party for Willy and myself. (Willy had played the second Brahms piano concerto and I had had my *Ideas of Order* on the program, conducted by Mitropoulos, who had commissioned it.)[3] Harrison was my guest, and while Willy was not hostile to me since he regarded me as a composer rather than a critic (I had accepted his request to write a piano concerto for him just before his tragic accident in a plane crash), he did tear into my colleague, taking him as a representative of the press. Just as the encounter seemed as if it would become physical our hostess had the presence of mind to summon us to the table, as if nothing were transpiring, for a midnight repast. That succeeded in restoring calm.

I often wonder how I survived my decade on the New York beat unscathed. Humphrey Burton, a biographer of Leonard Bernstein, has characterized me as "the most trenchant of New York reviewers,"[4] and as I look back, I myself am sometimes appalled at my nastiness in my younger days. (I take it that "trenchant" was used in the sense that my incisiveness could be cutting.) At one time for several days I had to use the back exit of the *Tribune* because an angry contingent, most of them with heavy mid-European accents, sat poised in the front waiting room ready to get at me because of what I wrote about the Austrian-born violinist Ossy Renardi, who had built a big reputation on his performances and recording of all twenty-four Paganini caprices. He had a pretty fabulous technique but his taste and musicianship in my opinion left a good deal to be desired when he appeared in intellectually demanding recital literature. (He was, among other things, capable of the indiscretion of adding piano to the unaccompanied Paganini on his recording.) When I began to review for the *Sun*, before I realized I should have an unlisted phone number, I was awakened in what seemed to me the middle of the night by an irate violin teacher (a very successful one) whose student's debut I had reviewed that very evening and who had evidently got the paper right off the press. He told me he'd make it impossible for me to write a word of criticism again but obviously failed to do so. (Thomson in a review once justifiably reprimanded that truly great Yugoslavian soprano Zinka Milanov when she developed a horrible tremolo. As a result he was challenged to a duel by a Yugoslavian who said Thomson had insulted his countrywoman. No duel ensued, however.)

My most consuming experience in this area, one that caused me years of inconvenience and exasperation, was a suit filed against the *Tribune* and myself in 1952 by the Yaysnoff sisters, a two-piano team entirely new to the local concert stage, who argued that I had libeled them in a review that appeared in the 30 July paper covering their performance the previous evening as soloists with the New York Philharmonic (or a summer version of it) at the Lewisohn Stadium.[5] I left the *Tribune* soon after writing the review for my long tenure at Brandeis University, and since the case dragged on until 1958, when the sisters finally dropped it, I had to fly down to New York on several occasions for questioning, though often I was represented by the *Tribune*'s attorney without being present.

It was the era of Joseph McCarthy's witch-hunts, and the sisters made much out of having a White Russian father. They insisted they were being pursued and persecuted by Communists and my review could be an example of it. The plaintiffs demanded that I produce "all cards, printings, writings or correspondence" which might "connect" me "with the Communist Party or any of its fronts and affiliates." The *Tribune* lawyer objected. In any case there were no such documents. Nevertheless on more than one occasion in a stifling interior (it was before air-conditioning was common) facing City Hall, where the *Tribune* lawyer had his offices, I was read the entire State Department list of organizations suspected of being subversive or acting as fronts, and in each case I was asked whether I was a member of said organization or had attended any of its meetings or functions. Even though the *Tribune* lawyer (acting also as my lawyer) would object to each one as it came up, the prosecution had the right to read that list as much as it wanted—a form of torture in a hot interior.

There were certain suspicious accidental circumstances that the prosecution found very incriminating and in support of its claim. For instance, the last sentence of my review read: "There are so many young performers around who would jump at the opportunity of a Stadium appearance that it is hard to conceive what obliges the Stadium management to scrape the bottom of the barrel as it did for last night's concert." Now it was not unusual, when reviews were reprinted in the early edition of the day after they originally appeared, for cuts to be made at the end because of other space requirements, since the item was no longer very important by then. But the fact that this admittedly nasty (but not libelous) sentence had been cut signified to the prosecution that the newspaper had thought better of it, thought that it should never have been printed in the first place.

A further complication was the fact that during the period of pretrial questioning I had left the paper for Brandeis. What else could this mean but that I was fired for incompetence? I received an urgent telegram from the *Tribune* music editor informing me that the paper's administration urged him to request me to submit a Sunday feature article on any subject of my choice to demonstrate that relations between the paper and myself were altogether amicable. No doubt the Yaysnoffs were disappointed that they received no publicity out of the entire caper, but newspapers don't normally advertise it when they are the ones involved in a disagreement, and the most they will do is publish a letter from the complainant in their pages stating the objections. Newspapers are formidable adversaries with all the research facilities at their disposal. The paper found that the Yaysnoffs were passionate litigants, and who knows how many subpoenas they might have been served if they turned up openly in court? Among other things it was found that they had falsified their ages on their passports.

Capping the whole preposterous affair was the contention of this duo-piano team that they were endowed with telepathic abilities that someone had once tested by listening to them play via a telephone connected to two different parts of the city, from which emanated their separate sounds in perfect unanimity without their hearing or seeing each other. Thus, a good deal of the pretrial questioning was devoted to the matter of whether a soloist in a concerto had to look at the conductor. The matter was never settled since the case never went to court. The plaintiffs withdrew after six years.

The proliferation of reviews of pop and dance events in the most recent decades has confronted the longhair music columnist with serious competition that did not exist in my day. In the *Times*, if not elsewhere, serious music seems to have held its own, though it still tends to be overshadowed by the other arts. When I was on the *Sun*, dance was not particularly important to the editors and it had not yet become commercially viable. So it seemed perfectly legitimate for me to be assigned its coverage as a sideline. I never felt comfortable about it for, while I had been an avid fan of the dance since I was a teenager, I really thought I did not know enough about it technically. But I was anxious to keep my music reviewing job and doing dance was the price.

The *Times* music pages are lively now, with quite a bit of attention given to contemporary music by well-informed writers. Music reviews often appear on the first page of the arts section. Feature articles (some of them what we used to call "think" pieces if they were speculative) appear not only on Sunday, but at times during the week. Since so many of the periodicals that used to carry pieces of this nature no longer do so or have folded, the *Times* makes a valuable contribution in filling the lacunae.[6] In addition to several magazines not primarily devoted to music, there are two music sources that are very much missed today: *Modern Music,* and also the *Musical Quarterly* as it originally was, since in its present metamorphosis it no longer runs reviews. A typical issue of the *Quarterly* at midcentury, that of July 1953 chosen at random, comprised no less than seventy-four pages of reviews, including several dealing with foreign events, and only seventy pages of articles. Other publications that ran reviews but no longer do so or no longer exist, to name just a few, include *Saturday Review, Musical Courier, Nation, New Republic,* and *Dial.* The *New Yorker* fills some of the gap with very solid feature pieces by Alex Ross, but not weekly and not such that you can depend on them to cover the scene as they used to.

In my day feature and news articles were in the minority. What appeared mostly were short reviews, some of them only three to six inches long, never written by the senior critic, and initialed rather than signed. If a reviewer had two reviews appearing the same day (rarely more), only one would be signed with the full name of the author; the other would be initialed. Except in the case of the senior critic, who always signed his full name, longer reviews might also be initialed if the event was considered not to be top drawer. The appearance of more than one review by the same author was likely to happen on Monday since Saturday concerts would be held over and on Sunday one reviewer, with a choice of afternoon, early evening, and night concerts, often did more than one. As a consequence of the fact that I so often had to use my initials it occurred to me that I should revert to my practice as a student of sporting my middle initial, "V" for Victor. "A. V. B." would be more memorable than just "A. B." Furthermore, in New York in the forties there was another incentive for using the middle initial: the Arthur Berger Valet Service, which had many branches in Manhattan. I thought it might discourage people from calling, as they did occasionally at all hours, to ask why their trousers had not been delivered. In any case, I alternated for a while between using my initials and not using them so that the music critic of the old *Boston Post,* Warren Story Smith, was once prompted to ask me if Arthur V. Berger and Arthur Berger were the same person.

I never cease to be taken aback when I find that a given newspaper re-viewer is represented in a single edition not simply by two articles but by several. On more than one occasion I have seen Richard Dyer's by-line in the *Boston Globe* as many as five times, its position varying from top of ar-ticle to bottom. One of the reasons we find this nowadays, of course, is that reviews are not published the day after the concert and there is no law spec-ifying the number of days they may be held over. So they accumulate, and finally the day comes when the paper decides to publish the whole backlog at once.

While it was customary to have many short reviews that were initialed when events were not considered important, the more important events had to have longer reviews whether you had enough to say or not. They could be signed or initialed (except, as I have already indicated, in the case of the chief critic, who never used just his initials). Bernard Holland, until recently the chief music critic of the *Times*, told me that he did not approve of the requirement that we had in my day to pad a story so that it would be commensurate with the occasion. At least once he ran into some difficulty in holding this view. It was the obituary of a world-class performing art-ist that he submitted only to be told it should be lengthened to underline the importance of the deceased. He refused and the editor had to find an-other way to fill the allotted space. Olin Downes had easily filled a column with a run-of-the-mill event. A review length of two columns was not un-usual for him (and the type was a little smaller than today's, allowing for more words per inch). It was one way a constant reader could identify him as the reigning critic. Thomson, his opposite number on the *Tribune*, would not have to depend on the length of the story to be recognized as first desk person since his name would be in bold type inside the ornate frame which read in caps CONCERTS AND RECITALS and which was only sometimes used for reviews of other members of the music staff. Holland tended to blend in with his staff, and so does his successor, Anthony Tom-masini, who has been known to have two reviews in one edition, something the first desk critics of the era of Downes and Thomson would never have dreamed of, since it was their policy to emerge like royalty only for the spe-cial occasion.

The debuts and seasonal repeat recitals of young performers vying for recognition and a career in music were usually consigned to the short, ini-tialed reviews. Debuts, as everyone knows, seem to have gone the way of the horse and carriage. One reason could be the current stratospheric prices of hiring a hall and engaging an agent. I came across a reminder of this trend in my scrapbook in a Sunday column I did in the *Tribune*, "The Musical Scene" (20 September 1948), in which I observed that there had been a falling off in the number of recitals since there had only been twelve so far the current month as compared with twenty during the same period the year before.

The indulgence since my day in the banner headline, a single line of three-to-five columns, makes the most routine concert seem important (though lately more and more reviews are grouped together with small single-line headlines). If there are almost no more young, aspiring recitalists, debutants, or returning unestablished young artists, there are still concerts on the same lower level that it seems to me get more attention than they deserve by being accorded reviews with long and large attention-catching headlines.

Current reviewers have no reason to regret the loss of the debutant or routine recitalist who returns year after year striving to hit the jackpot. What was there to say about any representative of the species? Your average recitalist could be counted on to have a fine technique but a poor range of expression, or a fine range of expression but poor technique, so it could scarcely be called news to have to constantly swing from one of these types to the other. Of the two requirements, technique, given normal physical resilience on the part of the performer, is more concrete and easier for the debutant or other young recitalist to achieve—namely, by long and arduous exercise, including relentless rote. I once heard of a French violin teacher who constantly used that old saw, "You must know it well enough to play it in your sleep," as an admonishment to his students. Among them was a young man, I shall call him Alphonse, who was preparing the Mendelssohn concerto for a debut performance. Surely enough, one night at about 3 A. M. the teacher shows up at Alphonse's Paris apartment, rouses his parents, and orders them to get Alphonse out of bed to play the concerto for him at once by heart.

Having to report over and over again the presence of good technique but a lack of the ability to cope with the music's expression, or a situation in the reverse, is not the happiest requirement of any critic's job. The repetitiveness was precisely one of the things that finally disabused me of the delights of criticism—or at least to a considerable extent resulted in making a decade of it on the New York scene sufficient for me for life. Even without the debutants the problem has not altogether gone away. Reviewers forever encountering the same virtues and faults have constantly to find new words for very much the same thing, and in addition there is the temptation to indulge in literary flights that may be quite out of proportion to the routine subject at hand. I take off my hat to the reviewers—and they do exist—who remain fresh and alert under these handicaps.

When technique and expression are both wanting in, for example, a debut recitalist or relative newcomer to the local concert stage, what a chance to let go with the language of invective! The reviewer should be cautious about this since often no one is being harmed. Such a response is especially uncalled for in the case of nonprofessional events. A review appeared in the *Globe* recently with one of those large three-column streamer headlines that read, "A Bach Mass Founders in Unpracticed Hands." The size of the headline in my day would have portended a fairly important occasion. It was the B-minor Mass in a joint performance by the chorus of one of the Boston region's top universities and an amateur chorale group. Since it involved nonprofessionals and, more especially, since it was out in Brookline at a church and not in the center of Boston or Cambridge, the paper was not obliged to cover it. That an amateur group should have difficulty with such a demanding work is scarcely surprising, but the reviewer seemed to thrive on the subject. It seems the paper had sent a stringer who was obviously reluctant to forgo one of the few opportunities to get a by-line in the paper. (I assume he would have gotten his fee whether or not he wrote a review.)

Another review in the same general category, but warranting kindness rather than criticism even more, was a *Times* report of a staged performance of the *Messiah* by psychiatric patients in company with their healers as part of a therapeutic experiment. It would certainly have made a deserving news story, and one would have been especially interested in the clinical effectiveness of the project. But the reviewer decided to evaluate it as he would any professional concert, remarking, for example, on the "extensive rehearsals, but you never would have guessed it from the quality of the performance." How much kinder not to have mentioned it at all! It was certainly harmless and making no pretensions. The usual readers of the music page would not have expected a review, would not have been looking for one, and were most likely not aware the concert had taken place.

In my day we were generous to occasions such as these that fell below minimum professional standard, and we would just describe the event without criticizing it. We found the simple unsigned news report that an event had taken place without critical comment to be useful in general, though currently there seems to be nothing like it. In the minds of the performers or presenters there could be more than one reason why a concert was covered only by a news item—even debut concerts, notwithstanding the fact that an evaluation was something performers and presenters looked forward to. The concert-givers could rationalize the absence of a review—perhaps there was no reviewer available for their event that night or perhaps there was insufficient space. So hurt feelings were minimized. It did not have to be known that the concert was not reviewed because it was so poor. There were times, also, when we went to parts of two programs that were in progress at the same time and decided which to review and which to report as news—or the reviewer (in rare instances, to be sure) would review both without concealing from the reader that he or she had heard only part of each. It may be wondered, why the news story, why mention it at all. To my way of thinking, while I had never been told by the business office that if someone advertised, a concert must be mentioned (or in the case of lavish advertising that it must be given special treatment), I always felt nevertheless that since the recitalists had put their hard-earned money into renting a hall and into advertising as well, the least the reviewer could do is mention them in the paper.

The time for indulging in the language of invective is when the world-class artist errs or becomes careless, and not because he or she has one bad night, but when the showing is faulty over and over again (like Pavarotti at one period when he was overworked). In such cases harm is being done to a large public that has invested its money. It was an unwritten law among us in the critical fraternity that this called for no mercy. Still another such law, sponsored by Noel Strauss of the *Times* and Jerome Bohm of the *Tribune* (who usually collaborated to make or break a pianist, singer, or violinist) was the admonition not to pass final judgment on soloists with orchestra in concertos but to wait until they appeared in solo recital. The soloist depends on the conductor to take care of aspects of the performance—the general flow, for example—but the solo recitalist is on his or her own.

It is a moot question whether journalistic reviewing is criticism. We need not, however, be condescending, for as Charles Rosen has been quoted as saying, "it was the journalistic critic who throughout the years has made the greatest contribution to the art. . . . critics from E. T. A. Hoffmann and Weber, through Schumann, Liszt, Berlioz, Shaw, and Thomson."[7] It is nice to learn that I can qualify for the title of elite critic wherever I publish. However that may be, the newspaper reviewer must remember he or she is a reporter as well as a critic. The reader expects information: the details of the program should be given, not excluding the first names of composers (except in the case of the three B's, etc.), and the names of the works played should be given so they are easily recognized. For example, it is not enough to identify a work as simply Mozart's Piano Concerto No. 25, something that we encounter often, since for many readers (even musicians) the number may not be enough to call it to mind without also the information it is in C major, or whatever the key may be. The *Tribune* in my day usually (not always) gave this information in agate type at the beginning of the longer reviews, leaving more room for discussion of the music (see page 235). Today this format is rarely encountered. Size of audience is relevant, and also the audience response if unusual (e.g., boos or an ovation) should be included in a review.

Editors do not welcome unfavorable remarks about the audience. Geoffrey Parsons had to wean Thomson away from a proclivity in that direction in his early reviewing days at the *Tribune*. When Shostakovich's *Lady Macbeth* had its first American performances in New York and Cleveland (February 1935), some critics berated the audience for cheering it and suggested it was merely taking vicarious pleasure in the opera's sexual explicitness. But beyond the matter of being careful about what is said with regard to the audience's behavior, the paper expects the reviewer to function like any reporter and be vigilant for anything newsworthy—though as reporters they rarely find themselves catapulted up to the level where a first-page news story is required. I once was, when the baritone at the old Metropolitan Opera House who was to sing Enrico in *Lucia di Lammermoor* was held up by a derailed Long Island Rail Road train, so that someone had to be found in great haste to sing his part in the first act until he arrived to assume his assignment in the second.[8] Nor is it often that the reviewer gets the opportunity to report the kind of incident that transpired at a concert of the International Composers Guild in New York in 1925 when, in the course of the performance of a work by Cowell, what was called a "thunder stick" (an ordinary stick with a string tied to it and the string grasped in such a way as to enable the "player" to twirl the stick rapidly to make a whirring sound)) accidentally slipped out of the hand of the twirler and flew across the hall just missing composer and critic, "so that both lived," as the *Times* reported cynically, "to the end of the concert." It was within the aura of such events (also, because of Cowell's attacking the piano keys with fists and elbows for his tone clusters) that Deems Taylor once persuaded the editor of his paper, the old *New York World*, to send a sports reporter to a Cowell concert.

To return to more pedestrian affairs, I miss the Sunday column of gossipy notes that was a regular feature in the *Times* and *Tribune*, covering little as well as big events. (Richard Dyer in the *Globe* has such a column on Fridays.) When I did the column regularly on the Sunday music page of the *Tribune*, being a composer I had special access to the contemporary music world, and I used to keep the *Times* music editor, Howard Taubman (before his promotion to senior critic), very much on his toes trying vainly to keep up with me, even though he had a unique flair for news.

The feature articles on speculative musical subjects or on big events and world-class artists, both daily and Sunday (many of them dealing with vital contemporary music), are certainly more numerous, longer, and more thorough now in both the daily and Sunday editions of the *Times*. Moreover, we may not find the gossipy notes, but coverage of Classical music, current and traditional, is quite visible in both the weekday and the Sunday arts pages, with many stories appearing on the first page of the section. The *Times* shows its high regard for the arts by having them covered in the second section (section B). My newspaper delivery people tend to correct this judgment and put them in what most Americans would consider their rightful place. That is to say, when they stack the sections they often put section C (business) before section B. (Following the attack on the World Trade Center on 11 September 2001, the arts were demoted for a period of about three months to section E, and a temporary new section, A Nation Challenged, was put in their coveted position.)

Not all of us are elated when we observe that coverage of pop music is likely to appear on the same Sunday *Times* pages as coverage of the serious. Rockwell, until recently editor of the Sunday arts section, favors "crossover." I found myself quite in disagreement with him on this matter as well as many others when he was reviewing concerts. My preferences in music also deviated sharply from those of Olin Downes, who pontificated over New York music events for a long, long period (1924 to 1955) from his powerful post on the *Times*. If ever we did agree I would be concerned and would reassess the matter at hand. But Downes was an honest, conscientious, and hard-working critic and I found myself comfortable with his liberal views on national and world politics. Where opera was concerned, he would make every effort to acquaint himself in advance with a new work. He would not only go to the dress rehearsal, as his fellow critics did, but he would attend early rehearsals before the opera reached the stage. An example of such devotion was his involvement with the preparation of Alban

Berg's *Wozzeck*, which had its American premiere in 1931 with Stokowski conducting, first in Philadelphia and immediately afterwards in New York at the old Metropolitan Opera House. By the time the day of the first performance approached he knew it well enough to partially prepare his review in advance, and he was ready merely to fill in the details concerning the execution. His reaction at this juncture was unfavorable. But the cumulative effect of his advance study was such that he was carried away at the performance, and as he reported to the public in his Sunday column on 15 March in a post mortem on his review, in "sixty minutes of inhuman pressure" he had recast his whole evaluation of the opera, which was now favorable, even enthusiastic.[9]

No such epiphany saved the day when Stravinsky's *Rake* was introduced to America in a New York performance by the Metropolitan Opera Association in 1953. Again Downes attended rehearsals even before the cast was on stage. I happened to accompany Stravinsky to one of these when we observers (along with orchestra, chorus, cast members, and conductor Fritz Reiner) were all crowded into a small, barren space, a rehearsal room on the top floor of the old opera house. Sure enough, Downes was there with his score. Stravinsky refused to acknowledge him, for after many reviews in which Downes had exalted Sibelius and (especially during the war when Russia was our ally) Shostakovich and had excoriated Stravinsky, the master was not on speaking terms with the powerful New York critic. I sat to the left of Stravinsky in the cramped space and Downes sat at my left. At one point Downes had the effrontery to urge me to ask Stravinsky whether he did not think a certain figure in dotted rhythm should be played more crisply. (I forget the exact adjective he used.) I thought it took a lot of brass to challenge the world-class composer and the world-class conductor and so I refused to deliver the message. Downes returned to review the *Rake* again the season after its premiere and still found it "empty" and "without consistency of style or inspiration," commenting on the poor attendance to which, of course, his earlier review may have contributed.[10] In much the same way his rave reviews of Shostakovich in the early forties had contributed to a frenzy so great that the performance material for the seventh and eighth symphonies had to be flown here on microfilm in order that audiences should be able to experience the latest utterance of their favorite modern symphonist without the suspense of waiting a few extra days.

One of the casualties the reviewer must be prepared for is the input of the headline writer who may have the inspiration to slant a review in an unintended direction, especially nowadays since what they write is more creative than it was in my day, when the performer's name and perhaps also the place would often suffice. The headliner's input can be particularly harmful when the critic is of two minds about the concert but the headline writer at best can encapsulate only a single evaluation in the allotted brief space. What I said about the reader remembering the photo more than the text also applies somewhat to the headline. It can weigh heavily in determining the impression readers carry away since it is not unusual for them to merely gloss over the start of the review and take in the headline, or to just remember the headline and nothing else.

When I was on the *Transcript* in the thirties, in an unusual departure from the staid old headline—just the performer's name and also the place of the concert—one of my reviews got me into quite a bit of trouble with chauvinistic Boston readers largely because of the emphasis the headline gave. It was a special case in which the senior music critic Moses Smith decided to take the responsibility of writing it. The concert was by a hometown Boston violinist of whom the city was especially proud. It seems she had had a successful European tour, but in regard to the concert she gave on her return in Jordan Hall I had reservations. My review appeared under the headline, "Home Again After Success Elsewhere." The sarcasm intensified the blow, for I myself had no intention of handing down so severe a verdict. I heard from quite a few Boston socialites who complained to me not how *désolée* the violinist Ruth Posselt felt over the review, but how much I had offended her patroness, the wife of ex-Governor Fuller of Sacco and Vanzetti fame—or should I say infamy? How poor Mrs. Fuller had suffered as a result of my review after having done so much for the violinist! I wonder how much my antagonism to her husband contributed unconsciously to my judgment of Posselt's playing that night since on later occasions I found it quite respectable. (Smith, who shared my political leanings, may also have been expressing his attitude.)

The kind of headline one could expect on the *Transcript* in the thirties was the same as that still favored in the forties and fifties on the *Times*, *Sun*, and *Tribune* when I reviewed in New York. The two-line headlines were typical: "Music of Busoni / Played by Petri," "Bernstein Leads / Diamond Symphony." Or there might be one line for the performer or organization, and two lines of a subhead in smaller type giving the place and perhaps an indication of the music played. (We still encounter this type of headline occasionally.) The streamers in large type for relatively modest concerts that started to appear soon after I left the field have been sufficient for the punster to go to work, as in this *Times* headline: "Gunther Schuller's 3 B's Rate an 'A,'" which I had occasion to mention earlier. Often the headline writer latches on to a single word or phrase that leaps from the page and gives a negative connotation to an otherwise favorable review, as in this example from a glowing *Times* account of a concert of Copland's film music: "Poignancy and Bombast in Film Scores by Copland."

But all such problems of a newspaperman were no longer a concern to me when I decided to leave the *Tribune* as of fall 1952 to assume a professorship and the position of chairman of graduate studies in music at Brandeis University in a department chaired by Irving Fine and with Harold Shapero on the faculty, my old pals and colleagues from the Harvard Stravinsky "school." How could I leave such a powerful position, my friends and colleagues asked me—and a position in New York no less where so many would sell their souls to establish themselves?

I had always wanted to go back to teaching but had never found just the right job. Then there were problems of my health which could be controlled better if I were not under too much pressure. I also had a certain intuition of the kind I had had at both the *Boston Transcript* and the *Sun* that the paper was on its last legs—admonishments to use the phone sparingly, unattended accumulation of dust and decay, light bulbs that expired and were not replaced, and the like. The *Tribune*'s demise would not have necessarily dislodged me from newspaper work in New York since Howard Taubman tried to get me at least twice to move over to the *Times* (with assurances that I would have the position of chief critic on his retirement). But the pressure on the *Times* would have been considerably greater than that on the *Tribune*, which was why I turned him down. While I knew getting out of New York would be disastrous to the career side of being a composer (because of the influence reviewing bestowed on one), I also knew the change would be favorable to composing itself.

It was not only teaching that attracted me, but the unique possibility Brandeis presented. At my arrival it would be the university's first year with a graduate program (the university was founded in 1948), and we would be three composers (Fine, Shapero, and myself) establishing the curriculum, whereas in other places in those years it was usually the musicologists who had some time earlier started the department, and composers were then brought in on sufferance, as it were. Of no little consequence in determining my decision was the awareness that Fine was a fabulous organizer, an admirable composer, and an individual of absolutely angelic character and temperament. He was also very persuasive in bringing me around to the decision.

It should not be assumed that the three of us at Brandeis, as close to one another as if we were bound by quasi-family ties, did not make every effort to assemble a strong musicology staff. What was important to us was to maintain a balance within the department so that musicologists would not tell composers how to run their affairs. Now that the composer is a familiar fixture in the university music department things, as far as I can determine, are quite changed.

Milton Babbitt and Arthur Berger at a meeting of the American Academy of Arts and Letters. New York, 1989. Photo by Sabine Matthes.

Critics at work meeting deadlines at the *New York Herald Tribune*, circa 1948. Left to right: Arthur Berger, Francis D. Perkins, Jerome D. Bohm, and dance critic Walter Terry. Photo by Ted Kell *(New York Herald Tribune)*.

Berger (seated third from right) conducting a seminar for students in composition in the living room of Seranak, the former summer home of the Koussevitzkys at Tanglewood, 1964. Photo © Heinz H. Weissenstein/Whitestone Photo.

Composers at Tanglewood, circa 1965. Front row, left to right: Randolph Cole-
man, Harvey Sollberger, Lukas Foss, Aaron Copland, Gunther Schuller, Arthur
Berger. Back row, left to right: Loren Rush, David Del Tredici, Mario Davidowski,
William Syderman, Charles Wuorinen, John Perkins, Donald Martino. Photo ©
Heinz H. Weissenstein/Whitestone Photo. All rights reserved.

Leonard Bernstein (center) with Aaron Copland (right) and Leon Kirchner on the grounds of Seranak, the former summer home of the Koussevitzkys at Tanglewood, 1985. Photo by Walter Scott.

Rehearsal for the New York premiere of Stravinsky's *The Rake's Progress* in a studio in the old Metropolitan Opera House, 1953. Conductor Fritz Reiner on podium. Seated at right, from left to right: Met chorus master (unidentified), Igor Stravinsky, Arthur Berger, Olin Downes. Photo by Serge Le Blanc, courtesy of the Metropolitan Opera House.

Harold Shapero, 1958.
Photo by Esther Geller.

Paul Fromm of the Fromm Foundation (extreme right) with editors and board
members of *Perspectives of New Music*, 1962. Front row: Roger Sessions (left)
and Aaron Copland, advisory board. Second row, left to right: Benjamin Boretz,
associate editor; Herbert Bailey, editor of the Princeton University Press; Gunther
Schuller and Milton Babbitt, editorial board; Arthur Berger, editor.

11 *PNM* and the Ph.D.

In the mid-fifties while I was on the faculty of Brandeis University, Benjamin Boretz was a graduate student of mine in theory and composition, and I once told him about the little music periodical I had edited while I was a graduate student at Harvard, *The Musical Mercury*—a magazine of modest proportions which could still be found tucked away on the least frequented shelves of a few libraries, but otherwise was pretty much forgotten. I have always been under the impression that after I told him about my own experience Ben found the idea of a student editing a magazine (other than just a school publication) while still in college very intriguing. Lincoln Kirstein's literary magazine, *Hound and Horn*, which he published and edited while at Harvard, provided a precedent for something quite prestigious, and after a very brief gestation period my student came up with a plan to do just that in collaboration with two fellow Brandeis music students, Barclay Brown and David Burrows.

But although he worked hard to find a sponsor he had not yet succeeded at the time he and his classmates received their M.F.A. degrees, and so they all went their separate ways. He continued his efforts, which looked promising while he was studying in California, but as the end of the decade approached he still had not succeeded, and when he entered the Ph.D. program at Princeton he persuaded me to agree to be editor of his projected periodical and he would be associate editor. I believe my prestige as a writer and my journalistic experience helped, and so did some lively promotion on the part of Milton Babbitt, for we succeeded in getting the patronage of the impressive Fromm Music Foundation.

With the foundation as our backer we had the further advantage of getting Princeton University Press to publish us. This was obviously not going to be a small operation like my *Musical Mercury*. We spent about two years soliciting articles and working out the handsome layout with the press. It is curious that each of my sponsors, Edwin F. Kalmus for the *Musical Mercury* and Paul Fromm for the present publication, wanted the periodical he was going to support to be named after his favorite magazine already in existence: For the music publisher Kalmus it was a popular magazine of the time, *The American Mercury* (which published H. L. Mencken), for Fromm it was the bulletin *Perspectives* of the Chicago FM station WFMT, which came on the air when the educational station was a new phenomenon.

When we adapted Paul Fromm's choice to our music magazine, *Perspectives of New Music (PNM)*, none of us, including representatives of Princeton University Press, caught the peculiarity of using "of" rather than "on" or even "in." Recently I came across a clipping in my files of a piece in the *New York Times* announcing the new publication as "Perspectives *in* New Music" (italics mine). Boretz and I have always thought we were responsible for the doubtful grammar. But since reading the *Times* piece I have occasionally had the fantasy that something could have happened en route to or from the press or maybe just at the typesetter's machine in the composing room that resulted in the preposition being switched without our noticing it. This was a kind of wish fulfillment. Perhaps it was merely that Eric Salzman, author of the *Times* report on the forthcoming periodical, just naturally assumed we must not have meant "of."

I still cannot get over my absolutely impromptu response when the editor of the press asked us if we had a logo and I came up on the spot with the suggestion we use Stravinsky's drawing in one of the books of his conversations with Robert Craft in answer to a request to make a visual representation of his recent music.[1] Promotional ideas of this nature are not my forte, but it turned out that not only, or so I have thought, is it a handsome piece of art, but it has mnemonic properties, and it is now, by people in the know, recognized more as an icon for *PNM* than as a visual representation of Stravinsky's music. Over the years not everyone connected with *PNM* (most of them serialists) has been exactly elated over the associations this logo brings in its wake. It once got us unexpectedly into trouble. Evidently Luigi Dallapiccola was not impressed by Stravinsky's conversion to serialism though it was pretty complete by the sixties. When the Italian master was approached for an article he was very indignant about our soi-disant avant-garde periodical having a neoclassicist's emblem on the cover and turned us down.

Fromm made a big point of assuring everyone that it was his policy to remain in the background where any of his benefactions (mainly, of course, commissions to composers) were concerned. But this was a commitment he did not really honor in our case. He was very much in evidence whenever there was a press photo opportunity. Also, on one occasion he sidestepped the proper authorities and solicited an article from Iannis Xenakis which Ben, who was sole editor at the time, found fault with. It was one of a number of events that precipitated a crisis. This particular crisis, which occurred after my retirement from the editorship, had a salutary effect which even Ben welcomed, since it brought Edward T. Cone in as coeditor to share the burden and exert the kind of authority toward our sponsor that Ben himself (still relatively young at that time and without a prestigious academic position of his own) admittedly lacked. (In 1969, when the crisis was sufficiently past, Cone became advisory editor briefly.)

Crisis was endemic to *PNM* on all levels and it was one of the provocations for my early resignation while the fourth issue was being prepared. I could tolerate neither the time required nor the emotional strain exacted to cope with the perennial objections. In addition to our sponsor there were others with whom I was obliged to contend. The publisher, for example, was vigilant lest we make improper inroads on the scholarly dignity of Princeton University Press. The editor of the press once tried to get me to strike out the phrase "twelve tonery" from a review by an English contributor on the grounds that it was too "cute." Then there was the editorial board—no list of names as window-dressing this. They were all composers, typically members of Fromm's stable, each with his (they were all male) own axe to grind and eager to impress his own view on the magazine. They were constantly vigilant for that moment when their own music might be an eligible subject for coverage. They were a board that wanted meetings to put their two cents in; they were not satisfied with being, in the usual way, merely a prestigious name on a roster (which is what I now am, by the way, on the *Musical Quarterly* board and I wonder why I persist). And of course, we also had the inevitable objections from the readership; there was still the highly debatable platform of serialism in the public arena as well as the studied linguistic obscurity that I discussed in chapter 6.

Not least of all my concerns were the time and energy I spent ironing out disagreements with Ben. Everyone knows that coeditors disagree and have always to reach some compromise (W. H. Auden had recently resigned from the prestigious British literary magazine *Encounter* because, I believe, he could not get along with Melvin Lasky). Ben had been passionately devoted to the aesthetic theory I had dispensed as his teacher at Brandeis (founded on D. W. Prall and Dewey). But by now he had transferred his allegiance to Babbitt (influenced by Rudolf Carnap et al., whose scientifically oriented philosophy was more au courant at that time but quite out of my line).[2]

I had trouble understanding, and therefore editing, some of the articles we were to publish, and it was a handicap living at such a distance from Ben and Princeton University Press—before the days, it is important to take into account, when we all had access to express and priority mail, fax, and e-mail. (I realize now with proper refereeing and editorial assistance an editor does not have to understand every article published.) Capping all the time-consuming matters I have listed, there was bitter disagreement as to the size of each issue. I had no idea when I signed on that issues would be over two hundred pages. I had the size of *Die Reihe* in mind (a far more compact German periodical). I certainly did not have time for the number of pages Ben wanted and I did not think that in those days we would find enough material of suitable quality to fill them.

I should not leave this recital of woes, however, without adding that underneath our disagreements lies a strong bond, philosophic and humanistic, between Ben and myself, and it lasts to this day. It seems to me this has been what enabled us to have the most bitter disagreements while remaining friends and loyal colleagues and never losing our respect for each other.

In any case, I had always felt it was Ben's periodical. He had had the idea and he was passionate about it. My publishing days were behind me and I now had to have time for composing and teaching. I had come on board, as I have said, mainly because I thought I could lend some of the prestige I had acquired by virtue of my writing and editing experience for whatever it was worth so that he could get backing, and also to help him get started with the benefit of my own know-how. (This was the fourth magazine I had edited.)[3] While I was altogether frustrated by the antagonistic forces surrounding me, it was not without reluctance that I decided it better to resign and leave it all to Ben. I had actually spent almost five years on *PNM*—about two years preparing for its appearance and about the same time editing it, and I was rather pleased with some of the results: the format we achieved and the general feel of the magazine. I did retain my association as a member of the editorial board.

In the early sixties around the time when *PNM* was being founded, the universities were beginning to recognize composition as a legitimate sub-

ject for the doctorate, which up to then had been the almost exclusive domain of musicology. While not explicitly supporting the doctorate in composition, *PNM* broached a number of subjects that would be of interest to
those establishing the new programs, commencing with the statement of
purpose in the very opening sentence of our Editorial Note in the first issue: "*Perspectives of New Music* has been established to provide a medium
for articles that seriously explore those aspects of contemporary music
with which composers find themselves most deeply involved." In other
words, *PNM* would be a vehicle for the learned articles that would be the
university composer's response to the administration's demand for the kind
of articles faculty members in most fields write to get academic advancement. At the same time there was in the first issue an important statement
in the form of an article by Charles Rosen—himself not a composer so
there was no conflict of interest—arguing that music is best taught from
the vantage point of the composer (whether one were a composer or not).[4]

PNM was published by Princeton University Press from 1962 up to
1972, and it was Princeton University's music department that spearheaded
the movement in 1961 for the Ph.D. in music composition in Ivy League or
Ivy League–level institutions. The leading figures in this movement were
Babbitt and the musicologist Arthur Mendel. One of the most cogent arguments was that the intellectual aspect of composition had been acknowledged when it was admitted into the university curriculum. (After all, as I
have already noted, in the medieval university music had been part of the
quadrivium, the four higher fields of learning: arithmetic, geometry, astronomy, music.) But once it had been admitted, it was treated as second-
class. Some time earlier, as a compromise, the Master of Fine Arts degree
had been introduced in a few places as a terminal degree for composers or
theorists as the Ph.D. had been a terminal degree for musicologists. People
did not always recognize the M.F.A. as a more advanced degree than the
simple M.A., however, nor did it meet the requirement of the Ph.D. that
universities and faculties strictly observed in hiring. Doctorates of one kind
or another were being offered here and there in the United States, and in
the Midwest it was as soon available to a tuba player as to a composer. This
new initiative proposed by the caucus of Ivy League professors aimed at a
degree that would not simply be any doctorate but a Ph.D. supported by
prestigious institutions.

Mendel, chairman of the Princeton music department as well as the senior composer, Roger Sessions, were at first opposed to the Ph.D. in composition, but they soon went along with the idea, and Mendel organized
and chaired a committee made up of the chairmen of a half dozen major

universities whose purpose it was to weigh the pros and cons of the innovation. Among the objections cited by the dissenters to the advanced degree was an unwillingness to be pressured by the mere contingency that those in charge of hiring needed a source of accreditation rather than relying on their own judgment. Also, they pointed to the Doctor of Music degree already available in some places, a doctor's degree for a musician that could be hyped up and made to take the place of the genuine Ph.D. despite its poor reputation at the time.

The institutions that joined Princeton to weigh the merits of the Ph.D. in composition and/or theory were the University of California at Berkeley, Brandeis, Columbia, Yale, and Harvard. Princeton instituted the degree while deliberations were still going on in the other places. Among the factors that favored its adoption at Princeton were the already existing Ph.D. for creative work in architecture and the testimonials from the mathematics department that it would never consider a dissertation in the history of mathematics appropriate for a Ph.D. candidate in its field: the candidate must "create new mathematics." Other universities in the, so to speak, caucus followed Princeton's example in their turn. This all transpired in the early sixties.

The objection to the Ph.D. for composers was of course a subset of the claim that composers had no place in the universities in the first place. There was a curious notion abroad that the more composers became a part of the university enclave the more they would be composing music that was difficult to hear and therefore to play, and the less they would be composing for the public at large, which was already sufficiently burdened by the intellectual challenge that new music imposed on its listening capacities. But what this notion seemed to ignore is that despite all the good will and free rehearsal time that the university can provide, its student performers for the most part, however talented and on the way to glory, are not professionals and would almost inevitably leave something to be desired in their performances, though things have been getting better. (Only in the few topflight conservatories do they approach the standards of world-class performers.) I have heard the contemporary American composer's relation to the university compared with that of medieval and Renaissance composers to the monasteries which provided the choirs and instruments for the performance of the music written during those times. Nothing could be further from the truth. The composers today work hard at teaching for their sustenance and do not have people with professional skills to perform their work such as the monasteries offered.

The composer in the university suggests the ideal situation of the "composer in residence" that enjoyed a brief vogue at mid-century but that too is a mistaken notion. Composers on university faculties now have enervating teaching hours and administrative responsibilities and have to do their composing in the spare time that other faculty members use for their own research and writing projects. And of course like other members of the faculty the composers must produce, and this means having performances and publications of their music, as well as, since the advent of the Ph.D., scholarly papers. Not that these scholarly papers were not sometimes required before the Ph.D. In the forties when I was reviewing for the *New York Herald Tribune* I was once approached by members of the music department of a distinguished southern university that was looking for a composer but had to have one with qualifications that would get him or her accepted by the university committee that passed on all appointments. Those qualifications included the candidate's having published scholarly articles *with footnotes.* It seems that since I wrote articles with footnotes they were confident that I was a composer with a good chance of getting past the university screening board. Department members urged me to apply though I was perfectly content at the time in my reviewing job.

PNM's affiliation with academe and with its Ph.D. program in composition in particular became unmistakable—in the unlikely event that it had previously escaped anyone's attention—barely a decade into the periodical's tenure when Boretz began to publish dissertations in installments of rather substantial length. I was apprehensive. I realized that often dissertations were published as books with very little revision. But in general the dissertation demonstrates knowledge and achievement, and literary fineness of style is not a requirement. Also, even in installments they are likely to be very long and top-heavy. As a member of the editorial board I made my objections known. A redeeming feature was that Boretz, who started the practice with his own thesis for Princeton, *Meta-Variations,*[5] was circumspect in his choice of the other authors of dissertations, namely, Philip Batstone and Godfrey Winham, distinguished minds and excellent writers. That Boretz ventured no further than this in the area was, I suspect, partly owing to the difficulty I had feared of his finding suitable material. What dissertations he had already published nevertheless contributed to the dissension in an editorial board that, as I have indicated, was not content with the usual role of providing a rubber stamp and did not feel altogether comfortable with the direction *PNM* was taking. As Boretz put it, in a "Conversation about *Perspectives*" that John Rahn invited him and myself to submit to the magazine for publication on its twenty-fifth anniversary: "People saw the 'style' of *Perspectives* as being antagonistic to their positions even if there was nothing in any way addressed against them. Like, they would feel that a context professing this high intellectual style would leave them looking less distinguished and glossy than those who would look particularly good within the terms of that style."[6]

In 1971–72 things came to a boiling point, and though there had been two or three earlier crises that Boretz managed to survive, this was a real stalemate since he was adamant about publishing (in installments) a piece about the same length as the dissertations that Fromm and several members of the board violently opposed. It was written by board member and Princeton professor J. K. Randall and its title was "Compose Yourself—A Manual for the Young."[7] Members of the board considered it a work of literature—not unlike a long poem, for example. But they thought of *PNM* as a journal devoted to theoretical, analytical, and critical writings on contemporary music, not a journal devoted to creative work, musical or otherwise. Randall pointed out that it was an "attempt to apply compositional concepts to words and to extramusical as well as musical issues and behavior." Publishing Randall's "creative literary piece," even if the subject and method were musical, the argument went, would be like publishing a lengthy musical composition, which was not *PNM's* reason for being. Moreover, what hit Fromm, in the eyes, at a time when it was far from the commonplace expression it is today, was the occurrence of the four-letter F-word. His reaction to this story, strengthened by his growing disaffection with Boretz and the confirmation of his resolve by a few board members, was such that just almost a decade into the life-span of *PNM* Fromm decided he would no longer support it.[8]

In sympathy a number of the original board members resigned,[9] though not enough of them to deplete the board noticeably since by 1970 the original core of eleven, who never lost their proprietary sense, were serving along with six new members. The spring-summer issue of 1972 (vol. 10, no. 2), which started out with the first installment of the Randall, contained a discreet note, the idea of the Princeton University Press editor, that read in part: "This is the first issue that appears without the direct sponsorship of the Fromm Foundation, which has decided to devote its efforts elsewhere in the future." One of Fromm's last acts as a benefactor of the periodical was to insist that the first installment of the Randall be held over and not published as scheduled in the double issue of 1971 (vol. 9, no. 2, and vol. 10, no. 1) devoted to the recently deceased Stravinsky. As Boretz put it in passing this information on to me, it was as if Fromm's decision was "out of respect to Igor Stravinsky whose memory would be mortally defiled by it."

The remaining board members were generally in a panic and were urged to use their academic connections to find support for *PNM*. But it finally turned out that with scarcely a glitch in the transition *PNM* continued under Ben's aegis, and as a subscriber you would have had to look very closely at the small print preceding the title page to learn that fact since nothing seemed to have changed. The move to the new venue was as smooth as it could be and scarcely evident to the world outside. The address soon became Bard College, where Ben at that time was starting his long tenure. (As well as the address the college provided office space.) Of no small consequence in contributing to the smooth transition was the fact that Ben was not unprepared for the turn that events took. We had both from the beginning been aware of Fromm's history as a benefactor of tiring of projects and people and of cutting off support without giving them sufficient time to recoup. Consequently Ben had the idea of establishing what he called a "survival fund." He would put away a little savings as the periodical received each stipend. Added to an annual donation from Princeton University that did not cease, it made it feasible to keep going.

With regard to board members who resigned during this crisis Boretz had this to say: "Of course some members of the Editorial Board saw their connection with *Perspectives* primarily as a connection with Paul Fromm, and when Paul Fromm left *Perspectives* they were eager to detach themselves too to demonstrate—to manifest—that connection. Those who didn't leave the Editorial Board at that time were conspicuously resisting the hierarchization of their loyalties. . . ."[10]

In spite of the defections, with the number of new appointees over the next four years the original number of eleven that constituted the board more than doubled by the time *PNM* moved to Bard; the editor was no longer constrained by a majority that represented the interests of Fromm and the composers qua composers. In the decade that Boretz continued as editor it gradually became obvious that he was being seduced by new directions in contemporary intellectual thought. I became most convinced of this after flipping through the double issue of 1981–82 (vol. 20, nos. 1 and 2) and being puzzled at first when I came across over fifty unnumbered pages with nothing but artful shapes created by inkblots and, in extra-large print, four to about fifty words per page (occasionally just the inkblot). The text started, "If I am a musical thinker . . ." and I assumed it was by Boretz since I was aware he was into this sort of thing, though there was neither a title nor an attribution. (I later found the title, simply "Talk," at the end and I became aware that it was listed in the table of contents where it was modestly attributed to "B. A. B.")

Once having become aware of this typographical inventiveness you inevitably noticed other, if at first less striking, instances of the same order: not only graphics but variegated type fonts. It became evident that this was part of a deliberate tendency, an aesthetic movement with a touch of Surrealism and one that could be traced back to "Compose Yourself" of J. K. Randall who with that explosive contribution had not only precipitated the schism between *PNM* and the Fromm Foundation but had established its author as one of a new movement's pioneers. In addition to Boretz the movement had as a prominent representative Elaine Barkin, who had been *PNM*'s mainstay as guardian of its superstructure since her appointment to the staff in the mid-sixties, first as editorial assistant and then as coeditor. (Barkin had been another of my graduate students in composition at Brandeis at the time when Boretz was there.)

Boretz has identified the new tendency as "non-verbal discourse," leaning heavily, to achieve its end, on the use of graphics and distinctive typography for the "performance" of each article. The practice escalated in 1979, and since Barkin remained as coeditor it still had a sponsor when Boretz retired and John Rahn took over the editorship. Though she in her turn decided to retire in 1983 it was not until 1985 that *PNM* returned to a single format with standard typeface for every article. It was inevitable that the transition took a while since there was a backlog of contributions that had been commissioned during the interregnum of "non-verbal discourse." Rahn retained the idea of some graphics in the form of reproductions in black and white of paintings and such by various artists. They helped relieve the gloom of the heavy, gray, scholarly articles.

I do not want to leave the subject of *PNM* without adding a few words with regard to the singular camaraderie among most of the original eleven board members and the hangers-on who were invited to join them within an environment that seemed to be charged with an energy emanating from Princeton and ultimately from Milton Babbitt. He was something of a guru to us in the sixties much in the way that Aaron Copland, proselytizing quite a different music, was to a different generation in the thirties. Despite the almost internecine behavior when there were disagreements on *PNM* we had a sense of belonging together that went beyond our experience as editors and, as Martin Boykan recently reminded me, we even had our games, properly esoteric and intellectually befitting our pretensions. The game he mentioned that we particularly favored was one that I myself may very well have introduced to the group, since I had encountered it back in 1940. I remember the circumstances vividly and with nostalgia. Archibald T. Davison of Harvard gave me a letter of introduction to Sir Donald Francis Tovey when I went abroad on my John Knowles Paine Traveling Fellowship from Harvard. Though I spent most of my time in Paris with Nadia Boulanger, I did manage to get to London and to phone Sir Donald for an appointment. He was perfectly charming and, true to English hospitality, he invited me at once to tea. I found myself in a cozy group of his acolytes and students who received me warmly as if I had always been one of them. There was some elevated discussion and then Sir Donald proposed a game. Despite hands that were by that time arthritic, he would play at the piano a single chord or even just one note, and ask what celebrated composition it was the start of—warning us if it was from a work other than solo piano. For example, he would play A below middle C and expect us to recognize it as the opening upbeat of *Tristan.* Or he would play middle C and the sixth (C-A) just below it and we would be surprised when it turned out to be Beethoven's "Razoumofsky" Quartet—a six-four chord so unusual for an opening of a piece. I had a very close friendship with Milton in the forties when the game Tovey played was fresh in my mind, and it was the kind of thing I would have certainly mentioned to my fellow composer. He, or some other member of the coterie, could of course have learned the game elsewhere, but I very much doubt it.

12   A Tale of Two Critics:
Rosenfeld and Haggin

I normally resist naming the "best" of anything in the arts where what matters most is not whether one work is better than another but the different qualities they purvey, so that someone who had a surfeit listening to Bach might find it refreshing to listen to a much less grand composer like Shostakovitch or Hindemith, or even one of the young composers starting out with all their faults at a composers' collective. I am no more inclined to pick out the best in any other situation, but were I threatened with physical harm by someone if I refused to mention the critic who I think has done the most for the promotion and, in his own way, explication of contemporary American music, I would not hesitate to remind my interlocutor of Paul Rosenfeld. I say "remind" because he has been a critic very much forgotten for quite some time. Indeed, in a collection of his writings published back in 1969, the editor, Herbert A. Leibowitz, bemoaned even then, "It is ironic and alarming that a man of Rosenfeld's 'myriad chivalries, drudgeries, and masteries' [words of Marianne Moore] . . . should have fallen into almost total eclipse." [1]

It is too facile to assert that the neglect of Rosenfeld is a function of our being disinclined nowadays to the heavy, purple prose, a distinctly psychological approach, and an Impressionist orientation. In my day we were sufficiently troubled by these aspects of his criticism, but we read him as if it were a foreign language and found our own translations rewarding and not at all difficult to make. For in its own way it was precise and it bespoke a most faithful apprehension of the music and a rare ability to go along with new forms and understand them. We did not, most of us, approach music in his way ourselves, we did not necessarily share his romantic notions of its relationship to personalities and society, which he touched upon, for example, in the following typical credo: "And music cuts away the foundations of ready-made Elysiums. Music is expressive, carrying us out of ourselves and beyond ourselves into impersonal regions, into the stream of things; permitting us to feel the conditions under which objects exist, the forces playing upon human life."[2]

But what was more difficult to take was the convoluted prose, sentences like the following which obliges us to hold our breath as we wait for the object of "perceive": "The music world may think to perceive in the isolation in which members of the Viennese group about Schoenberg have been living with their intimates and their pupils, acquainted each, it has been asserted, with at most eleven persons outside his actual family, the sign of their divorce from common humanity and self-indulgent concentration of interest in a private world; and choose to detect in the apparently fantastic monotonal system, the twelve-tone technique original among them, the proof of a retreat from life."[3]

We persisted because the rewards were considerable. For it was in Rosenfeld's columns in periodicals like *Dial* and the *New Republic* that we were introduced to the names of the most significant composers writing at the time—American composers in particular—names that one rarely encountered any place else. His own regard for them was contagious, and we learned to be patient with a style we were brought up to view with considerable skepticism. We had to admit, nonetheless, that it communicated the quality of the music in no small way.

Rosenfeld wrote appreciatively of Schoenberg quite close to the beginning of the composer's career though he became apprehensive as early as about 1916 with regard to the direction the music was taking. The trend away from the intense, febrile, post-Romanticism was something that endowed the music with an air he characterized as "mechanical."[4] Still, this did not discourage him from continuing to be attentive to the composer ("there is no living German whose music we want more to hear than Schoenberg's")[5] and to convey his penetrating impressions, demonstrating that he himself was thoroughly abreast of current developments while his fellows in the critical fraternity not only despised Schoenberg's music but were thoroughly in the dark where it was concerned, finding it not only totally enigmatic but even laughably arch and eccentric. On the basis of the few early works available to American listeners around 1920 Rosenfeld already recognized that Schoenberg was a composer who could claim a place in the line of the masters even though basically, as we shall see, he was not sympathetic to the direction the German composer was taking. Here is an example of the glowing terms in which Rosenfeld wrote of him at one time:

> Each of his pieces that we have been given to hear is a separate and distinct experience; and we can guess what awaits us in the second string quartet, in the monodrama *Erwartung,* in the new *Kammersymphonie,* and the oratorio *Die Jacobsleiter,* and in the rest of his unknown works. Even though some of his compositions, the piano pieces Opus 11, the last of the five for orchestra, and certain numbers in the melodrama, refuse obstinately to come close; the greater portion of them grow upon one. The early *Verklärte Nacht* pleases upon deeper acquaintance. At the first hearing of the work in its orchestral dress, we perceive its resemblances to *Tristan.* But in a second or third, the resemblances, obvious as they are, do not disturb us as they used. We are delighted with the sincerity of the experience, the delicacy of feeling, the daintiness of the violin color.[6]

Notice how Rosenfeld strives to put the works in context. He already knows what the works are that he can look forward to—a knowledge not so easy to come by then as it is now. Notice too how careful he is to distinguish a bona fide influence, a participation in a tradition, from some illicit pilfering for which the composer should be reprimanded. As he continues he points to another influence that some observers still miss because they are so overwhelmed by the Wagnerism:

> There is a strain of Brahms in Schoenberg, too. One hears Brahms in the famous three piano pieces; the ghost of Brahms in the final poem of *Pierrot Lunaire,* with its touching promise of recrudescence. Something of the closeted atmosphere which sometimes irritates in Brahms is in the modern too. The smell of the lamp is never entirely absent from Schoenberg's music.[7]

This brings us after a while to the reservation Rosenfeld had in mind that I mentioned above:

> There must be some over-theorizing habit of mind in the man, threatening him always to snap his intuitional grip upon the universe. And still, it is as one of the exquisites among the musicians that he comes to us. Since Debussy, no one had written daintier, frailer, more diaphanous music. The solo cello in *Serenade* is beautiful as scarcely anything in the new music is beautiful.[8]

How skillfully he softens the blow.

Still, Rosenfeld's most important contribution to music—music being only one of the arts about which he wrote—was his explication, appreciation, and promotion of twentieth-century serious music of the Americas, North and South. In 1929 a small book by him—almost pocket-size and consisting of one hundred and seventy-nine pages—appeared under the title *An Hour with American Music.*[9] For some of us interested in new American music it was a bible. Rosenfeld started out with a disquisition on jazz and how it was not American music, or not the whole story. In the course of the chapter he presented his notion of what serious music is and, without being disrespectful to jazz, how jazz did not share the most essential properties of the other music: "Jazz is an 'entertainment'; and an entertainment, in very simplest Bœotian, is something which temporarily removes people from contact with the realities. Perhaps it is a little ungracious of us, to analyze what, like an entertainment, pretends merely to please?" (p. 15).

At the time the little book was published, the year of the shattering Wall Street crash, composers that we now consider the most important Americans of their time operated in an underground; you could not find their names in the newspapers or the most popular music magazines, but you did find them in Rosenfeld's book and his articles in the "little" magazines. For some of us it was like being admitted into an occult, elite, and altogether special world. Rosenfeld's pantheon of composers who were establishing an indigenous American school included, along with the avant-garde, the conservative Edward MacDowell, whom he singles out from among all the epigones devoted to the middle European symphonic tradition (Chadwick et al.), as "the first American to deserve the name of composer" (p. 40). The others included Leo Ornstein, Dane Rudhyar, Adolph Weiss, Sessions, Copland, Carl Ruggles, Thomson, Harris, Gershwin, Chavez, Edgard Varèse, Ruth Crawford, Theodore Chanler, and Colin McPhee—a remarkably inclusive list for that early stage in the evolution of the modern stem of American music. Commenting on the American music scene and speaking with authority because of his cognizance of the various arts, Rosenfeld admits, "As a whole, the musical movement is still slighter and of less importance than either the pictorial or the literary, in proportion to its comparative recency. But it exists; it swells. New creative talents appear with every year . . ." (p. 26).

It is not altogether obvious why Rosenfeld's star declined so precipitously by the mid-thirties, but according to one of his most devoted chroniclers, Charles L. P. Silet, it had something to do with "the collapse of genteel cultural criticism and the loss of faith experienced by American intellectuals during the period between the wars."[10] Even when his influence in the art world was at its lowest ebb, he could draw some consolation from the respect with which the most distinguished writers regarded him. Rosenfeld died in 1946, and in 1948 a book was published under the apposite title *Paul Rosenfeld: Voyager in the Arts.*[11] Because his fellow music critics thought so little of him, considered him an amateur, the contributors were mainly men and women in literature (poetry and criticism): ten composers but about three times as many writers, one name from dance and a couple from the visual arts, and significantly only one music critic (Alfred Frankenstein of the *San Francisco Chronicle*, who himself had a distinguished record as advocate of contemporary American music). About half the book consisted of collected essays, but many of the contributors submitted short tributes, contributors who were top drawer, names like e. e. cummings and Edmund Wilson. For the reviewers of the daily press, on the other hand, it was as if no such critic as Paul Rosenfeld had ever existed; he was simply not in their club.

What would I, an ardent advocate for the preservation and promotion of new music, be doing writing about Bernard Haggin, and in praise of him as a critic no less? He could be pretty nasty in his treatment of most new music except when it was a matter of Stravinsky of any period, whom he came to admire in his capacity of dance critic because of his passionate devotion to anything that George Balanchine choreographed. Balanchine's use of so many Stravinsky scores, as I had occasion to remark earlier, gave many of us the opportunity to hear music of the master that we could probably not have heard in any other way (except, of course, at the concerts of Craft).

During his most active days as the critic of the *New Republic* and later of the *Nation*, Haggin had a sincerity and single-mindedness that I doubt very much any of us in the critical fraternity can honestly claim to surpass or even equal. On one occasion during my early days at the *New York Herald Tribune* I confided in Thomson that I sometimes tossed in my bed and found it hard to sleep, worrying about whether I had been fair to the artist I had reviewed that night. Did I make a mistake in judgment or even on the most trivial level, if it had been the opera, had I mistakenly called a baritone a bass? Thomson told me he wrote a review and then completely banished it from his mind. He thought that was a good example to follow. But Haggin was even more of a worrier than I was. He was incapable of banishing a review from his mind. He once reviewed a piece of mine, not altogether unfavorably in view of his stand on contemporary music, and soon after the review appeared I received a letter from him expressing concern that I might have misunderstood what he had written. Had it come across that despite the reservations the thrust had been favorable? He was equally concerned about my reaction to an article on composer-critics that was published in the *Hudson Review* and that claimed poor composers make poor critics. He wrote me a letter dated 21 March 1948 saying he hoped I did not get the wrong impression the way a friend of his did; he hoped I realized that he had not included me in the category "bad composer = bad critic" since I should know he admired my music which he found "diverting"—the kind of guarded compliment he would have for a contemporary work. He wanted to assure me that he thought me a good composer and therefore someone with all the potentiality to be a good critic, which in his view I certainly was. His friend had told him she thought he should assure me of this. Picking on his fellow music critics, something considered a No-No by members of the fraternity, was one of his favorite occupations. An exchange with Boretz over the esoteric "Princeton school" language particularly comes to mind.

A unique accomplishment of Haggin's, admirable in a way but highly questionable, was his grading of a substantial portion of standard music literature from Bach onwards. The results he shared with his small but absolutely faithful readership in his book *Music on Records*, published in the days before the long-playing record when a book on recordings had a reasonable chance of not becoming outdated on publication as it would in the days of LPs and especially lately with the proliferation of constantly newer CDs duplicating and outdating previous versions of the same work.[12] Of course the book did ultimately date, and by now it seems perfectly antediluvian. But it is still of interest as an example of Haggin's preoccupation with grading serious music. Let me take the Mozart entries as an example. There are some one hundred works of this composer listed, including complete performances of the four best-known operas and quite a number of operatic excerpts. A single sentence usually suffices for each recording, including a succinct evaluation of performance, the latter taking the form, for example: "the music is devitalized by the care taken to achieve impeccable technical finish," or "superb performance . . . recorded harshly," or "insensitive performance." (When there was more than one recording of the same work he would naturally consider the relative merits, but at that period duplications were nowhere near what they are now.) That would be about as far as he would go in coping with performance and recording.

What is most striking in the book is the way works are classified in terms of the value Haggin placed upon them. Thus, of Mozart we have "The Great Works," "Important Works of Lesser Stature," "Minor Works," "Uninteresting or Unimportant Works" (yes, the great Wolfgang Amadeus was capable of such though for most people he could do no wrong), and to cap it all, "The Greatest Works." On the subject of Brahms we meet again the snobbish attitude of Paul Henry Lang. Brahms brings in his wake the category "Bad Works," and Shostakovich is a victim of both "The Poor Works" and "The Worst Works."

In the days when Haggin wrote for the *Nation* it seemed very much like the *New Republic* if one did not go too deeply into their politics. The austere format was the same and they appealed to more or less the same kind of public, so there seemed to be a certain rivalry between them. When I reviewed Haggin's book *Music for the Man Who Enjoys "Hamlet"* for the *New Republic* he was surprised, harboring a touch of paranoia as he did, that I should be so favorable, notwithstanding some reservations.[13] The reason was that he considered the *New Republic* the enemy. As the title suggests, the book is addressed to an intelligent reader and the rationale behind it is that just because he or she is an amateur and beginner in the mastery of technical musical knowledge was no reason to be addressed as an elementary school pupil.

To overcome the obstacle facing the nonprofessional intelligent readers he was addressing, an obstacle created by their inability to decipher what is to them the unbridgeable code of musical notation, Haggin adopted a procedure that was quite innovative in the early forties. He provided his readers with a gadget that gave exact measurements to enable them to locate on the (mostly) twelve-inch seventy-eight rpm breakable wax disk of those days any passage illustrating a point about the music that he wished to make. For example, the reader would be told to listen to "side 3 of the Columbia recording of Egon Petri's performance [of Beethoven's Opus 111] to the point one and nine-sixteenth inches from the first groove. . . ." In this way the reader was in a position to follow the author when he cited crucial details and their musical consequence. Toward his readers he assumed the role of genial schoolmaster, advising them to listen to some particular strand over and over and then hear it with a secondary strand. He thus avoided the sin of the purveyors of what Thomson called the "appreciation racket," for example, perpetrating such inanities as having the student listener lie in wait to catch the second theme of a *sonata allegro* so that he or she could name it, and glossing over everything else—this despite the fact that Tovey had issued an important corrective, a warning to observe two *groups* of themes, first group and second group, rather than merely first theme and second theme. What distinguished the approach overall was that Haggin was not satisfied to send his readers away feeling very smart about their musical knowledge because they had a few new terms under their belts, which seemed to be the aim of any number of effusions of the "appreciation racketeers." Haggin felt that it was the effect of the music on listeners and their own actual experience of it that was important, not the terminology. It seems to me his example is still something to bear in mind when dealing with the amateur music lover.

Today Haggin's book suffers among other things from the circumstance that almost no one would play seventy-eight rpm records any more, even if they were available. But anyone who reads music can consult the score; the observations are interesting not only to the amateur but to the professional as well. It was surprising that the innovation of using the ruler to locate the music illustrations did not catch on. Perhaps it was because Haggin was considered marginal, writing as he did for a magazine that many found politically left. The device, moreover, seemed somewhat pedantic and eccentric. Now, of course, we have the CD, which makes it easier to find a specific place in the music since it is clocked. Also, its compactness does have a distinct advantage since it can easily be slipped into a flap inside the back cover of a book, and some writers have taken advantage of this.

As a corollary to his rating the works of the great composers Haggin admonished his readers to beware of sharing in the all too common belief that masters always write masterpieces. It is a subject on which he expressed himself as follows, using J. S. Bach as an example, no doubt because of that composer's unchallenged reputation for genius and a vast output that included numerous short occasional pieces often for religious or teaching purpose:

> I would like to point out that those prodigious powers of invention and construction which were unceasingly in action—if not on ideas of his own then on the ideas of others, if not on good ideas then on poor ones—gave us great works like the Passacaglia and the D minor Concerto [for clavier or violin and orchestra], but also works in which they appear to have operated on their own momentum, unfueled by inspiration. Ernest Newman was led to write once that "no man can keep on turning out music day by day, as Bach and Mozart for instance did,

and not fall very frequently below his own highest level. No man can produce a work of genius any day and every day; a great deal of his music is bound to be no more than merely fluent chatter and good workmanship." [14]

Haggin goes on to cite concertos "without real organic musical life," among them the Violin Concerto in E major "and even the Concerto in A minor for flute, violin, and clavier that Tovey considers a great work." That Haggin resists the temptation to add some wry comment with regard to the judgment of his distinguished colleague in the domain of musicography bespeaks his directness as a critic who sticks to the point and does not particularly indulge in the literary niceties that make criticism of an abstract art more appealing to the general reader.

III

AESTHETICS AND MUSICAL ANALYSIS

13   Do We Hear What
       We Say We Hear?

Until not so long ago the cleavage between adherents of absolute music and program music could become at times as wide as the more recent one between adherents of tonality and the serialists. It would appear that one could take the program (i.e., the plot or story) of a given work and apply it just as easily to another. The hopelessness of seeking a one-to-one correspondence between the music and the story line has been demonstrated again and again. Donald Francis Tovey refers to "the human foolishness of a *priori* thinkers" and remarks: "The experience of Beethoven's 'Pastoral' Symphony shows that that foolishness is most stimulated by the imitating of sounds. Beethoven's thunder rouses more righteous indignation than his rainbow; and the indignation descends to the childishness which it would rebuke when it points out that Beethoven makes the lightning follow the thunderclaps."[1] And still more foolish: ". . . the notion that the 'Eroica' Symphony should be a chronological biography of a hero and should therefore put the funeral march at the end."[2]

I remarked earlier on the hazards of using words for a nonverbal medium, and I hesitate to dwell on the subject since nowadays it is fairly commonplace knowledge. Tovey advances a nice precautionary measure when he suggests we substitute "the notion of untranslatability for that of absoluteness." Indeed, "absolute music" is an unfortunate locution though it continues to be used despite the excellent possible alternatives proposed by the visual arts: "abstract" or "nonobjective." Of the two I should opt for the latter since "abstract" like "absolute" is somewhat forbidding; it can even suggest a music that is low on the emotional scale, whereas there are "absolute" Romantic symphonic works that are as fiery and intense as anything you will find in a Richard Strauss tone poem.

It is more difficult to find a replacement for the locution "program music." Nowadays the Romantic tradition of outright program music is less to be observed than the equally Romantic tradition of using fanciful or evocative titles, not to tell a story but to attempt rather to embody the feeling aroused in the composer by whatever the title refers to. In the heyday of program music (the second half of the nineteenth century and the early decades of the twentieth) the assumption that music could do what words can do was the order of the day, with all the naiveté that goes with it. But even in vocal music, as it need scarcely be pointed out, however much the composer strives after it, there is no identity between the feeling and content of combined words and music, and we are perfectly free to take them separately—which is something to be thankful for when the poetry is poor. Or when the words express sentiments distasteful to us. I remember as a youth, when I took my Jewish background seriously, I was terribly torn between my profound love of the Bach *Passions* and my horror at the representation of the Jews until finally I realized that I was not, in being deeply moved by these works, being complicit with the perpetrators of the iniquities depicted. For the music embodied Bach's emotional reaction to the text, an emotion that one could appreciate without believing in the story itself. I am not saying the text is of no importance at all, but there are times when the emotion distilled from it is of more consequence than the text itself. In my case it helps if the *Passions* are sung in the original German, since I have a limited knowledge of the language. I am similarly grateful for this limited knowledge when I listen to the masterpieces of German *Lieder*, many of which have texts of a quality that leaves much to be desired. Having made this confession, I feel I should add that I am not at all immune to the special pleasure that ensues when poetry and music come together in an ideal marriage as in Francis Poulenc and Guillaume Apollinaire, Virgil Thomson and Gertrude Stein, and, if for nothing else than the setting of "Chamber Music," Israel Citkowitz and James Joyce.

A legacy of the era of program music still with us is the impulse to look beyond the edges of a work of musical composition or behind it to determine its meaning or essence, ignoring the important principle that it is only the work of art itself that can give up its secret. The example still at times followed is of a practice that was once carried to extremes of absurdity as in the case of the nineteenth-century behaviorist author of *The Power of Sound*, Edmund Gurney, who declared that the pleasure we experience on contemplating a mountain was due to the fact that we are "traversing and surmounting with facile sweeps of the eye something the traversing and surmounting of which might be, in another way, a matter of time, toil, and danger."[3]

One can only stand in awe at the imagination that led its author to such a conclusion. Coming closer to home and to a realm of the commonplace, I am sure we all find ourselves going beyond, in D. W. Prall's sense, the directly presented aesthetic surface to account for the effect of music we hear—sometimes foolishly and quite illogically. For example, the Austrian musicographer Hans Gal observed, in somewhat redundant writing about Brahms's symphonies, "The four are completely different in character, different in style, and different in effect. Herein lies a part of their greatness." [4] Strictly speaking this could mean in order to thoroughly appreciate the "greatness" or apprehend the totality in which the relations of any one symphony are involved, you have to hear all four symphonies, preferably, I should assume, at a single sitting, in order to grasp the unity in its temporal parameter. From an aesthetic point of view, simply remembering the other symphonies is not enough. They have to be immediately present as a sensuous experience, though I doubt we will change our habits in this matter of dwelling mentally on what is not present. (It is very likely the plot line more than the music that enables us to grasp the unity of the *Ring*.) This is something to ponder. It is undeniably a credit to any composer that he does not write the same piece over and over, and some of us as listeners, who do not share the large public's contentment with hearing the same few masterpieces until they are so familiar as to become opaque, naturally profit from a composer like Brahms, who can so skillfully vary his approach to the creative process. But the relations along the parameter of each work are not affected by all this. If all four symphonies were the same, hearing and knowing them all might result in our tiring more quickly of each one individually. But strictly speaking in some abstract sense each one individually would be just as great as it now is without all four being so distinct and without the others existing at all. Nor would I deny that how we listen to any given work does depend in some sense on our total listening experience. That experience is something that sharpens our perception of any one work and turns us into listeners of broad and varied exposure. But it is not a matter of having to know a specific other work to appreciate the present one.

As a graduate student in musicology at Harvard I was exposed to the ruminations of a real *Spinmeister* in the *Mittel Europa* Romantic tradition of music's capacity for word-painting. Hugo Leichtentritt, my teacher in musicology, was another of the European refugees who found a haven in the United States. He had a pretty thorough knowledge of social and cultural history which enabled him to deal with music in a broad context: for example, his studies in iconography led him to observe that singers in me-

Ex. 11. Mozart, *Don Giovanni*, Overture (opening of *Moderato*) (reduction)

dieval and Renaissance paintings had screwed-up noses, which suggested to him that their voice production was nasal, and thus indebted to Eastern (including Hebrew) sources. Ad hoc decisions like this did not endear him to American musicologists, who tended to be more specialized and dedicated to a philological rigor.

In the classroom he would be sure to mention at almost every session "Volume IV of Ambros' *Geschichte der Musik* vich I myself hev edited." [5] His favorite subject was word-painting; when a rapid sixteenth-note scale passage you could find anywhere occurred in Mozart's *Don Giovanni* it would represent for him the Don's "flowing plume." Once he asked the seminar what the D-sharp in the third bar of the faster part (*Moderato*) of the overture suggested to us (Ex. 11). I volunteered the epithet "defiant." He was ecstatic, it was perfect for the Don. He kept coming back to it and asking, "Mr. Berger, vat vas that vord you used?"

One day Leichtentritt was striving to back up his claim that word-painting was ubiquitous and important in vocal music by claiming that it had been evident as far back as the recorded history of Western music extended—for example, in the music of the Greeks as evidenced in a tiny surviving fragment of the music of *Orestes*, the play of Euripides. Notice, he admonished us, how in otherwise fairly conjunct motion at the word "devil" there is a sudden rise of the interval of a fifth. It happened that I had been investigating Greek music at the time, and I learned somewhere that precisely this spot was a lacuna filled in by a modern editor. Instead of discreetly keeping this information to myself I had to parade my erudition and disabuse my instructor before the whole class. Leichtentritt was thick-skinned and my arrogance did nothing to ruffle him or affect our warm and close friendship, which persisted for many years afterwards.

When we pass from the subjective discourse and metaphysical uncertainties that prevail in dealing with music from the angle of its emotion and the story it tries to tell us, and proceed to the cool and calculating realm where we confront it theoretically and by means of the most advanced twentieth-century analytic equipment at our disposal, the expectation may be that we are finally on the firm ground of objectivity and even, I might add, sanity. Oddly enough, however, we run into some of the same problems—problems that arise out of the application of verbal criteria (for music analysis is not altogether bereft of them) to a nonverbal activity. Analysis at its best is a very useful tool for understanding what a composer has accomplished and to apprehend in all its fullness what we otherwise take in through direct nonverbal aesthetic experience. It is most rewarding if and when we subsequently make the transition to the essentially perceptual part of our listening insofar as it is feasible. But it requires caution. Above I remarked that one could take the same program and apply it to a different work without anybody knowing the better. It's not quite the same thing but in a related manner one can have two different analyses even when dealing with the same parameter of the music. Your neopositivist theorist, if I understand the position, seems to be telling us that one of these analyses must be wrong. But whether or not the difference flows from the fact that we are dealing with two different aspects of the same music, or two different ways of analyzing that music, they can both be perfectly valid.

This is not to say that there are no "wrong" analyses when two conflicting ones deal with the same parameter. Thus, with regard to the following statements we are perfectly justified in asking whether their promulgators heard the same work. (Also, it is highly questionable whether either statement is apposite to the work under consideration): 1) the harmony of *Sacre* "emphasizes a definite tonality" (Alexander Tansman);[6] 2) "When Stravinsky used the language of atonality in his middle period, particularly in his *Sacre du printemps,* he seemed to take his place alongside Schoenberg as a pioneer of a new type of music" (Ernst Krenek).[7] Here is an absolutely clear case of contradiction in the statements of two reputable and knowledgeable composers. Perhaps it could have been avoided by treating the work *sui generis* instead of trying to force it into available categories. The *Rite* was written during the last stages of Impressionism when there was a sudden burst of innovation for which its composer was largely responsible. Some attempt to relate the work to that tradition might possibly have helped. Krenek's statement is more plausible if we can think of a broader context for "atonality" than the Second Viennese School.

If one approaches the *Rite* from the direction of tonality one can illuminate it by indicating what it does *not* do—namely, how it does not conform to the specifications of tonal functionality. But this is circuitous. The most devout Princeton serialists would not be likely to take this direction even though ironically when dealing with Classical music they are dedicated to the teaching of Heinrich Schenker, who considered any music misguided that does not conform strictly to the rules of functional tonality (i.e., the rules prescribed by the major triad, the "chord of nature"). Most of us who use Schenker's analytical methods do not believe this. What appeals to us in Schenker's system of structural analysis, and certainly also appeals to the neopositive Princetonians, is its superb organization and an objectivity that lends itself to choosing the "right" note in your chart or arguing over it as if the analysis were as sacred as the composition itself. What also must appeal to the neopositivist is that the analysis of any given work is not an interpretation of it, involving opinion and hypothesis (the kind of approach that is the prerogative of the critic), but something that is rigidly organized. Those of us who lean toward interpretation but also find many aspects of Schenker extremely useful must find ourselves engaged in some prestidigitation to balance the rigidity with our dedication to freedom of choice in analysis.

I remember being introduced to Schenker's system in lectures at Columbia University during the early thirties by one of his chief disciples, Hans Weisse—lectures in a course, it should be well noted, designated "Musical Criticism," which I audited though I was attending New York University. With suggestions from the floor, Weisse would make a veritable construction (actually a reduction) on the blackboard and would light up when the "right" note was volunteered. The "construction" was virtually another work of art, because everything had to be just right. As in a piece of music, if you alter any note it will affect the totality of relations.

I found "prolongation" very revealing—the idea that certain notes were essential, a kind of skeleton on which the fleshy substance hung. But I wondered about what I regarded as significant things that were ignored because they were *merely* on what was condescendingly designated the "surface."

A very few years later, as a graduate student in music at Harvard, in a seminar in aesthetics given by David Prall, who was responsible for the formation of my thinking about the arts, I learned that "surface"—"aesthetic surface" or "qualitative surface"—was extremely important. Indeed it was the differentia of art! All the relationships within the work were felt, perceived by virtue of the fact that they came to us through the sensuous surface.[8]

In his review of Felix Salzer's *Structural Hearing*, the book to which many of my generation had recourse for the tenets of Schenker's methodology, Babbitt observed, "The hearing of music is always organized perceptually according to some analytical conception, be it verbalized or not, and the test of the validity of Schenker's conceptions is not whether 'one hears that way' but whether, after having become aware of these conceptions, the listener does not find that they may not only codify his previous hearing but extend and enrich his perceptive powers. . . ."[9] I have some reservations about Babbitt's use of "perceptually" in the first part of the sentence since I regard "percept" and "concept" to be in many ways opposites. (I discuss the subject in some detail in chapter 14.) But I like the way he puts the matter of the value of analysis and its capacity to "enrich" subsequent hearing. I should hope it were clearly understood that in the view to which I subscribe the process of conceptualizing should ideally not take place during the listening process, where it might prevent the listener from an uninterrupted and immediate transaction between full and unanesthetized attention to the presented aesthetic object. In the best circumstances aesthetic apprehension is direct and immediate; we do not hold a conversation with ourselves about it while listening, thus distracting ourselves from hearing the music.

Yet with full absorption in the sounds we hear we can find having a concept somewhere at the edge of our minds enormously helpful. Or we could justifiably hold a conversation with ourselves and listen discursively the first time we hear a difficult new work in a difficult new idiom. This may only be preparation for more aesthetic listening in the future. Then again there is no ideal way of listening. It may not be the highest stage of listening, but sometimes it is not altogether unrewarding or unprofitable to merely sit back passively and act as a sounding board for the aesthetic surface to which one is exposed—one hopes, in a receptive mood. This may very well be the stance one is obliged to assume at a first hearing without any forewarning, and indeed one may never recapture the precious experience of hearing a piece for the first time. Given a reasonably good piece—it need not be a masterpiece—we may find ourselves experiencing a special thrill at the slightest show of novelty—a feeling that we can never have again in listening to the same piece.

Concentrated, unimpeded listening is not at all easy. One must clear one's mind of distraction and keep it fixed upon the aesthetic object. The British analytic philosopher Gilbert Ryle warned us of the traps that are strewn upon our way to this ideal goal when he wrote about a listener "putting his mind" on music: "He need not, though he may, be murmuring to himself comments, strictures, instructions, encouragements, or diagnoses, though if he is doing this it is again a proper question to ask whether or not he is thinking what he is murmuring. Sometimes an addict of discourse, like Hamlet, is thought not to be applying himself to a given task just because he is applying his mind to the secondary task of discoursing to himself about his primary task. . . ."[10]

I would not want to leave the impression that I believe the mind is absolutely clear of any other thought when it is fully apprehending a work of art. (I wonder what the concert reviewer hears who is sketching his review either in his head or on the printed program while the music proceeds.) Words and thoughts may enter one's head, but without requiring the time-consuming intellectual effort of dealing with the choices and ambiguities of a painstaking analysis. Such analysis is not always called for. A poet as severely intellectual as T. S. Eliot once remarked somewhere something to the effect that poetry can be appreciated before it is understood. And what is it that the critic who wrote the following means to say? ". . . in an episode that serves as a rueful slow movement, Mr. Reich becomes fixated with counterpoint, sometimes writing for twelve separate string lines. This is beyond what the ear can take in, of course, but the effect is haunting."[11] Is it that we cannot hear twelve separate lines at once and therefore cannot savor the total work as the reviewer suggests? No, the object is not to hear twelve separate lines but what is conveyed by their relationship. Music, as I have already observed, is relationship. What point would there be in writing music that could not be heard, and if such is the case is it indeed music? I do not think Reich ever went as far out as the Fluxus gang, which claimed that "just to know of a work" was to experience it (see chapter 8). Contrapuntal music has always presented listening problems whether there are two voices or a dozen. One solution often suggested is to pass quickly from one voice to another, back and forth constantly to be sure they are all there and you hear them. But actually relationship is such that even if you think you are hearing one isolated voice, you cannot help but hear it in its relationship with all the other voices, unless, of course, you manage to block everything out by singing just the one line along with the music subvocally. The point of all of this is that if your hearing is not faulty and you are in an unanesthetized state you can hear a lot more than you think you can. What is required above all is merely that you *listen*.

You might say that ideally the form of a musical work is felt (see chapter 4). But even if your listening is exemplary, even if you are completely receptive to the directly felt qualities that are coming to you through the aesthetic surface, ideas may come into your head with regard to either the music you are hearing or any other matter. Usually these can be easily disposed of. But if they become obsessive they will naturally deflect you from the music. A conservative listening to a far-out contemporary work may be totally consumed by questions in the mind that in essence amount to "Where the hell are the tunes?" If you allow your received notions (concepts) to get in the way, you may become simply a conduit for sounds pouring over you, hearing the music but not really listening. Thus, there are times when someone is justified in claiming that you are listening in the wrong way. If it is a bona fide contemporary work it is advisable for you to stop listening for tunes, and to concentrate, rather, on texture, line, densities, etc. Reviewing a work of Pierre Boulez in the *New York Times*, Tommasini wrote: ". . . if you rid yourself of concern for the methods used to pick the pitches and listen for color, shape, character, and darting, skittish rhythmic writing, the music is hard to resist." [12] (This checks out somewhat with a remark Boulez himself once made after a detailed explanation of the technique of his *Marteau sans Maître:* "Now forget everything I just told you," he said, "and listen to the music"—an admonishment that should be taken with the proverbial *granus salis.*)

Another thing of importance is that you must differentiate between generally interesting knowledge and knowledge that is distinctly relevant to hearing. The desire for knowledge is universal and musicologists spend their time in pursuit of it. But how does it advance hearing to know that the minor triad is an inversion of the major? Do you think Beethoven knew this, or paid any attention to it? Then too, if you listen conceptually, there is the matter of interpreting harmonic events when they are not exactly clean-cut. Theorists have been known almost to come to blows over their disagreement as to what the name, and therefore function, of a certain given chord is. (Schenkerites may disagree over a structural note on a Schenker graph, but they would be unlikely to argue over a vertical harmony since their analysis is linear.) Are you going to argue with yourself with regard to the name of the chord while the music is progressing?

The recriminations one might be regaled with when theorists argue about matters like this would no doubt take the form of, "But I don't hear it that way!" The *Allegro* of the "Dissonance" Quartet which I cited above provides a good example. In m. 116 there is a V⁷ of B-flat major in root position (see above, Ex. 4b). Consulting the printed page we observe the "same" chord continue up to and including the second beat of bar 117, but on the second part of the second beat instead of an E-flat (seventh of the dominant on F) what we hear as the same pitch is notated D-sharp, and we continue to get it to the end of the bar in place of the E-flat. The harmony is no longer spelled F-A-C-E♭ but, according to the convention of spelling chords in thirds, D♯-F-A-C, though this chord (an augmented sixth) always appears in first inversion, so the F remains in the bass. (The inversion does make a difference but pitch content remains the same, and given our ability to abstract as we listen the degree of identity is patent.) The question is do we hear a new harmony? One has no difficulty with this if one accepts the premise that E-flat and D-sharp are the same pitch as far as our hearing is concerned. But there are those who still insist that despite the universal acceptance (certainly in Classical music) of equal temperament the two notes are different, and therefore one should be hearing a different harmony in bar 117. I once knew a very fine cellist who ran herself ragged trying to play a D-sharp differently from an E-flat, and she claimed it was precisely what she was doing but none of us could hear it. She was totally unimpressed when I drew her attention to quite a number of instances in Mozart and Beethoven and their contemporaries which attested to their assumption of equal temperament, even to the extent, in many cases, of notating the C string as B-sharp (the viola, for example, in bar 39 of the *Andante* of Mozart's String Quartet in D major, K. 575, or the cello in bar 64 of the *Adagio affettuoso* of the Brahms Sonata No. 2 in F major for piano and cello, op. 99). The brief excerpt in Example 12 from the *Adagio* of Mozart's Sonata for violin and piano in E-flat major, K. 481, looks polytonal for half a measure, with a signature of four flats in the violin and a signature of three sharps in the piano. It is simply that the violin arrives at the new signature before the piano and accommodates itself to the piano with a G-flat that stands for A-flat. Passing from one of these keys to the other happens three times in the course of the movement.

Ex. 12. Mozart, Sonata for violin and piano in E-flat major, K. 481, *Adagio*
(bars 59–62)

To return to the "Dissonance" Quartet, it is only in the passage from bar
117 to the next bar that we hear the chord in a relationship of augmented
sixth. Strictly speaking, it may be said the chord is a dominant seventh that
has been used in the relationship of an augmented sixth. We do not know
its function as an augmented sixth until we are past it. So it is debatable
what we "hear" in bar 117 at the very moment it occurs and whether we
can say the chord "is" this or that. If the music were cut off at the end of
bar 117, and we heard it without seeing the score, there would be no doubt
of the whole measure being in the relationship of a dominant of B-flat major—but of course we'd be listening to a different piece. The metamorphosis of that dominant into an augmented sixth chord depends on its relationship to the totality, something we will know for sure at the end. When
we analyze the work, what is significant is not that the dominant seventh
chord "becomes" an augmented sixth chord, but that the dominant seventh
chord that we hear for two full measures (despite the premature notational
alteration) will "function" as an augmented sixth chord leading us to the
dominant of A minor, a half-step lower than the "expected" B-flat major.[13]
It is important to be wary of concepts formed *after* hearing a work to be

sure they take into account what you have heard and how you have heard it at a given point in time. In other fields of learning, linguistics for example, we sometimes encounter a locution that would be quite useful in musical analysis and might prevent many arguments. Instead of saying the chord *is* this or that, we "assign" a structural function according to its relationship at a given time.

When technical matters of this nature are spelled out it must sound formidable to nonmusicians who find their Beethoven wonderful without knowledge of them. Indeed, it is enough to discourage them from any attempt to listen seriously to "serious" music. The mavens somehow give them the impression that listening to music on a properly high intellectual level must involve murmuring to oneself the description and the names of the structural attributes of the music as it is being heard. This can be quite distracting and I sometimes wonder whether those average listeners are not in a better position to apprehend what is truly aesthetic in the music they hear without having its true nature occluded by a wall of theoretical speculation and sheer jargon.

14 New Linguistic Modes and the New Theory

The essay that follows is a free adaptation of a contribution I made to PNM *3, no. 1 (fall-winter 1964). Writing in a journal that was promoting the scientific orientation that music theory was assuming (something abetted by the new Ph.D. in composition), I was, as it were, boring from within, approving the intellectual maturity that theory and its possible relevance to criticism were achieving, but at the same time questioning the scientific assumptions — and doing so on territory where they were held in the highest esteem.*

Joseph Kerman had not seen my article when at approximately the same time (27 December 1964) he delivered his thought-provoking address, "A Profile for American Musicology," at a plenary session of the thirtieth Annual Meeting of the American Musicological Society in Washington, D.C. But when the lecture was printed in the spring 1965 issue of the Journal of the American Musicological Society, *he remarked in a footnote, "Berger's article was published at around the time this address was read — striking evidence, it seems to me, of the ferment currently being felt in all quarters about our received intellectual and academic views about music" (p. 65).*

He went on to say in the same footnote: "This quiet article makes many very important points and hints at others; not least among these is the formal academic recognition of theory and analysis. Professor Berger draws a direct analogy with 'the establishment of musicology as a legitimate scholarly discipline in our universities'; he makes up a good title for the new discipline — all the better if it evokes Ransome and Babbitt (Irving) — and he concerns himself with the relation between the New Theory, musicology, and criticism. . . . Berger takes note of the possible interpretation of theory as a branch of musicology, but he backs away from the suggestion as 'not quite consistent with the spirit of the current theoreticians.' The way Berger sees the New Theory is as 'essentially a form of criticism.'"

Kerman enlarges upon the subject in chapter 3 of his 1985 Contemplating Music (60 ff.), in which he presents penetrating profiles of innovative American theorists of the last half of the twentieth century. It may be of some significance, since the matter of musicology and criticism is at issue, to point to the fact that the important paper of Milton Babbitt's that I quote in chapter 6 was read at a session of the International Musicological Society, and it is also significant in the matter of analysis and criticism that the seminar on Heinrich Schenker at Columbia University in the early thirties presented by Hans Weisse, a disciple of this revered innovative theorist, was called "Musical Criticism," as I have already indicated.

When my 1964 article is viewed from the vantage point of the present, it naturally requires to be put into the past tense where I draw on it literally. Although the main purpose of resuscitating it is to demonstrate what the thinking was at the time, I could not resist inserting some observations that touch upon what we know now and editing out observations less relevant today. Also, I have used some materials already presented in earlier chapters of this book (e.g., chapter 6) since the repetition seemed necessary for continuity. Another comment I might make is that inevitably after so many years my perspective on certain matters has changed, causing me to revise some statements and delete others, so finally it may be said the revisions are substantial. But I hope the article still has the thrust that prompted Kerman to observe that it reflected the "ferment" in the sixties. Incidentally, my designation for the new tendency ("the New Theory") with its overtones of the New Criticism failed to catch on. Also, I was disappointed that the two approaches to theory, the scientific and the "other," have not lived peacefully side by side, and that the scientific approach has tended to dominate the field.

A faithful account of the musical thought that was current in the sixties must necessarily reflect the diverse ways in which some of us were searching, at times tentatively, clumsily, or inscrutably, for a new theoretical approach, motivated by a profound reaction against the woolly, otiose attempts at explanation and the inflexible definitions that had been allowed to achieve the sanctity of divine law through the sheer inertia of almost everyone concerned with music. What seemed to be taking place in a domain to which the designation "theory" or even "analytic theory" could be applied only provisionally, is curiously reminiscent of the gestations that some three decades earlier had preceded the establishment of musicology as a legitimate scholarly discipline in our universities. I have in mind not only the skepticism directed among other things toward the choice of so stern a label for any pursuit having to do with one of the arts but also—and mainly—the tendency to equate a rigorous approach and clear, logical thinking with scientific method. (In his article cited above Kerman suggests "we better abandon the word 'musicology' altogether—who ever heard of 'artology' or 'literology'?")

The recurrence of the old symptoms may be fortuitous. But it may also suggest that there was a certain parallelism in the problems the two disciplines encountered at their formative stages, or—a possibility that seems less likely and not quite consistent with the spirit of the theoreticians—that an affinity was maintained between what I called at the time the "New Theory" and musicology, a family relationship, as it were, in which the former figures as an outgrowth of the latter. This second possibility would have been welcomed by those who would like to fill the slot for "music theory," "theory of music," "theory of music theory," "speculative theory" (call it what you will) in Guido Adler's original ground plan for musicology—not in the historical part, which has emerged in the course of years as the principal orientation of the field as a whole, but in the "systematic" part, where it would make curious bedfellows with ethnomusicology. Indeed, in a paper read at a Symposium on Music Theory at Ohio State University in 1962 William Poland went so far as to infer that the gradual infiltration of the concept "science" into musicological thought was in itself something in the nature of an adumbration of those preoccupations with music theory that in the sixties were becoming more and more evident as a significant force. Citing the allusion to "scientific method" in Glen Haydon's *Introduction to Musicology*, Poland concludes that "considering it was made in 1941," it "approaches the prophetic. Haydon's use of the word science is congruent with current usage." [1] The observation is interesting in the context of the present discussion, but somewhat exaggerated. The earliest attempts to translate *Musikwissenschaft* and *Musicologie* (for which our "musicology" did double duty) repeatedly raised the question of a choice of denotations for the suffix of the former, viz., between "branch of learning" and "science." This must be why Haydon began his book with an effort to settle the matter, and that he made no claims to being the first to bring up the S-word with reference to musicology was evident from a footnote deploring the incongruities that had resulted from translating *Musikwissenschaft* sometimes as "musicology" and at other times as "musical science." While Haydon rejected the translation "musical science" he did agree to use the locution to characterize musicology—only, however, through a bit of legerdemain whereby "science," understood in ordinary language by ordinary mortals as having to do with technological or rigorous systematic processes, is accorded the highly generalized connotation of "research in any given field."[2]

The foregone conclusion that scientific method is endemic to theory places a needless bugbear between it and those—how shall I put it?—who cherish music's sanctity as an "art," an "aesthetic" genus. Now it is perfectly true that mathematics and physical science are tools in both the practice and theory of electronic music; and the advantages of numerical calculations, group theory in particular, for dealing with serial organization and predicting its results have been repeatedly demonstrated. (Let us not forget, too, the tonal theorists with their Information Theory.)

But it does not follow from this that scientific method is the only one open to theorists who want to brush the cobwebs off the traditional methods that are badly in need of updating and cleansing of waste and irrelevance. Nor does it mean that the rationale behind serially organized and electronic music prevents these genres from being apprehended (listened to) via some of the same perceptual channels through which we apprehend (and listen to) any music. Neither does that rationale render it faulty to analyze such branches of music composition in the same way that we have analyzed any other music—provided the specific terms of analysis, of course, are rendered suitable to the new idiom and new constructs. Not all of us who are involved with a new approach to theory and analysis follow Babbitt's directive, which it will do no harm to quote again, that "there is but one kind of language, one kind of method for the verbal formulation of 'concepts' and the verbal analysis of such formulations: 'scientific' language and 'scientific' method."

It may very well be that system construction reveals facets of musical structure that cannot, or can only with difficulty, be otherwise revealed. But other analytic methods effectively cope with other facets that are just as significant, and despite the claims or implication of the system-builders that theirs is the only valid way, I am convinced that these other methods—rigorous in their own terms—can perfectly well be encompassed by the new theoretical approach cultivated in the sixties without coming into irreconcilable conflict with the program of the system-builders. David Prall would remind us again and again in his Harvard seminar in aesthetics that if you are considering one aspect of a given object—say, in music, the pitch content independent of its rhythmic investiture—in one particular way it explicitly assumes that there are other aspects of the object as well as other ways of considering the same thing. Many of us had our fill of motive analysis and its emphasis on derivation (putting us in the role of another type of tune-detective), and even the refinements of Rudolf Reti did not dissuade some of us from the conviction that it was a relatively lower level of music analysis. Still, the fact that it was overdone and for a long time represented the chief analytical tool is no reason to banish it altogether, no reason to no longer resort to it as something useful in its modest place.[3] There is also an approach to analysis that is germane to musicology, embracing identification, description, and analysis of style in respect to period, conventional (textbook) form, or both. This is not particularly important to theory, in which style description, if it occurs, is mainly incidental to determining how specific relations yield structurally significant points within a work or account for similitude and differentiation within a given technique. But it should not be denied its place.

Unique or new analytic techniques demand unique terminology, and in this there should be nothing untenable or upsetting to the historian's comprehensive evolutionary plan when the aim is not to classify techniques as to period-style or compositions as to conventional form, nor to relate one instance to the whole of music literature. Earlier I demonstrated how the loose application of the term "tonality" can lead to conceptual confusion, and it also, I might add, can lead to irrelevant associations damaging to proper apprehension of heard relations, though I venture to suggest, fully aware that it is a highly debatable statement, that what appears to be a "wrong" analysis need not always contribute to wrong hearing of a given piece of music. At other times, however, it could affect proper hearing: for example, in a case of strongly tonally biased individuals listening to Stravinsky's *Serenade in A* and so thoroughly impressed by the collection of F major (which is used in this work with the pitch order of a Phrygian scale on A) that they would keep yearning for a resolution on F and in this way receive the wrong message from the music. A performer has many opportunities to reify what may be simply an analytical device. On the simplest level, an ornament is a cluster of very short notes that literally ornament a longer note, the main note. This suggests they do not support the structure as the main note does and a performer is likely to gloss over them, not articulate them, since analytically they are not important entities. Another simple example is the accompaniment. The very name assures us that it is not the main event, and performers need not concern themselves too much about making it be clearly heard though there may be so much beauty and musical content in it. Try playing the opening measures of the *Allegro* of the "Dissonance" Quartet without the main tune in the first violin and you will see how much substance there is in the accompaniment alone. (See above, Ex. 4a.) It is enough to absorb attention without the theme. And finally, on a higher level there is the question of what to do with the structural tones in a Schenker analysis. Do you emphasize them in performance? I think not.

Musicologists are not likely to get involved in problems of this kind since their preoccupations lead them in any discussion of a musical composition to be attentive to historical context, which is perfectly understandable as long as it is not insisted that we are all required to do so, for in such a case neither can we ignore the physical source (acoustics), the listener's nervous reactions (neuropsychology) and bodily states (physiology), the influence of social forces (sociology), etc. None of us has the right to legislate a priori that this or that parameter, this branch of knowledge, or that dimension of phenomena must be given its due in every theoretical speculation.

If anything beyond the pure quest for knowledge propels the speculation of composers (knowing about their own music is like knowing about any other music), it is their need qua composers to know how they are functioning. Was it not E. M. Forster who said, in a much quoted phrase, speaking as a novelist, "How can I know what I think before I see what I say?"[4] And Paul Valéry has referred to ". . . mille accidents de mémoire, d'attention, ou de sensation, qui surviennent à mon esprit, apparaissant enfin, dans mon oeuvre achevé, comme les idées essentielles et les objets originaux de mes efforts" (. . . a thousand accidents of memory, attention, or sensation that occur to my mind, appearing in the end, in my finished work, as the essential ideas and original objects of my efforts).[5]

No doubt some listeners will feel that composers talking about their own music is shoptalk, and in a way it is, though nowadays shoptalk is becoming more and more a part of the marketable theatrical element of a concert (the panel of composers before the musicians start playing, for example). So what if it is? Granted it may seem more appropriate for composers to be talking about the nitty-gritty of music-making to one another rather than to their audience, which is precisely the complaint one hears from those who say composers are now writing music for one another. But it should be kept in mind that while some things will be clinically interesting to composers alone, their quest for understanding what they themselves accomplish as creators should also yield conclusions of concern to anyone who aspires to such understanding.

At the same time it is important not to lose sight of the fact that most composers prefer to have the public's need for better understanding satisfied by intelligent theorists cum critics. The most verbally articulate composers, and there have been a plethora of them in the past century, are dominated by ultimate allegiance to expression in a nonverbal medium and should welcome someone else to represent their viewpoints, even to help solve their problems: theorists, for example, who have special insight into the compositional process. Such theorists, alas, are rare, and rather than settle for anything less, composers may prefer, especially in this self-conscious age of ours, to turn out their own hasty, incipient statements of their ideas at the price of moments jealously guarded for writing music. ("Oh! What a bore! I better get those program notes ready in time for the upcoming performance.") It is perfectly legitimate, however, for composers to insist they have said everything they have to say in the music and it's therefore pointless to say anything more. A composer might even recite to you that old saw about Beethoven having played a piece for the listener who asked him when he had finished what it meant, and how the master's answer was alleged to be to play the piece all over again.

It is idle to predict that all composers would abstain from theoretical speculation about their own music if the kind of theory they now produce were sufficiently provided by thinkers in other branches of the music field. Perhaps there would be less of it on the composer's part, but the current predilection for self-searching and persistent self-analysis—why be apologetic about it?—is for some composers more than an adjunct: these activities stimulate creativity and may be essential to successful functioning of those composers qua composers.

In chapter 6 there was some mention of what I called the "intuitive" composers who insist that the work of art remain inviolate. In their view it was something of a desecration to impose an analysis on it. Also, the truly inspired composer feels the music in an almost unconscious way as a complete whole. Analysis, being a function of the intellect, involves cruelly rending it into its component parts. Curiously enough the other kind of theorists, the cerebral ones, are capable of an analogous religious fervor to maintain the inviolability of their analytic mapping of the total structure of any given work. Their own analysis, they insist, is the only way. Granted that the awareness of total structure, the effort to encompass the totality in analysis—be it only a matter of the pitch or harmonic content—is a major advance in our day. At the same time any effort to deal with details, the "surface," is discouraged with an equally religious fervor that is so devastating that I myself long ago gave up fighting it since the fight was hardly worth the effort, though I had what some may have conceivably found interesting ideas on the subject of analysis of what Schenkerians would have dismissed as "mere surface." An intelligent analyst should be aware that to call attention to a brief configuration of tones is to dwell on an experience different from that configuration in its context. Yet the configuration when it came into the relationship was not altogether a *tabula rasa.*

In the configuration we already have a musical entity of some kind. This is different from contemplating a single sound, which can indeed be close to a *tabula rasa*—though a sound (one that might be better called a "noise" if it has no pitch) is not a toothbrush, it has potentially a musical existence. Its meaning may depend almost entirely on the relationship in which it occurs, and in a music composition it will relate to other sounds. In the early thirties I attended lectures at the New School for Social Research by the eminent Austrian musicologist and tone psychologist Erich von Hornbostel and he performed for us the following naive but revealing experiment: He took a piece of wood about the size and shape of a six-inch ruler and dropped it on the desk, satisfying himself that none of those present heard a pitch in the sound it made—or if they "thought" they did, they admitted it was difficult and they were not sure. If different people thought they heard different pitches, they also admitted it was difficult, and they were not sure. He then produced a second piece of wood like the first one but somewhat shorter. When the two sticks were dropped in succession we clearly heard the first one as a sound at a definite pitch somewhat lower than the pitch of the added stick. Thus, pitch may be said to have been in the relationship *between* the sounds rather than in the single sound as such, and the usual talk of "indefinite pitch," whatever that may be, is entirely unnecessary and does not settle the matter of what a noise is.

A familiar case in which some musicians, not so much today as formerly, tend to reify a relationship is in the matter of parallel fifths, that bugbear of every student of traditional tonal functional harmony. There are musicians who train themselves to detect parallel perfect fifths in harmonic exercises or actual Baroque or Classical music, and to hear them as something offensive. The rule outlawing parallel fifths has to do with certain requirements of voice-leading in tonal music and is really not a matter of sounding bad unless one conditions oneself to that response since what is involved is a certain kind of relation in a certain kind of context. But take the perfect fifth out of the tonal context and none of this pertains to it since the problem was not a matter of the interval itself but (I repeat myself for emphasis) the context in which it was placed. Thus, I had to look again, convinced that my sight must be betraying me, when I read the statement by the distinguished late nineteenth-century historian of music theory Hugo Riemann that the well-known thirteenth-century double canon "Sumer is icumen in" is "even today listened to with pleasure despite some parallel fifths and octaves."[6]

When we start from a configuration of tones we are starting with a miniature composition, and there is much more to it than there is to a single sound. There are things to be learned from contemplating that isolated configuration while keeping in mind, first, that it is not the whole story, second, that we are abstracting it from a much larger context, and third, that the configuration's meaning, as I have said, will be modified when it is restored to the whole. The point is it is not meaningless by itself: a melody, perhaps, or a basic cell on which subsequent lines or harmonies are built. It does not tell the whole story but it tells us quite a lot. Were I to say of a person (X) entering a room that the person limps and uses a cane, scant information about X would be conveyed—for example, whether X is man, woman, or child. Nevertheless what we would now know about X would not be insignificant. Even the total Schenker analysis does not yield the whole story after all since there are still the parameters of rhythm, density, color, etc. What so often passes for "mystery" in music is nothing more than our inability (aided though we may be by a powerful computer) to stipulate the whole complex of relations in an art work, which is no reason not to try to stipulate some of them.

The zeal to encompass the total art work in any discussion or analysis of it has led, among other things, to a genre of criticism attempting to communicate the music's flow, its feeling, its excitement, its color—what Impressionist critics attempted by means of empty, often embarrassing rhetoric. Your neopositive theorists would throw up their hands in horror at this. But their ways of trying to encapsulate the totality, to incorporate everything we know and consider important about a work in every statement we make about any part of it, betray a serious failure to distinguish between "concept" and "percept," between "the idea of a quality" and the quality itself, as Arnold Isenberg would put it[7]—or, as John Dewey admonished us (I am not sure it's intellectually respectable to quote him now in view of all the hard-line philosophers who have appeared since his time), between "recognition" and "perception": The difference between them is "immense," according to Dewey: "In recognition there is the beginning of an act of perception. But this beginning is not allowed to serve the development of a full perception of the thing recognized. It is arrested at the point where it will serve the development of some other purpose as we recognize a man on the street in order to greet or avoid him, not for the sake of seeing what is there."[8]

I touched upon this subject in chapter 12 when I brought up the matter of whether we hear a change of harmony in bar 117 of the "Dissonance" Quartet, and I pointed out that you may *know* (have the "concept" or "recognize") that the chord assumes a new function and new spelling but at that moment what you *hear* and are *supposed* to hear (have the "percept" of) as an essential aspect of direct aesthetic apprehension is the same harmony that was operative in the previous measure. You may even *know* what's going to happen to it, that it is notated differently, and how it will be used in a somewhat surprising way. But it requires a certain suspension of disbelief to *experience* the surprise rather than merely *know* it, each time over and over again. It must have been in the thirties that there was a film about Irish revolutionists, *The Informer*, with pretty routine movie music by Max Steiner, and while I recall very little of it, I have a vivid recollection of an episode in which a captured and wounded revolutionist is being ushered out in a wheelchair and is looking very happy. He is being taken to a firing squad, but we are not supposed to know this. It is supposed to be a surprise; though once we find out we realize that of course Irish revolutionists are happy to die for the cause. The whole thing was spoiled when the music launched prematurely into the funeral march, so there was no more surprise for us. Similarly, to know the new function of the chord in the Mozart, or to hear it as the new chord or describe it as such even though, having heard the quartet before, you can easily do so, is to miss the main point. It may be difficult to prevent knowledge from getting in the way of hearing. But there must be a way of accomplishing it so that each time you hear the work you listen as if with an innocent ear, trying to recapture that essentially unavailable experience of a first hearing.

Isenberg's subject was critical communication, and whether theory is to be called "new" theory or not, what I envisaged in the 1960s for its future was essentially that it assume the form of criticism, particularly in that strand of the new harmonic organizing principles that were not the scientific ones.

What Isenberg had to say on the subject of criticism should therefore be of special interest to us:

> "What can be said" and "what cannot be said" are phrases which take their meaning from the purpose for which we are speaking. The aesthetics of obscurantism, in its insistence on the incommunicability of the art object, has never made it clear what purpose or demand is to be served by communication. If we devised a system of concepts by which a work of art could be virtually reproduced at a distance by the use of language alone, what human intention would be furthered? . . . The scientific *explanation* of aesthetic experiences would not be accomplished by a mere change of descriptive terminology. There remains only the *aesthetic* motive in talking about art. Now if we set up as a condition of communicability that our language should *afford* the experience which it purports to describe, we shall of course reach the conclusion that art is incommunicable. But by that criterion all reality is unintelligible and ineffable, just as Bergson maintains. Such a demand upon thought and language is not only preposterous in that its fulfillment is logically impossible; it is also baneful, because it obscures the actual and very large influence of concepts upon the process of perception.[9]

We have been considering concept and percept as, in a very important sense, distinct from each other, and we observed that the confusion between theorizing and creating instilled fear in "intuitive" composers, because they could think only in terms of one type of behavior arrogating the place of the other; it also put the practice of music criticism or of any writing on music in constant danger of being made too much of—that is, of being, indeed, used as an excuse to get rid of frustrated creative drives. Now, however, it would appear from Isenberg's last thought in the quotation above, that there can be a transaction between concept and percept, an influence of the one on the other. (It does not alter what I have said about keeping concept and percept separate.) Everyone has had the experience of seeing a new relationship or pattern in a familiar object, or hearing a new aspect in a familiar constellation of tones after someone else has elucidated it and explained its presence (and I don't mean simply by pointing, as can be done with a painting, since it may be intricately woven into the whole). Such experience obviously, for example, may arise out of correlating concept and percept. "Reading criticism, otherwise than in the presence, or with direct recollection, of the object discussed," Isenberg admonishes us, "is a blank and senseless employment—a fact which is concealed from us by the cooperation, in our reading, of many non-critical purposes for which the information offered by the critic is material and useful."[10] Music, if it is unpublished or unperformed, creates insuperable obstacles in establishing this "presence," but we can go far toward providing at least some of it with as many musical examples as practicable as well as charts explicating structural aspects, much as we may regret excluding intelligent readers incapable of deciphering the notation. (There are some promising beginnings of a practice of providing an accompanying CD on which the examples can be heard.)

Pages with musical examples are fodder for the familiar complaint that the reviews or articles are too "technical." How very odd it is that those who object most vociferously to the atomization of music by the analyst should be most voluble in decrying the examples when these aim precisely at restoring the reader to the musical entity. The examples, besides refreshing the memory, enable the reader to reassemble the dissected parts (which is not, by the way, and in a very real sense cannot be, the analyst's job), to check details against context, and to assess new concepts that, in the words of Stuart Hampshire, "place a frame upon the object and upon its parts and features . . . by an unnatural use of words in description." [11]

If a branch of theory is to embrace criticism, it should be allowed the "unnatural use of words" and room for speculation. The term "modulation," for example, used to distress some theorists so much, for quite a long time as I recall, when applied to what they prefer to call "tonicization," that one would think the most heinous sin had been perpetrated. There would be no place in the new theory cum criticism for such rigidity. One would be free to espouse any valid analysis that illuminates a work, and not be bound to the analysis that happened to be in the composer's mind or the most fashionable current system. An age like our own in which composers are analysts—their own analysts as part of it—imposes a special burden upon the noncomposing analysts who find themselves, in competition with the composers, under constraint to do the "right" thing and determine how the composers would analyze their own music. But let us recall that priceless admission of E. M. Forster's which I should hope the reader will agree is important enough to warrant repeating: "How can I know what I think before I see what I say?" Composers need not have the last word with respect to their own works. There may still be things they may have conceived as creators that they fail to conceptualize as observers even in their own music, things they must dig up on their own. This does not mean they did not know what they were doing and this should not be held against them. It means there is a different sense of "know."

15   The Octatonic Scale

Parts of this chapter, in particular the discussion of the statistical octatonic instances in traditional sources, are adapted from a lecture presented at Harvard University as part of the music department's Colloquium Series, 26 October 1998.

During the course of the last three centuries or so, with significant and well-known exceptions, the prevailing scales have been the major and minor. Indeed, a good case could be made for the contention that Western music of all genres (pop, folk, and serious) has been dominated by one scale, the major, and that minor has figured prominently only by virtue of its borrowing substantially from the major. At the end of the nineteenth century and the beginning of the twentieth, "new" scales started to appear (often of ancient or Far Eastern origin) at first in an auxiliary role, that is, without displacing the major and usually used in conjunction with it. While this development was taking place there was to be observed in the ranks of what were regarded as the more radical composers a chromaticism we sometimes call "atonality," which was quite free, and then, side by side with it, "serialism" (a form of atonality) with a reputation for strictness everyone knows by now.

For both atonalists and serialists it was no longer necessary to extract a scale from the total chromatic (the semitonally divided pitch continuum); one went directly to this collection and employed its constituents either quite freely or in terms of a newly conceived row-technique. To put the matter in perhaps a crude, oversimplified way, it may be useful to be aware of a bifurcation defining the music scene. On the one hand, there was the maintenance of the traditional major-minor pitch content (among neoclassicists and conservatives), part of the time liberated from all constraints of traditional functional harmony with its required voice-leading, and on the other, the exploitation of the total semitonally divided pitch continuum in which each tone is exonerated from the obligation to any other tone—an obligation that had been prescribed by traditional functional tonality. The music in which a residue of the old scales and chords could still be heard (music that answers to the calling "diatonic") usually incorporated the scales I have termed auxiliary (neoclassic Stravinsky and his school, for example).

It is not a good idea to assimilate this music to tonality by virtue of the superficial resemblances, as is so often done, and consequently to designate it "tonal," simply because it draws upon traditional scales and triads. It has liberated itself from subservience to restrictions of functional tonality sufficiently to be considered "atonal" or, at least, "nontonal" in the view of many observers. Indeed, tonality involves much more than just using the major and minor triads and the traditional scales. It involves a stringent conformity to the rules of functionality. This is a case in which my insistence on music as relationship is particularly relevant. Traditional scales and chords are there but they are not being placed in traditional relationships.

Of the auxiliary scales, surely the most prestigious was the whole-tone consisting of six members—every alternate degree of the familiar chromatic scale—favored by Debussy and Impressionist composers in general. The Impressionists also got some mileage out of a scale imported from the Far East: the pentatonic.[1] In addition a backward look to the Middle Ages led to a reinstatement of modal scales which could be obtained merely by reordering the notes of the major scale (i.e., changing the interval order of the whole- and half-steps).

I confess I was not particularly aware of how much of a contribution I was making to our knowledge of the twentieth-century repository of the marginal scales in "Problems of Pitch Organization in Stravinsky"[2] when I discoursed at some length on Stravinsky's liberal use of a scale in which semitones alternate with whole-tones (or vice versa), yielding a collection of eight steps—a scale to which I assumed it was only natural, since it had eight tones, to refer as "octatonic" by analogy with the already existing pentatonic, which has five. I made no claims of "discovering" it. I stated that Messiaen had included it among "modes of limited transposition,"[3] and the Italian composer Roman Vlad, taking his cue from Messiaen, had cited an octatonic passage from Stravinsky's music in his book on this composer without comment.[4] Further, I vaguely remembered having seen some mention of a succession of whole- and half-steps in, of all unexpected places (to me at least), Rimsky-Korsakov's *My Musical Life* many years earlier. Perhaps I should have looked up the passage but my approach was not historical.[5] I suppose the reason I was treated as if I had practically discovered the scale is that I gave it the name "octatonic" (it's as if a thing does not exist if it has no name), and I also said something about its origin in the diminished seventh chords and about its structure and potentialities. I was not elated at the thought that what most readers got out of my article was a new locution and a new scale formation. My concern was the significance of tone center in nontonal music and how it was established. The octatonic scale was at issue insofar as it interacted with the old diatonic scales to surround the tonic with a relational situation that I hesitate to say rendered it ambiguous (since earlier I expressed doubts about the use of that locution) but certainly placed it in question.

I thought I had made it clear that the general tenor of the whole article was to throw out ideas that had occurred to me over my many years of intimate acquaintance with the music of Stravinsky, ideas that I nurtured as a composer myself who had never denied a profound debt to his example (though I had never deliberately employed this particular scale myself—and still to this day have not). My final sentence was: "I leave these considerations as a query in the hope that a new branch of theory may someday provide an answer." To my delight, sooner than I had expected, there arose out of the ranks of the most distinguished younger theorists the knight who was to pursue and defend my cause in an impressive volume devoted to the music of Stravinsky: Pieter C. van den Toorn.[6] Later came Richard Taruskin's two hefty volumes on the master's earlier music, *Stravinsky and the Russian Traditions*, filling out the picture with historical origins that had not concerned me and brilliantly finding antecedents of the master's octatonicism in the music of Stravinsky's teacher Rimsky-Korsakov as well as the latter's Russian acolytes.[7]

The octatonic is capable of two scales with different interval orderings depending on whether it starts with the whole-tone (whole, half / whole, half, etc.) or the semitone (half, whole / half, whole, etc.)—e.g., E-F♯-G-A-B♭, etc., or E-F-G-A♭-B♭, etc. (Ex. 13a and b; T = tone, S = semitone). Quite a commotion was made among my devotees (if I may presume to call them that) over the circumstance that I underplayed the role of the first of these two interval orders. Thus, van den Toorn found it necessary to "correct"

Exs. 13a and b. Octatonic interval orders

Ex. 14a. Two manifestations of the "Petrushka" chord

Ex. 14b. "Petrushka" chord, referential gapped octatonic scale (numbers indicate number of semitones between scale degrees)

me, and that maven of Stravinskyana, Robert Craft, who should have known better, after crediting me with naming the scale, adds the caveat, "Berger's description did not include the sequence of major and minor seconds."[8] This, though I quite explicitly introduced the whole subject of octatonic by way of two examples built on the whole-half type: *Les Noces* and the *Petrushka* chord[9]—a chord I argued could be better explained as a product of a gapped octatonic scale *starting with the whole-step*, rather than as a blend, according to the composer's own interpretation, of two "polytonal" major triads on C and F-sharp (Ex. 14a and b).[10]

I was not writing a formal theoretical tract on the octatonic, but demonstrating rather how its interval ordering can come into a reciprocal relation with the traditional diatonic to influence the disestablishment of tone center in nontonal music. It so happens that *Psalms*, the main work I used to make my point, employs the octatonic scale with the interval order starting with the half-step. In addition, I quite frankly stated a preference for this form. The whole- and half-step ordering does not sound to me nearly as fresh and intriguing. It is easily derived from the old Dorian mode merely by mildly skewing either of the tetrachords (first four notes or last four notes): pushing the upper one down a half-step or the lower one up a half-step, so that the tetrachords are tritone-related rather than fourth-related. Finally, I remarked that "the succession of consecutive scale degrees would yield nothing different from any referential ordering of intervals in the familiar white-note vocabulary until the fifth degree was reached—and even this, in terms of Classical practice, could be a so-called 'tendency tone.' It is the new 'rhythm' in the ordering of intervals that defines the uniqueness of the relations Stravinsky employed, namely, an ordering that gives up its secret, not at the fifth, but at the fourth degree. . . ."[11]

I did not feel at the time I was writing "Problems" that the historical context in which the octatonic scale originated, as I have already remarked, was germane to my discussion of Stravinsky. But I believe I can now take credit for what practically amounts to a scavenger hunt in recent decades for octatonic occurrences in music of the Classical and Romantic periods. The search has not been without reward since it casts some light on a harmonic device that we had not conceptualized in just this way before. From time to time we hear advocates of new music claim that an understanding of it and familiarity with it can enhance our comprehension of the music of the past. Here certainly is corroboration of that claim.

The pitch collection of an octatonic scale can be found wherever two of the three possible diminished seventh chords occur. In its simplest form the members of one diminished seventh chord will be capable of providing neighbor-notes to a given diminished seventh chord, as in Example 15a, from the finale of Beethoven's Piano Concerto No. 5 in G major. But the furthest thing from one's mind or ear would be the hearing of an octatonic scale in this very typical tonal passage. Thus, the irony of the octatonic scale is that despite its origin in the diminished seventh chords, the more audible the chords themselves are the less the context will have the characteristic octatonic sound. A vast ocean can separate the statistical presence of the octatonic pitch collection from the actual ordering of the collection as an octatonic scale. Example 15b shows a skeleton form of the harmonies of the Beethoven example and it will be observed that of the two diminished seventh chords, the main one (F♯-A-C-E♭, indicated by half-notes, stems up) is merely being embellished by the other diminished seventh chord (E♯-G♯-B-D, indicated by quarter-notes, stems down) in the form of neighbor-notes of the original chord-tones a semitone below.

Let me attempt to demonstrate the decisive role that the articulation of the diminished seventh chord plays in the maintenance of tonality or the

Ex. 15a. Beethoven, Concerto for piano and orchestra, No. 5 in G major, Opus 58, Rondo (bars 252–55)

Ex. 15b. Same, harmonic scheme and referential (octatonic) scale

occlusion of octatonic sound. Given the passage from Chopin's *Ballade No. 4* in A-flat major, Op. 52 (Ex. 16a), let us suppose we had only the music that is in the right hand (treble clef) without the opening dyad G♯—F. The heard roots of the right-hand chords are tritone-related: D—A♭ (G♯) (Ex. 16b), like those in *Petrushka* chord: F♯—C. A rigid positivist may

Ex. 16a. Chopin, Ballade No. 4 in A-flat major, Op. 52 (coda)

Ex. 16b. Same, harmonic scheme

Ex. 16c. Same, referential scale

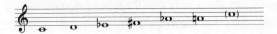

make something out of the fact that the harmonic content of the two passages is not absolutely equivalent and thus there cannot be a parallelism: namely, the Chopin has seventh chords and the Stravinsky only triads; and there is the further detail that the chord inversions are different: second inversion in the Chopin and in the Stravinsky a case of root position for the C triad and first inversion for the F-sharp triad. More troublesome, perhaps, is the detail that what we may hear as A-flat in terms of the two seventh chords is notated G-sharp (more of that later).

If we reduce the Chopin to scale formation we can find, as one of our choices, a *referential* scale that is the same as the one we proposed for the *Petrushka* chord, transposed a whole-step lower and gapped in the very same places (Ex. 16c).[12] Taken out of context the chords in the right hand yield the octatonic sound, but notice how, if we restore the left hand (still without the downbeat), even though we are adding no new pitch classes, a curious alchemy takes place. The two dominant seventh chords become part of a total sonority and the amalgam is now one pervasive diminished seventh chord, A-C-Eb-Gb with D and G-sharp as lower neighbor-notes. (It now becomes clear why what could be heard as an A-flat, root of one of the seventh chords, was notated as G-sharp, it being a neighbor of the A.) Though the pitch classes of this diminished seventh chord in the left hand were always there in the right hand as well, distributed between the two dominant seventh chords, once we isolate those pitch classes and articulate them as a chord, the one diminished seventh chord they define dominates the procedure with its tonal implications. We are now ready to reinstate the F chord on the accent. F fills one of the two gaps in the collection where the octatonic is concerned. But its function on the tonal side is hierarchically of maximum importance because its role is to serve as the root, the foundation of the entire aggregation of notes—the F being the root of an extended dominant ninth chord—which has no doubt been obvious all along to some readers who may have been wondering why a dominant ninth chord is being worried in the way I have been worrying it (if they are unsympathetic, that is to say, with the point I want to make).

The octatonic is a symmetrical scale since the dyad, whether whole half (TS) or half hole (ST), repeats itself throughout the system, just as the single whole-step does in the whole-tone scale. But there is an important difference. If you put your palms down on the keyboard and sound all the scale degrees of the whole-tone scale at once it will have the characteristic sonorous ambience of whole-tone practice in the form of a tone cluster. If you similarly depress all the notes of an octatonic scale at once, you will scarcely be able to detect anything of the octatonic sound, but you will hear, rather, a cluster comprising an undifferentiated mass of notes out of the chromatic scale. I believe this has some significance, and I suspect that a young new theorist may be able to make something of it.

One cannot expect that any simple octatonic scale passage presenting the referential order unmitigated is going to suffice to create the octatonic ambience just as we encounter it in Stravinsky. Note how in Example 17 from Liszt what might have been heard as a straightforward octatonic scale in thirds retains its tonal investiture by virtue of the notes plucked out of the scale (every second note) in the uppermost voice outlining the diminished seventh chord. The passage is from the *Mephisto Waltz* and we should be reminded that Liszt's exploitation of the octatonic served as an inspiration for Rimsky-Korsakov, who in turn passed a certain preoccupation with it on to his student Stravinsky—especially in the latter's "Russian" period, as Richard Taruskin establishes with impressive scholarship in *Stravinsky and the Russian Traditions*.

Ex. 17. Liszt, *Mephisto Waltz*, octatonic scale passage (measure before second *Presto*)

Taruskin was not unaware that the manifold instances of ornamented diminished seventh chords that in traditional music are fashioned out of the octatonic collection or part of it have really little to do with the ordered octatonic scale as such, except in some statistical way. He gives a priceless example from a Bach "English" Suite (Ex. 18a). It has the harmony of countless passages one has heard from Bach's time without its ever having crossed anyone's mind that a system other than the traditional diatonic is involved, and yet, being free with the relationships in which the notes obviously are, we can find in it the referential scale in Example 18b. However, having made the point that every embellished diminished seventh chord, though it may have the required pitch content, need not have octatonic structure, Taruskin adds a corollary I'm not sure I sympathize with: "As long as the diminished seventh chord so embellished is eventually resolved by leading-tone progression, that is, in the conventional tonal way, the use of the term octatonic to describe the scale is unjustified."[13] I think this is to throw the baby out with the bathwater—if I may be permitted an indulgence in that old saw. Why, once we get beyond the simplest form of embellished diminished seventh chord (that is, beyond such neighbor-note activity, for example, as we observed in the Beethoven in Example 15), should there not be degrees of octatonic in which the characteristic sound we hear in Stravinsky merely starts to manifest itself but never altogether materializes? Notwithstanding the deployment of tonality in the prolonged hor-

Exs. 18a and b. Bach, "English" Suite No. 3, Sarabande (bars 17–19) and referential (octatonic) scale

Ex. 19. Robert Schumann, *Faschingsschwanck aus Wien*, Op. 26, Finale (bars 253–55)

izontalized diminished seventh chord in the Chopin *Ballade* there still resides a vestige of an identifiable aroma of octatonic in the tritone-related dominant seventh chords. The Schumann excerpt in Example 19 may be precisely what Taruskin had in mind. The scale is a diminished seventh chord with passing tones and I assume he would say that as soon as we hear the resolution on F we realize—retrospectively?—that what we heard as a bona fide octatonic scale really was actually not one. As I remarked much earlier, this notion of retrospective hearing is quite common but I've always had difficulty with it. It is a good instance for the query "do we hear what we say we hear?" (see chapter 13). When we arrive at the F-major chord in the Schumann, or better, when we reach the end of the movement, we *know*, if we analyze what we have heard, that the figuration in F major is not being exploited the way Stravinsky would in an octatonic context. But as we listen to it, before it arrives at the cadence, we *are* hearing octatonic relations of the same type, broadly speaking, that we would hear in Stravinsky.

One of the most remarkable occurrences of octatonic pitch content that I am aware of in traditional music, a rather brief one, is found in Variation 20 of Beethoven's "Diabelli" Variations, Op. 120 (Ex. 20a and b). The

Ex. 20a. Beethoven, "Diabelli" Variations, Op. 120, No. 20

Ex. 20b. Same, referential (octatonic) scale

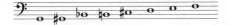

C-major triads in bars 11 and 12 turn out to be subdominant in a conventional G-major cadence in their relation to bars 13 to 15. But when they first materialize they are strange and wonderful, more like Debussy than Beethoven. Part of the freshness may be due to the C not having been a scale degree in the octatonic collection in evidence for over six bars: G-A♭-B♭-B-C♯-D-E-F.

When I anointed the octatonic scale with the label that is now conventional, gave some idea of its structure, and demonstrated the degree to which Stravinsky elicited from its relationships a personal quality that I was later convinced no practitioners before him succeeded in eliciting from it, I had no idea how much mileage van den Toorn and Taruskin would get out of it, and it was beyond my wildest flights of the imagination that so rigorous an analyst as Allen Forte would condescend even simply to have recourse to the term in analyzing Webern (though what he does with the interval collection has nothing to do with what I do with it).

I was, I must admit, on first observing the scale, sufficiently excited to allow my "speculation" to take flight in a direction in which I felt just a "simple step" would lead "to the conclusion that short of twelve-tone and 'atonal' procedures" nothing would provide the conditions for "the denial of priority to a single pitch class" (music without tonic or tone center) better than the octatonic scale.[14] When I wrote this I realized that it was indeed highly speculative, almost a fantasy, but I fear it did not come out as such. It was a burst of unwarranted enthusiasm on my part, and I regret it. One does not play around this way, I suppose, with the rigorous tenets of theory, especially when they are regarded in some circles as science. I suppose I should have put out a shingle reminding my readers I was a composer-critic and I should also have asked them to bear in mind my admonishment much earlier in the course of these essays that there is more than one way of dealing with any given subject. In donning so many different hats: critic, journalist, educator, composer, theorist, and even at one time, musicologist, I have not always been sure which professional code I have been bound by. In any case I do regret the burst of enthusiasm and any idea I may have conveyed that I was assimilating octatonic procedure to Viennese atonality.

In looking back I am also inclined to think I should have made more of the octatonic's nature as a symmetrical scale, something it shares with the chromatic and whole-tone formations, though it has two intervals and they each have only one.[15] The traditional major and minor (and the modes) also have the same two intervals: whole-tone and semitone, but they are asymmetrically placed rather than simply alternating (viz., whole, whole, half, whole, whole, whole, half) in the major rather than whole, half, whole, half, whole, half, whole, half in the octatonic. The consequence is that the old scales (the "diatonic") have significant structure whereas in the symmetrical scales being in one part of the scale is much like being in another. (People with absolute pitch may argue differently since they do not depend on the scale structure to know where they are. But they miss the point that the matter is one of relationships, not absolutes.)

It is important to bear in mind that as a result of this the symmetrical scales are contextual. That is to say, they derive their structure from the way in which they are treated within any given composition. Joseph Straus, who has made excellent contributions to the theory of contemporary music since, barely beyond his student days, he wrote about the octatonic scale,[16] did not seem to understand the implications of this, and at that time consequently faulted me for maintaining that there were four potential tone centers (pitch priorities) in an octatonic scale because of the symmetry of the conjunct trichords: E-F-G, G-A♭-B♭, B♭-B-D♭, D♭-D-E. But I was assuming that within any given composition, when this was the referential scale, as it was in Stravinsky's *Psalms*, the E would be contextually established as a tone center and because of their intervallically parallel positions the first note of each of the other three trichords, G, B♭, or D♭ (3, 6, or 9 in semitonal counting) could be a clone of E and sound *like* a tone center without being one. But Straus objected, "The octatonic scale is symmetrical not only at 0, 3, 6, and 9, but also at 1, 4, 7, and 10. This being so, the scale may be said to have *eight* potential tone-centers of equal weight and independence." But the context provides no evidence for this and indeed, E and F cannot have pitch priority at the same time unless some scheme of polytonality were to be imposed, and this is a procedure that never entered into the discussion. Straus complained also that though I spoke of four potential pitch priorities, "B-flat and D-flat have at best secondary importance."[17] I found this rather surprising. Once you establish what your referential collection and order are, you do not even have to use all the notes of your key (whether in C major or anything else) to clearly affirm it.

IV

RETROSPECTIVE

16 Backstage at the Opera

Opera, as everyone knows, is a colossal undertaking with activity in its preparation on many levels. Reporters do well to keep alert for any wisp of scandal, which is as likely as anything else to be a case of the acting up of a diva or world-class tenor declaring her or his privileges. I seem to have accumulated some memorable experiences that have little or nothing to do with the music or anything else essential that goes on during performance. (Opera by virtue of its libretto and stage business can be involved with worldly events and come into conflict with them, for example, Shostakovich's *Lady Macbeth* and the attack on it by the powers that be which I mentioned in chapter 1.) I had intended writing them up as unconnected paragraphs, each devoted to a given work, person, or subject, but I was surprised at the number of instances in which two or more successive ones actually connected with one another.

My most vivid recollection from my earliest experiences as an operaviewer is that of attending my first contemporary opera, which happened to have been nothing less than Alban Berg's *Wozzeck* at the old Metropolitan Opera House in New York in 1931, presented not by the Met, but by the Philadelphia Orchestra under Leopold Stokowski, who had also conducted the League of Composers' *Rite of Spring* the previous year in the same place. (The opera was not done in England until 1952!) The story I have to tell (a very inconsequential aside) concerns the soprano Anne Roselle, who sang the leading female role of Marie. It seems my rich aunt and uncle (those who had given me, when I was eleven, their upright piano when they acquired a grand and had thereby made my musical career possible) had on several occasions invited me to occupy a seat in their box at Carnegie Hall at Roselle's recitals or to meet her socially at their home. She was among several important musicians they knew, and my aunt thought that since I was a musician myself it would be good for my career. (The guests included the distinguished Italian conductor Tullio Serafin and, though I was snobbish about pop music then, I now regret not having met Rodgers and Hart at their house.) As a poor relative I cultivated a superior stance. They might be rich financially but I was rich intellectually, and thus superior to them. Any singer they would patronize could be nothing more than a folksinger. I never accepted their invitations. Imagine my astonishment when I encountered Roselle in the role of Marie in the Berg opera. My uncle was appalled and bewildered and walked up and down the corridor saying "*Turandot* she should be singing, *Turandot!*"

Another occasion involving *Wozzeck* had to do with a Columbia Records LP of Marie's long solo in the form of variations conducted by Eugene Ormandy with his Philadelphia Orchestra. I do not know how many of my colleagues in the critical fraternity owned the score, pretty difficult to read in the late forties when the record came out. But I was proud owner of both the piano version and the orchestra score. Listening with a score I was suddenly perplexed; surely I was not listening to Elgar's Enigma Variations. Was I being confronted with another set of variations which, like his, had a trick to it? The enigma here was how to find the theme. Where was the missing theme? This somewhat smart-alecky approach on my part was the burden of my review in *Saturday Review*—I was eager to display my one-upmanship by pointing out the mistake.[1] Not unexpectedly, all hell broke loose, as the saying goes. The A and R man at Columbia, David Oppenheim, was someone with whom I had enjoyed a long and warm friendship, dating from well before his accession to such a powerful job. "Why didn't you call me before you spilled the beans?" he remonstrated on the phone. Columbia naturally had to withdraw the LP. If they could find the missing piece of tape to splice in, it would be no more than a relatively straightforward matter of transferring the corrected tape to disks. But if they could not find it, they would be obliged to have the whole thing played and recorded all over again. (I was never privy to the information of what they did, they were too angry at me.) To this day I still wonder whether I should have done precisely what I did. What is the place of the moral obligation in friendship when duty dictates otherwise? Should I have called David first so that he could quietly withdraw the recording?

A brief work—fifteen minutes in duration—of quite another kind, sometimes referred to as an opera, was staged along with the *Rite of Spring* at the latter's 1930 American premiere, also at the Metropolitan Opera House. It was Schoenberg's *Die glückliche Hand*. (I suppose it translates "lucky hand," but that sounds so trivial.) It is his Opus 18, and though it is atonal it predates his emergence as a genuinely serial composer. The chorus and soloists were in the pit with the orchestra; the characters on stage were dancers and mimes. Next to the Stravinsky with its length and its high dynamic quotient the Schoenberg, delicate, ever so tenuous and elusive, was completely overpowered, and yet it was this work and not the *Rite* that had the profoundest effect upon me and determined the direction that my composing would take during the next few years until I declared a moratorium on that particular approach. As a result of experiencing this little opera I definitely threw in my lot with the Second Viennese School. All I had was the vague knowledge that Schoenberg had started writing something called "twelve-tone" composition some years after 1913 when he had finished *Die glückliche Hand,* and I wanted to follow whatever direction he was pursuing. I began writing in a manner that was my own notion of what twelve-tone music must be. (We did not call it "serialism" then.)

It is a long way from *Wozzeck* to Stravinsky's *Rake's Progress.* What they have in common is their status in the repertory as surely two of the greatest operas of the twentieth century. I was in touch with Stravinsky during the gestation period of the *Rake* and also during the preparations for the American premiere at the old Metropolitan Opera House on 14 February 1953. I had met Stravinsky in Paris just before World War II, and by September 1939 when he fled Europe things were such that he had to travel light. Consequently there were old records and some publications difficult to find here that he did not have, and I was happy to be able to provide him with copies. The first thing I heard about the libretto of the *Rake* while it was still being written took the form of a rumor that was circulating within the "inner circle" to the effect that the librettists, W. H. Auden and Chester Kallman, had implicated the unaware Stravinsky in a homosexual in-joke. It was said that Hogarth's bearded lady would be laughed off the stage. In fact, the costume department made her look quite fetching with her short marcelled beard, and she turned out to be a most sympathetic character, especially in Act 3 at the end of the auction scene, when she renounces Tom Rakewell and bids Anne Truelove to return to him.

Naturally there was much interest among Stravinsky's acolytes and fellow musicians in the progress of the *Rake,* his first large-scale opera. It must have been about 1948 when he agreed to an evening at our apartment on East Twenty-eighth Street in New York where he would read at the piano the first act and barely completed second with the aid of Nicolas Nabokov. The audience was to be a small and, of course, chosen group from the circle of his closest friends and admirers. Since it was a warm spring day people had their windows wide open, so we thought we should prepare our neighbors, especially those across the courtyard, in order to anticipate any complaints that might interrupt the procedures. We assured them we would close our windows and suggested that they do likewise. To our surprise without exception they urged us to keep our windows open. They would not think of closing theirs. "Just imagine," one of them said. "If this were the eighteenth century it could be Mozart playing his unfinished *Don Giovanni.*" The hypercritical observers in our living room, after hearing the reading through, wondered whether the simplicity and a certain dryness of the first act were meant to symbolize the innocence of country life in contrast to the wild and colorful life of London in the second act.

Stravinsky had a successful visit to Germany around the time of the *Rake* and people there were talking of "Oedipus Rake's Progress." Perhaps his stay in middle Europe left its mark on him, for in casting about for a soprano to sing the role of Anne in his new opera he was impressed by a performance of Hilda Gueden at the Metropolitan in Strauss's *Fledermaus.* I happened to be reviewing the performance for the *New York Herald Tribune,* and during the intermission he asked me whether I thought she would be a good choice for Anne Truelove and wasn't her high C great? (He was thinking evidently of the big *Cabaletta.*) She did not seem to me quite right for the part to the extent that I knew it. (Perhaps it was her accent— something which in view of his own he was not sensitive to.) But I had to agree about the high C and that she was turning in quite a good performance. She did sing the role of Anne at the Met. I myself did not change my mind about her suitability for the role, but I have to admit she sang well.

Sir Rudolf Bing was the company's director when the *Rake* was given. He was quite outspoken and could be nasty at times. When he had the occasion to talk informally to the critics, which was quite often, he would let slip some hints with regard to what displeased him in the running of the opera house in the hopes they would get into the papers without his being officially responsible. In those days contemporary operas were very much token affairs, something the Met had to do to retain its prestige, and in the case of Stravinsky's opera, as with others, Bing would have welcomed unfavorable comments in the press so as to have some support for doing even fewer of them. (Things are very different now with James Levine as music director.) It was not beyond Bing, moreover, to bad-mouth some of his top-flight singers, especially the world-class prima donnas and celebrated tenors, in the hope that our reports would help bring them down a peg or two. He was very strict about having the regular Met singers available even during an entire extra-long season. In 1951, for example, one of the Met's finest baritones, Robert Merrill, went to Hollywood to make a movie instead of joining the company on its spring tour, and to his surprise Bing promptly dismissed him from the roster of singers. It took almost a year before, with an apology, he was allowed to return.[2]

In the forties and fifties the Juilliard School of Music had an active Opera Theater under the direction of Frederick Cohen which did operas not in the usual repertory and experimented with staging. We exchanged words in the *Tribune* over his direction of Verdi's *Falstaff*. I could understand that Cohen must have been discouraged by the way in which opera singers assumed a statuesque stance in those days, conveying visually no sense of the action and feeling about which they were singing. But he went to an extreme, maintaining that since he was employing the empty stage characteristic of Shakespeare's day, the singers, as he put it, "had to create the illusions with their acting alone." "Accordingly," to quote my own reaction from the *Tribune* article the Sunday following the first performance, "the participants were required to provide a visual continuity of constant gesturing, lurching, flopping, jumping, and parading. Up to Falstaff's soliloquy opening Act III, there was scarcely a moment when anyone sat or stood still." It was my opinion as expressed in my report that the authentic "empty stage" did not warrant the rationalization that it had to be compensated for by such antics.

Shortly after World War II there was also an attempt at the Metropolitan Opera to put some zing into the stage action and get rid of the drab, ancient sets. One of the first operas to undergo the new treatment was Mozart's *Cosi fan tutte* with pink sets to italicize the opera's sexy content. Reviewing it in the *Tribune* I found it entirely too cute and too much like a Broadway musical. The decor reminded me of a chain of restaurants called "Longchamps," which was dedicated to dainty repasts. Not long afterwards my wife and I were invited to dinner at the home of a fairly well known traditional poet, Jeanne Starr Untermeyer, with whom I had struck up a friendship when we were both guests at the MacDowell Colony. Lo and behold, the other dinner guest turned out to be the very same Fritz Stiedry who had conducted the Met performance of the Mozart. Obviously, the whole point of the occasion was for him to try to convince me that Mozart operas in the composer's own day were regarded in the same way that we regard Broadway shows. He failed to do so.

Paul Hindemith extracted a very fine symphony from his opera *Mathis der Maler* consisting of the music for the Isenheim triptych of Alsace. It was played with a certain success in Nazi Germany in 1934. Around the same time, however, the government was coming around to the view that the composer was not in the spirit of the *Weltanschauung*, and his symphony, conducted by the eminent leader of the Berlin Philharmonic Orchestra, Wilhelm Furtwängler, figured prominently in the official denunciation of Hindemith. In protest Furtwängler resigned from his post and from several other high positions he occupied; and in sympathy so did another eminent conductor, Erich Kleiber, as well as a number of VIPs in the German music world. The opera itself was not to be performed until three years later in Switzerland, but the fact that Hindemith's idiom, with its neoclassic leanings, was not nearly so difficult as Schoenberg's did not keep the Nazi government from branding it *Kulturbolschevismus*. Their main reason may very well have been the composer's own libretto, which was evidently a veiled criticism of the dictatorship, dealing as it does with the oppression of the sixteenth-century painter Matthius Grünewald in the struggle between Lutherans and Catholics.

The Boston Symphony Orchestra under the direction of Richard Burgin gave the first American performance of the Symphony *Mathis der Maler*, consisting of excerpts from the opera, about the same time as the crisis over Hindemith's music was unfolding in Germany. The opera itself was not done in America until 1956 in a nonprofessional performance by students of Boston University, which was surprisingly good since it was directed by the indefatigable Sarah Caldwell. It was truly amazing how much came through despite all the handicaps. Economically staged against an all-purpose backdrop, with movable props for scenic changes, the production could no more than suggest the rich *tableaux vivants*. Moreover, the pit could only hold an orchestra half the size of the minimum requirement, and so the resourceful Caldwell conceived of the idea of putting herself and the full orchestra backstage, while the singing was piped back to her podium. Invisible to the singers she could not propel them forward at intense moments, and the muffled orchestra, a product of the relatively primitive electronics of those days, was delinquent in the highs and generally incapable of the necessary weight. But with some imagination one could get a pretty good idea of the opera, and the impression I carried away was that it is one of a handful of the great twentieth-century operas. I find it hard to understand why it is not in the active repertory. It moves swiftly and has the story and visual appurtenances of successful grand opera: a street fight between Lutherans and Catholics; a real battle (the Peasant War); church pageantry; the burning of Lutheran books; and an allegorical vision. Part of the reason may be that Hindemith is out of fashion. He did himself great harm when he became involved, later in his career, in a pedantry that led him to make a catalog of what he did right and what he did wrong in his own past works. In some cases he proceeded to "correct" them—sacrificing, for example, the inspirations in his music of the twenties such as could be found in the original *Das Marienleben*.

Mishaps are naturally legion in opera performances since so many different departments are involved, but the public is unaware of most of them. Occasionally, however, it does notice them. Earlier I mentioned the singer who was trapped on the stalled Long Island Railroad during the first act of *Lucia di Lammermoor* when he should have been onstage singing. The Met management has to be prepared for things going awry. On quite another wavelength there was the pristine white horse on which Lohengrin was mounted that decided to empty its bladder in full view of the audience at an instance of high drama. In a crowd scene in *Aida* I saw a chorister faint and other members of the chorus precipitously change their formation to create a screen so she could be carried out with as little notice as possible, while the performance continued without a hitch. Then there was the custom of the house to create the illusion of the magic fire at the end of Wagner's *Die Walküre* by having steam highlighted with red lighting so that spectators in the first few rows would feel as if it were drizzling.

Schoenberg worked on *Moses and Aaron* for two years ending in 1932 and returned to it in 1950, completing the music for only two of the three acts before his death in 1951. He was quoted as saying fifty years would pass before it would be staged. Surprisingly, it had a concert performance in 1954 by the Northwestern German Radio Orchestra under the direction of Hans Rosbaud, who also conducted the first stage performance in 1957 in Zurich. This performance was recorded by Columbia Masterworks, which sent out a news release with a diagram of the twelve-tone set of the opera and its transpositions from "the album notes" of Milton Babbitt. The twelve transpositions were listed in the customary rectangular box by letter-name. Incidentally, Babbitt was still in those days using a numbering from one to twelve, and had not yet instituted the convention of labeling the first note zero. Analytic information of this caliber was altogether unusual for a press release from a commercial establishment. Perhaps Columbia realized that an album of this sort was for connoisseurs. In general, while it cannot be said the opera has been a roaring success I have found the degree of tolerance and interest unexpected, especially in the recent performances at the Met. Perhaps the newly installed surtitles help, because Schoenberg's libretto, which he himself wrote, is absorbing and thought-provoking.

Some of us may have a special place in our memory for Margaret Harshaw's Isolde because she usually sang alto roles. It seems the first time she sang it was with the Philadelphia Grand Opera Company. Four members of the cast were from the Met and they noticed there was no one in the prompter's box. Seasoned members of the Met were always solicitous of new young singers, shepherding them to the right position on the stage and turning them toward the audience so that they could be heard better, for example. In that tradition Harshaw's fellow singers in Philadelphia were much concerned that in her debut in such a difficult role she would not have a prompter. Since Kurvenal is off the stage during most of the time during which Isolde sings, Paul Schoeffler, who was cast in that role, undertook the assignment. Harshaw, well prepared though she was, appreciated the gesture and learned on this occasion what every opera singer knows: the prompter is essential however well you know your part.

17 A Tale of Two Conductors: Koussevitzky and Mitropoulos

During Serge Koussevitzky's lifetime I would find fault from time to time with the freedom he would take with the scores he conducted, but as I look back I think those transgressions were immaterial relative to his essential contribution and I find I appreciate him more. As a newspaper reviewer I was in a position to make my feelings known, and I became aware of his absolute intolerance of criticism of any kind. But as a composer I now am convinced that he was a big man, and it is difficult to find anyone of his stature and influence who is currently dedicated as he was to the cause, to the sheer crisis of survival, of the American composer. He was not the first Boston Symphony Orchestra (BSO) conductor to promote the avant-garde. Even before 1920 the conductor Max Fiedler terrified New Yorkers when he descended upon them for the orchestra's regular visits. As Paul Rosenfeld reported somewhere they "woke critical agonies" with Vincent d'Indy. The orchestra's programming was the subject of many "sarcasms over the 'rarefied taste' of the cultivated city opposite Cape Cod."

Koussevitzky paid some obeisance to the new music from Europe, but this did not keep him from his dedication to American music. He made Boston a tremendously exciting place musically, aligning himself with the creative talents of the region and actually making the city his home. His style as a citizen of Boston offers quite a contrast to the recent maestro Seiji Ozawa, at the time of this writing on the way to retirement from the BSO. Ozawa's primary commitment has remained to Japan. When once required to mention the name of a prominent young Boston composer in a radio interview, in connection with the fact that the orchestra would later play his work, he had to be prompted before he could come up with it, though he was scarcely old enough at the time to be pardoned on the basis of old-age memory loss. But Ozawa's record as a Boston citizen is on the high side compared to that of Kurt Masur (also on the verge of retiring from the New York Philharmonic) when it comes to having some identity with the city in which he conducts. Masur does not even have something like Tanglewood to keep him in the United States beyond the season.

However much Koussevitzky became part of the Boston scene, after a quarter of a century in the area his speech still sounded as if he had migrated there recently. His malapropisms provided a rich store of conversational material for the orchestral musicians whose normal dialogue leaned heavily, as it still does, on the supply of jokes. One of Koussie's pronouncements that I particularly like was delivered at the Berkshire Music Center, the orchestra's summer school at Tanglewood, during the meeting of a conducting class he was presenting. Listening to students demonstrating their conducting skills in turn, he was particularly incensed by one of them I shall call Johnny. He stopped him in midstream and with a red face that made him appear on the verge of apoplexy, he shouted, "Johnny, took it a tempo and kept it." (In case you need a translation—some people do—"take a tempo and keep it.")

Conductors need charisma, as everyone knows, and they have to develop some semblance of it if they have none to start with. Koussevitzky was an individual who had somewhat more than average. This enabled him to forestall the disapproval that would normally emanate from the conservative wing in reaction to his programming. It also helped him to get extra rehearsals when he needed them to cope with the demands of new music. Despite receiving the added time for preparing new works he had trouble with difficult passages because his technique was limited. Toscanini also had the charisma to get extra rehearsals. But he used them to worry the same limited number of traditional pieces to such an extent that Thomson found himself "lulled to sleep by the perfection of the machine." Koussevitzky's distortions, one may be surprised to hear a composer like myself say, could be endearing.

Once, for a review I was writing, I compared several LP versions of Copland's *Appalachian Spring* and found Koussevitzky annoyingly slowing up in certain spots because he was evidently having difficulty negotiating measures of seven beats. But despite this I thought his the best, even though it was a reissue of an old seventy-eight rpm. What redeemed him was not only the sound he got from the orchestra but the conviction that somehow communicated itself over the loudspeaker. His dedication to new music was not just a token gesture; one had the feeling he believed in it. He also believed in the modern movement. A statistical report of how many premieres he gave was insufficient indication of his contributions to it. It was not simply a matter of how many new American works he programmed, but how much he did for a composer like Aaron Copland, for instance, to usher him into a position at the forefront of American music. To accomplish this entailed more than a few premieres, which another conductor might easily have gone through the motions of presenting to satisfy demands of a PR nature since a premiere is news. Not that Koussevitzky did not take advantage of PR; he lost no opportunity to avail himself of it, using it not to promote himself, but to promote the composer, and not hesitating at all to indulge in Madison Avenue exaggeration. Or perhaps it was not calculated to any extent but was merely enthusiasm. Lenny Bernstein, who, as a rapidly rising protégé of the maestro, already visualized himself as future Messiah of American conductors, was in the audience at Columbia University to witness Koussevitzky present a citation to Howard Hanson, and in the course of his remarks the veteran conductor told the audience that the honoree was "die grea-eatest American conductor." Lenny confronted him after the ceremony with the greeting, "How could you say such a thing?" The maestro answered, "Well, Lyenyshka, you know, I was just carried away." I wonder if Lenny had that in mind when he set those very words in a song for his Broadway musical *On the Town* and if he in fact suggested the phrase to the lyricists Betty Comden and Adolph Green.

Koussevitzky was prone to exaggerate. He thought nothing of saying one week that he would play "die grea-eatest" symphony of our time, Copland's third, and the next week saying exactly the same thing of the latest Shostakovich essay in the genre. And there are some estimable individuals in the contemporary music world who believe "exaggeration" is an epithet that may also be assigned to the whole reputation of Koussevitzky as savior of the American composer. It is argued that the insistence on the Boston maestro in this role occludes the remarkable contribution of someone like Dimitri Mitropoulos. The year that Koussevitzky retired from the BSO Mitropoulos acceded in New York to the conductor's chair of the Philharmonic. Koussevitzky regarded Mitropoulos as a kindred spirit and while he (Koussevitzky) was still in Boston invited the still young Greek musician as guest conductor. Mitropoulos admittedly played a lesser role than Koussie in advancing new music. Better public relations would not only have enabled Mitropoulos to give his support to new music on a scale comparable to that maintained by Koussevitzky, but would have enabled him to avert the fate that prematurely deprived him of the very minimum conditions for offering that support—namely, the continued occupancy of his post as Philharmonic conductor. As it was, he was relieved of the post after only a decade owing in no small degree to a relentless attack from a powerful branch of the press for, among other things, essentially his predilection for the most advanced and least friendly new music.

Whenever Koussevitzky is lauded to the skies for his contribution, some of us think of Mitropoulos, whose name is scarcely recalled. I am, of course, biased since Mitropoulos was one of my benefactors. But this gave me the opportunity to watch him from up close and to reinforce my admiration for him. The circumstances of a commission he gave me are revealing. In 1950 he was present at a chamber music concert the program for which included my early Quartet in C Major for woodwinds—a typical "neoclassic" work if you used the expression. It was undoubtedly the first work of mine he had ever heard, and at the intermission he asked me right then and there to write a piece for him to conduct at the Philharmonic—stipulating substantial terms. Now it is well known that Mitropoulos's leanings were in the direction of the products of the Second Viennese School, so my immediate response was, "You can't mean it, my quartet is in C major." He assured me he recognized quality and craftsmanship in whatever idiom they manifest themselves and since Milton Babbitt was present and conversing with us and I still looked skeptical at such an impromptu decision, he said that Babbitt would be our witness. I had had so many empty promises from instrumentalists and conductors in intermission exchanges like this that I did not really believe him until the confirming letter that soon arrived. I understand he took the money for such commissions out of his own salary. A new work would give him some publicity in return, but this was not his goal, since the serial works he habitually programmed were what contributed to the unpopularity that led ultimately to the termination of his contract. He did not have Koussevitzky's PR skills for dramatizing the adventurous components of his programs.

Some readers may wonder why I have not brought up the name of Pierre Boulez sooner in the present context. Quite properly he declared that symphony audiences should be introduced to the traditional twentieth-century repertory before being exposed to the newest music. I was nonetheless not altogether happy with the way he implemented this objective. There was condescension in his remarks (he did do a lot of talking to the audience) when he conducted Berg's *Three Pieces* Op. 6 for orchestra (1914) in the spirit of one bringing culture to the natives. Moreover it turned out he was less a pioneer than he thought, since Mitropoulos had brought us this work as one of the high points of his career.

Like other foreign conductors in America, Boulez spent too much time abroad to have the kind of close relation with young local composers that Koussevitzky and Mitropoulos had. Neither of them was a world-class composer but they did, as part of their music education, compose—Koussevitzky light-weight pieces for his instrument, contrabass, Mitropoulos more serious pieces, I am told, though I never saw any. This accounted for a certain sympathy with composers and the ability of both conductors to identify with them in the United States. Both conductors were available to nurture composers who were writing pieces for them.

I took my unfinished commission *Ideas of Order* to Mitropoulos from time to time in his modest room in the Great Northern Hotel a few doors down from Carnegie Hall where he purposely chose an austere lifestyle. His suggestions were useful. He was still making suggestions when the piece was in rehearsal, and at lunch after the first rehearsal, which was to be followed by the second rehearsal in the afternoon, he made a proposal that was unheard of then and would be even more amazing today: namely, to take some precious and costly rehearsal time to try a little revision that he thought would improve the music's flow. It seems there was a string line that was interrupted by a widely spaced wind chord before continuing. Mitropoulos wanted to try leaving out the wind chord, so that the line would not be interrupted. I explained that I did not consider it an interruption but a means of siphoning out a salient sonority at which the string counterpoint had arrived in order to dwell on it briefly, just as one might italicize or otherwise draw out an important and striking phrase in a sentence. Well, he would try cutting the chord out and see how we liked it. (Another conductor might have just peremptorily made the change without consulting the composer and over all his objections, rather than use precious rehearsal time to try it.) But at the rehearsal nothing of the sort took place, and when I asked him afterwards why not, he said that in terms of his own indoctrination this type of music was something in which he was not well informed. It was not his forte. He was a stranger to it. However, with the aid of my explanation he had been able to understand the reason for the chord. On another occasion he spent over an hour of rehearsal time reorchestrating a passage to achieve a more convincing ending in a score of one of my fellow composers with the collaboration of the composer. I was equally struck by how much Koussevitzky was involved with the young composers he commissioned when I heard from Copland how the maestro would have him come and stay at his house when a Copland premiere was being prepared.

Koussevitzky and Mitropoulos were both approachable human beings for a young composer whereas the average conductor with an international reputation was like royalty who could be approached only through his (or her) vassals. My experience with Erich Leinsdorf was particularly frustrating in this regard, though I must admit that in the end his performance of my *Polyphony* with the BSO was quite creditable. When he was rehearsing a new piece with the composer present he always consigned the latter to silence during the entire proceeding. I could not make any suggestions to the conductor or players, which is what a composer usually does at a rehearsal. Leinsdorf asked me to save my comments and after the rehearsal we would have a conference. (I suppose with the limited rehearsal time a conductor usually gets there is a perfectly good rationale behind the practice.) The conference was very businesslike with a recording secretary, the assistant conductor, the orchestra librarian, and of course myself. If I said a given passage or instrument marked *f (forte)* was too loud he would instruct the librarian to revise the parts to read *mf (mezzo-forte)*. The secretary also kept a record of any of my comments Leinsdorf thought should be conveyed to the orchestra. If it was after the last rehearsal he would have the secretary put notes on the stands conveying my remarks and anything he thought of. This was not surprisingly the subject of many barbs on the part of the musicians.

Boulez conveniently disengaged himself from his obligation to new American music early in his Philharmonic conductorship by denouncing what was currently being written by American composers. He still programmed American chamber works at what were called, with a nod perhaps to the avant-garde periodical in Princeton, Perspective Encounters. (They became known as "Rug Concerts" because with the limited number of seats the overflow was provided with rugs to sit on the floor.) At these concerts Boulez could take advantage of the public relations device of having the composers present to discuss their work.

One of the most disastrous blows to American music's support in the second half of the twentieth century was Leonard Bernstein's decision to devote his not inconsiderable musicianship and conducting prowess to Mahler. Like Koussevitzky he had clout, he could win the public over to any cause he desired, and most of all, twentieth-century American music

was very much his thing. He had been somewhat in the position of a protégé of Copland. In addition, his boyhood associates had been Irving Fine
and Harold Shapero. He continued to maintain a close friendship with
them during all his Harvard years, at which time I myself joined this musically avant-garde coterie. From the very beginning of the movement on-
ward he had been, like each of us, a member of the group of Harvard or
New England neoclassicists. But like Boulez he exonerated himself from
the obligation of playing a good deal of new American music by announcing in mid-career his ideological objections to the atonal and serial approaches, which accounted for much of the best music being written in this
country. For the prestigious Charles Eliot Norton Lectures that he was invited to give at Harvard University in 1970, he went pretty far afield, to
Noam Chomsky's notions of a universal grammar, in order to prove that
tonality was as natural as the innate modes of forming sentences.[1] (Chomsky told me that Bernstein did well in encapsulating the essentials of his
theory for a general audience, but he refused to comment on its application
to music since he felt he did not know enough about it.) Ray Jackendoff, an
ex-student and disciple of Chomsky's, in collaboration with the composer
Fred Lerdahl has developed the kind of Chomskian methodology to which
Bernstein pointed the way.[2] But none of this gain in the realm of music theory compensated for Bernstein's defection as a conductor.

Among Stravinsky's last pronouncements was advice to today's composers that in view of the public situation in music they would do well to
"go underground," and many of us have. Such being the case, I wonder
how Boulez could have known enough to make such a blanket condemna-
tion of our music. But even if he was right, not performing the music was
not the proper response. Good or bad, the music must be played to keep the
tradition alive. Any improvement would have had to come from performers and critics ferreting out the most promising manifestations and en-
couraging them, in the hope that composers would use them as a starting
point for improvement. Not performing the music at all is the best way of
allowing the tradition to die. That tradition is kept alive even in the most
mediocre creations.

I can very well understand that there should be those who will want to
deflate Koussevitzky's image because of the more inaccessible and difficult
music that he neglected. We should be grateful that there was at least
Mitropoulos who favored the composers that Koussevitzky failed to do jus-

tice to, and we are perfectly within our right to regard Mitropoulos's orientation as nobler since the composers he favored (the serialists) had less audience appeal. It should be said on Mitropoulos's behalf that he tried to be catholic in his tastes, even finding merit in a piece of mine in C major, my little woodwind quartet which I wrote in the heyday of neoclassicism. He also did a good deal for David Diamond, a composer whose music could be difficult at times but who is not serial, and Mitropoulos tried out some pretty poor composers, one of whom enraged him so with the deficiencies of his score that at a rehearsal he threw it on the floor and stamped on it.

With regard to Koussevitzky's omissions, it is difficult to forgive him for the fact that in the total of one hundred eighty-one American works presented by the BSO from 1924 to 1946—some of them conducted by Richard Burgin or the composers themselves—there is only one work by Roger Sessions, and by no means a representative one: his early Symphony in E minor. Sessions was not a serial composer but he could be mistaken for one. His music is demanding and has a certain unyielding seriousness in a middle European way. Moses Smith, in his book on Koussevitzky, explains that the conductor's attitude toward the music of the Second Viennese School was that "it was more difficult than any with which Koussevitzky had had to do," but Smith quickly adds that the necessary pains he would have had to take "must have seemed especially unrewarding because he probably found most of the music unsympathetic to his temperament."[3]

While I was at Harvard in the thirties I witnessed two rare occasions on which Koussevitzky did performances of works from the Second Viennese School. Not surprisingly they were both by Berg, the least severe of the Viennese triumvirate: the violin concerto and music from the opera *Lulu*. The soprano in the opera excerpt was a fine Russian singer, Olga Averino, who had settled in the Boston region. I would meet her socially from time to time. On one occasion I brought up the subject of her Berg performance, but she shushed me and said she wanted to forget it ever happened. Neither the maestro nor the players, she said, knew what they were doing and she simply had to improvise. But this was not unusual for atonal and serial music in those days. Even knowledgeable musicians associated with the founding of the movement had trouble. The late Eugene Lehner, former violist of the BSO, told me that as a member of the celebrated Kolish Quartet he had played in the premiere of Berg's *Lyric Suite* in Vienna. Given no doubt to exaggeration in his agitation at recalling the event, he shouted, "Not a note was right!" But it was a huge success and Koussevitzky, who happened to have been in the audience, invited him on the spot to become a member of the BSO.

A curious corollary to the position of conductors as dictators on the contemporary music scene is that although they are obliged to make their programs catholic as to taste, it is perfectly clear what music they prefer, and their preference is likely to influence the quality of sound they elicit from their orchestras. This, in turn, may very well have an effect on composers who want their music played by a given conductor and orchestra, and it is also in this way that conductors will dictate the direction in which music progresses. Koussevitzky set before composers as a persuasive model the gorgeous tone he elicited from his Boston ensemble as well as his own leanings toward the broad Romantic symphonic style. I wonder if Copland did not tailor his Third Symphony to Koussevitzky's BSO manner, since a sinewy leanness is more common to the character we had come to admire so much as defining that composer's individuality. (But of course, there was also Copland's long-standing regard for Mahler.) As for other prominent figures in Koussevitzky's stable—Walter Piston, Roy Harris, William Schuman, and David Diamond, for instance—the imprint of Koussevitzky and the BSO on their music seems very apparent to me. There is nothing unprecedented about composers tailoring their music to performers for whom they write. I recall one composer who was quite elated by the Koussevitzky rendition he received, even though it imposed a Romanticism on his music that he had not intended and it was doubtful whether it was apposite. He commented "the air was so thick you could cut it with a knife," and it turned out he found this was something he actually relished. It was not surprising that the next time he wrote a piece for orchestra he bore this rich, full sonority in mind and indulged in it.

If there were no pressure on conductors to present programs representative of all tendencies, calamities would be less likely. They would each specialize in their chosen domain and know thoroughly the portion of the repertory in which they specialized. Ideally, taste should not be arbitrated by the conductor in power; there should be music of different tendencies with sympathetic interpreters being found in each given instance. (It would mean orchestras would have to alternate conductors even more frequently than they do now.)

That composers are not on symphony boards is deplorable. No composer relishes the fact that conductors have so much power to arbitrate taste and that they play such an important role as disseminators of any given musical style they fancy. In their dealings with the typical conductor, composers also find themselves intimidated by the personality and the imperiousness even if their music has been selected by him or her for performance; they may find themselves during rehearsals tongue-tied when they have to communicate details and instructions relevant to the manner of performance. Koussevitzky may not have assumed the royal pose like other conductors, but he was by nature an aristocrat not only in the way he lorded over the Boston music scene, but also in the way he delighted in having the young composers as part of his entourage, his courtiers—quite unlike Ozawa who was completely oblivious of our existence. Because he respected us as a knowing audience, Koussevitzky assumed we would regularly attend his subscription concerts and come to the green room afterwards. But we were not interested much in the staples that inevitably constituted the bulk of his programs, and unless he was playing a new work that we wanted to hear we would arrive at the end of the concert and go directly backstage. I remember in particular the cold nights when we would have to vigorously rub our hands and blow on them so that when we extended one of them in greeting he would not be able to detect that we had just come in from outdoors. Memory of those occasions goes a long way toward encapsulating my nostalgia for the Koussevitzky interregnum. He cared. It was important to him that the young composers were there.

It would be hard to find a personality who better fits the description of the antithesis of Koussevitzky than Mitropoulos who was monklike, almost shy, retiring. He gave his money away to needy composers, lived very modestly, as I have said, and seemed completely bereft of the capacity for public relations. Nevertheless he decided to do everything he conducted without the score in front of him. It was not a matter of poor eyesight as it has been for other conductors as they get older. It was just some extra trick, as he once confided in me, to give the audience an additional show of virtuosity in order to raise its confidence, and also to enhance its image of the conductor as trapeze artist. He would even memorize if it was a contemporary work that he was never to conduct again. At rehearsal he might very occasionally have recourse to the miniature score for rehearsal numbers, but often he even memorized these.

I remember consulting with the Philharmonic's first violist after a rehearsal of my piece and telling him a certain line he played did not come out sufficiently. He suggested that if it were an octave higher it would be heard better, and he said he would transpose it at the next rehearsal so I could see how I liked it. I answered that I better tell the maestro to change it in the score. The violist assured me the way Mitropoulos memorized a score did not take octave position into account, and sure enough in the next rehearsal the maestro did not stop to correct the violist. His memory was perfectly satisfied to accept it in its admittedly insignificant revision. (I do not wish to convey the impression that all octave transpositions would be insignificant. It just happens that this was.) At first my enthusiasm for Mitropoulos and his fabulous memory were dampened somewhat by this piece of intelligence. But I soon got over my disappointment and realized his memory was still pretty fabulous. Not having his head bent over the score gave him freedom of motion. I remember when I first saw him—it was a rehearsal of the BSO which he was invited by Koussevitzky to conduct in the mid-thirties. Without a baton and with fists clenched he seemed like a prizefighter, the orchestra his adversary. (I was doing a story on him for the *Boston Evening Transcript* to introduce him to the Boston public.) It is still the way I most remember him when I think back to how regrettable it was that we could enjoy his ministrations on the New York scene for no more than a decade.

18   From My Diary: Brief Encounters

The harpsichordist Sylvia Marlowe invited Esther and me to dinner with the Stravinskys (Vera and Igor). Many were the travails associated with the occasion. He had called earlier to ask what kind of wine there would be, and she told him there would be a very fine Chianti. "I will bring my own wine." He carried his bottle of Burgundy (his favorite type of wine) with him when he was not at the table. Sylvia served a leg of lamb of superb quality and cooked to the proper shade of pink-red, but he pushed it away, "Je mange pas d'ail" (I don't eat garlic). Ditto with the fine salad of endives. When the dessert came on, a delicious *mousse au chocolat*, and the maestro came up with "Je mange pas de chocolat," it was just amazing that our hostess was able to maintain her composure and not burst out in tears or develop a temper tantrum, which she later told us she felt on the verge of.

Stravinsky once confided in me that when he was orchestrating and he came across a musical line that would traditionally be scored for violin(s) he would very likely put it into the trumpet or some other wind instrument. This must surely be one of the things that give so unique a quality to his orchestration.

Around 1940 when Stravinsky arrived in America from France, at a time when he was still speaking French, he was addressing a small group of nuns and I was present. When he asked for questions from the floor it was not surprising that the first one was about Shostakovich, whose star at that time in America was at its highest. What did he think of Shostakovich? The response was quite negative. What did he think of Prokofiev? "Ça, c'est tout autre chose" (that's an entirely different thing).

———————

A group of us, part of Stravinsky's entourage, were leaving a Columbia Recordings studio in New York in the West Fifties with him just after he had conducted a piece of his for a taping, and we emerged into a bright, clear day with the temperature unusually low, perhaps around fifteen degrees Fahrenheit. It was lunchtime and the maestro, who had a passion for lobster, said he knew an excellent place for it over on the East Side. We suggested getting a taxi, saying it was a pretty long walk for him to take in such cold weather. He said not at all. He breathed deeply to fully savor the cold clear air, and declared nostalgically, this was just the way it would be in St. Petersburg.

———————

I was sitting with Stravinsky at a rehearsal of his *Requiem Canticles* in Princeton where it was to have its premiere. In the "Libera me," where the chorus recites freely what the quartet is singing to convey the impression of an actual noisy church situation, he nudged me with his elbow and with a very broad smile said, "People should not talk while music is being played." Making fun of his own work was part of a larger syndrome: his ambivalence toward the speaking voice with music. He was never happy with the Gide words recited in *Perséphone* though I myself think they are quite wonderful—superbly integrated with the music. He contrives music and words so that they never interfere with one another.

———————

Stravinsky was having a conversation with some young people about his Mass and the subject of the disproportionate length of the *Credo* arose. "There is much to believe," volunteered the maestro in a very solemn voice.

———————

An old friend of mine, the pianist Elly Kassman Meyer, also, incidentally, a friend of Robert Craft, decided to play Stravinsky's piano concerto at her Town Hall recital in the forties. Since the orchestra was made up only of winds there was no problem of fitting it onto the platform. And though it involved an expense that her husband, a successful psychoanalyst, could well afford, it was still nowhere near as costly as a full orchestra. I was somehow involved in the preparations, perhaps because my recommendation had been one of the things that had convinced her to do the work at a time when neoclassic music was quite in ill repute. When the date for the performance was almost upon us the concerto's publisher, Boosey and Hawkes, phoned me in great agitation to say they could not find the harmonium part! It seems their score and parts bore the original title with the French word for winds: *Concerto pour piano et orchestra d'harmonie.*

NADIA BOULANGER

In 1937 with the John Knowles Paine traveling fellowship from Harvard under my belt I married and my wife and I sailed to France for what was to be the first part of my two years of study (the other part of it to be later in London). At the beginning of September it must have been, I made my way to Montparnasse, to the establishment of Nadia Boulanger at 36 Rue Ballu. There was a bell to buzz in a rather small vestibule, and after several attempts with no answer I gave up and decided to wait. I became aware that quite a large number of people my age were gathered outside, obviously doing the same thing, and they were talking to one another in English, so I joined them. Soon a car arrived and Boulanger emerged majestically, indicating endless bundles of music which she expected us all to carry to her apartment (she was just returning from her summer place). We were put into a stuffy little room with walls every inch of which were covered with dusty framed photographs—relatives, celebrities. After about an hour I was summoned into the studio and "Mademoiselle," which was what we called her (perhaps to emphasize that she never was nor would be married) declared, in excellent English with a marked but charming accent, "I should have been a man. A woman cannot have a career." (She did have one, of course, and a brilliant one.)

In 1938 while I was studying with Boulanger in Paris we had a visit from one of my closest Harvard classmates, Oscar Handlin, later the well known Pulitzer Prize–winning American historian. He was accompanied by his wife and they were on their way to a winter vacation in the Alps. They tried to persuade us to come along with them but I told them I had a Monday lesson with Mademoiselle (it must have been a Thursday or Friday). After we all had a good deal of wine they broached the subject again, promising us they'd get me back in time for the lesson. Under the influence of the alcohol our resistance was shattered and we agreed. Throwing our things down from our studio balcony, I allowed them to pack our bags. After an overnight trip in third class, sleeping on hard wooden benches which our companions did not seem to mind at all, we arrived in Salanches. As I sobered I realized I was thoroughly unprepared with proper attire for the snow, and I easily catch colds. It was a very stressful weekend for me, but they got me back to Paris Sunday night, just as they had promised. Boulanger expected a student to be in the city and available at any time for a change of schedule. There was a *pneumatique* under our door telling me not to come Monday, come at 10 P.M. Sunday. (It was that already!) My heart sank a notch. How would I explain myself? But there was something else under the door that we had not noticed at first—a communication, a telegram that said don't come Sunday night, come Friday at 8 A.M. I was much too relieved to complain that I was not, and still am not, my best at that hour.

DARIUS MILHAUD

As a visiting alien during World War II, Darius Milhaud while teaching at Mills College had to go to the courthouse in Oakland to sign papers or something on more than one occasion, and there would be a long wait—an hour or two—which he would spend in his wheelchair. None of the waiting fazed him. On each occasion he would take along one of his elegant old French small pocket-sized music-writing notebooks, and by the time he returned home it would be filled with some little newly composed chamber piece, usually for a combination of two or three strings.

———————

When I arrived at Mills College in 1939 to assume the duties of composition teacher, it was at the end of a period during which I had taken a furlough from composing for a number of reasons, including an indecision as to the proper direction to take and self-doubts as to what kind of contribution I could make. I still had those doubts but I had resumed composing on a modest scale. During my second year Darius Milhaud joined the faculty and my fellow composition teacher Charles Jones started to show our celebrated colleague his compositions on a regular weekly basis. So I followed his example. When I brought Milhaud the music I was writing for a Mills dance group he threw up his hands, shouted "merveilleux," and embraced me. To have such a reaction from a world-class musician was all I needed to restore my faith in my composing. It was only later that I became aware that Milhaud was unburdening himself of a favorite locution that he would as readily use for the most primitive attempt of a freshman.

Milhaud traces his lineage back many centuries to French ancestors of Jewish persuasion who inhabited Provence, especially the area around Carpentras where a lovely old synagogue still exists. So when I was teaching at Mills College and the Milhauds invited my wife and me to Passover dinner we were quite curious. The Passover story was read in what Milhaud has described as a "jargon consisting of Hebrew and Provençal" but it did not sound to me at all like Hebrew. It sounded like nothing I had heard before and the ritual was quite different. As on other occasions when I had visited, little Daniel, who was under ten, was noisy and unruly and not at all the disciplined youngster I had expected a "bien élevé" French boy to be.

AARON COPLAND

In March 1950 Copland and I were invited to participate in an annual Festival of Contemporary Arts at the University of Illinois in Urbana, each of us to have our music played and to lecture. I had not started to fly yet and I was apprehensive at the prospect. So although Copland was reluctant I succeeded in persuading him to make the trip by rail. It so happened there was a coal strike and the delays were inordinate, so that for the return trip Copland was adamant about not taking the train. He persuaded me to return by plane, and assuming the fatherly, protective stance for which he was well known among composers of my generation, he gave me a silver dollar as a token to guarantee my safety. The flight was as smooth and calm as it could be, with a clear sky revealing a full moon and with a tail wind.

I don't know how serious he was but Copland used to say he hated to give his autograph since some stranger might have it in his or her head to use it to forge a check.

When Copland came to dinner at our apartment in New York in the forties as he did on several occasions he sometimes helped dry the dishes in the days before dishwashers and dryers were common. On one occasion he said to us in jest, "Don't tell Stravinsky." In those days men were not expected to share in housework or child care.

In the early thirties Koussevitzky gave the American premiere of Stravinsky's *Perséphone*, a work that to my mind stands beside the Bach *Passions* as one of the choral masterpieces of all time. I was sitting with Copland, always a staunch admirer of Stravinsky, at a rehearsal for the occasion in Boston's Symphony Hall when he turned to me and in a voice indicating a sense of disappointment remarked, "So French." He was obviously referring to the perfumed atmosphere of Impressionism.

VIRGIL THOMSON

I first visited Virgil Thomson in his New York apartment at the Chelsea Hotel some time in the mid-thirties. He cultivated a Victorian decor that was consistent with the character of the hotel. At the time it did not seem too extreme. It was well before the general influx of Bauhaus-type furniture and I came to take it very much for granted. Around 1970 when I brought my wife Ellen to meet Virgil I suddenly saw it through her eyes. It was, she said, like walking into a different century, the nineteenth: the heavy drapes and rugs, the loveseat in which each of the occupants faces in a different direction, the cartoonish painting by Florine Stettheimer with the Statue of Liberty and the American flag. The Victorian decor was quite chic at the time, cultivated especially by folk in the arts.

Thomson was discussing a soprano who had made a simple German *Lied* sound grand and operatic. "It's as if she were taking the Queen Mary to Brooklyn," was his assessment of the affair. I do not know whether he ever used the observation in a review. It seems too good to squander.

OTHER COMPOSERS

Shostakovitch was having a piece played in Carnegie Hall and he was here in the United States for it. I remember neither what piece nor when. On opening the program book he was shocked to see the standard (in America among other places) torso of a woman advertising a brassiere.

Some time during World War II Elliott and Helen Carter invited Esther and me to visit them for a few days at their rented summer place on the Pamet River in Truro on Cape Cod. Esther and I decided to spend one afternoon window shopping in Provincetown about ten miles away and we took the bus to get there, since gasoline was severely rationed so even if people had cars they used them sparingly. We thought we could solve the problem of a house gift if we brought back some lobsters since we knew there was doubt what we would do for dinner. Naturally we brought them live, and it was with some difficulty that we kept them from creeping out of the cardboard boxes on the crowded bus. When we arrived at the house Helen said we had to leave immediately for a cocktail party. We knew we could keep the lobsters alive on ice. There was an ice chest that opened on top that was perfect for this, except that out of force of habit Helen closed the lid. When we returned the lobsters were no longer alive but we were not ready to dispose of them before calling the marine laboratory in Woods Hole. We were told they would be poisonous and to discard them at once, which was something we could not get ourselves to do since lobsters were an even greater luxury then than they are now. We then called some natives who pooh-poohed the experts and said the lobsters had been dead too short a time for it to matter. Of course that was the advice we took and here I am over half a century later to tell the tale.

It must have been some time in the mid-thirties when the writer and musician Paul Bowles, the expatriate member of the Young Composers Group that Copland had created, was on one of his trips to New York from Morocco or Paris. We were walking back from a meeting of the group and when we arrived at the apartment house on West Fourteenth Street where he was staying he invited me up for tea. When I entered his apartment I was struck by the objects that adorned his walls: knives and whips. I dismissed the notion that these were the paraphernalia for unnatural sex acts and I summoned up the courage to ask what made him opt for such gruesome decor. He told me he had more than the ordinary fear of violence and having these objects around him helped him face it. When he served tea he brought out some cookies but he warned me they were laced with hashish. If I was not used to it I should know "they make you feel like flying," and while there was no harm in that in Tangiers where living quarters were at ground level, here we were in a penthouse fourteen stories up. Since I decided not to take the chance he offered me some cheese in a glass jar. When he opened the jar it was swarming with creeping objects but he was quite unperturbed and simply took a spoon and removed them. All this in those days was a pretty heady mixture, very far out for me.

———————

One would have taken the pipe-smoking Walter Piston to be a businessman or perhaps a lawyer. He was someone who seemed to be completely self-possessed, without any of the flightiness or unpredictability that we expect from an artist. He spent almost four decades on the Harvard music faculty (never held a regular position anywhere else), and during most of that time he almost never missed a concert of the Boston Symphony Orchestra and could be seen Thursday nights year after year in the same seat, a preferred area for acoustics in the first balcony right and quite near the front of the hall. (It is a convenient place for composers to get on to the platform quickly to take a bow.) As a teacher he was soft-spoken and placid, and in the sessions one on one with him I had to pry the words out to get him to talk. It was well worth it since he always spoke good sense.

———————

Alvin Lucier was one of my earliest graduate students in composition at Brandeis. He came from Yale where he had written a Broadway show and his style for serious music was dyed-in-the-wool neoclassic. I helped him make his music sound more contemporary within that idiom, but when he went to Italy on a Fulbright and studied with Boris Porena in Rome, his teacher criticized the first work he brought as "troppo tradizionale!" Lucier inserted a few extra dissonances in his next work and increased the fragmentation. Porena said, "poco meglio ma ancora troppo conventionale" (a little better but still too conventional). This process continued for several weeks until Porena was satisfied with the modernity of Lucier's composing. The experience makes one suspect that perhaps Lucier continued the process on his own until he finally arrived at the nonmusic genre that is sometimes called "Sound Art."

———————

David Diamond dedicated a song to me, but after I wrote an unfavorable review of his music he came to the door unexpectedly and practically in tears demanded I return the manuscript. He rescinded the dedication. It was too bad since we were very close friends and I admired his music in general. Our friendship was ultimately patched up but not his annoyance at my review.

———————

In 1939, while I was teaching at Mills College, Henry Cowell was not very far away in San Quentin, where he was in about the third year of a fifteen-year sentence on a morals charge as the outcome of an appalling miscarriage of justice. (He was released in 1940 and granted full pardon in 1942.) Cowell was very active and successful in educating the large prison population musically, and he established an orchestra and chorus, at the same time composing fluently. Among the pieces he wrote were some for the Mills College dancers in the form of modules that could be put together in various ways by Cage and Harrison (anticipating Stockhausen's *Klavierstucke XI* by quite a number of years) tailored to the dancers' needs . (These two young composers, as I said, provided the music for the college dancers.) One day it occurred to me that it might be a good idea, if a bold one, to take my graduate composition seminar to see Cowell. It was a great success. Cowell was in a good mood and talkative, and the students were exposed to a creative personality with some extraordinary ideas.

VARIORUM

Nathan Milstein was playing the Glazunov violin concerto with the Pittsburgh Symphony under the direction of the guest conductor Paul Paray, who was desperately looking for a permanent post and coveted the one open in the orchestra he was guest-conducting. (I was at the concert because Paray was doing a string orchestra piece of mine on the same program.) At one point Milstein stopped dead and went over to examine the score on the podium music stand. He later told me it was impossible to know a piece better than he knew the Glazunov, he had played it about a thousand times. (If such was the case why should he not be bored with it?) Paray corroborated this, saying he had conducted a Milstein performance of that very piece when the violinist was a boy. The sad part was that the Pittsburgh audience thought the great Milstein could do no wrong, could not possibly forget what he was playing, and so it had to be the conductor who was responsible for the mishap.

A pianist by the name of Hortense Monath gave a concert in Town Hall in 1932 or thereabouts at which she played Schoenberg's Suite Op. 25, a most unusual choice at the time (it is still not a repertory piece). I borrowed the score from the library (it had not been bound yet) and took it along to follow the performance. The pianist got lost several times and just floundered around though most listeners were unaware. I went to the green room to

pay my respects at the end of the concert, carrying my score rather osten-
tatiously as if I wanted people to know how up on things I was. When I
greeted Ms. Monath she could not fail to notice that I carried the music.
She turned pale and said to me, "Then you know!!"

The American Composers Alliance gives a prize annually known as the
Laurel Leaf to an individual or an organization in recognition of a contribution to the advancement of contemporary American music. In 1955 the
conductor George Szell was the recipient, and according to one observer,
"the poor man was utterly nonplussed since he hadn't played any American music that season." Indeed, he almost never played any contemporary
works, and in Cleveland, which was the scene of his main conducting post,
he would farm them out to guest or assistant conductors to balance the season's programs.

When I was at Townsend Harris High School in the twenties I founded and
was president of the Fine Arts Society, and I was quite enterprising. I
thought the school ought to have the new phonograph that you did not
have to wind laboriously, but the machine was costly and there evidently
were no funds for it. It might have been 1926, but no later than 1927, when
I decided that in my capacity as the club's president I would approach the
manufacturers of the new Orthophonic machine directly and persuade
them to donate one to our club—one that would remain as a fixture in the
school. We invited the student body to a demonstration on its arrival—as
many as would fit into the assembly hall—and on the platform, a lonely
eminence in the middle of the large vacant space, stood this elegant rectangular box, new to practically everyone, magic in its capacities, and as awe-
inspiring as an altar before which one worshipped. I wish I could remember what we played, but it hardly mattered, we were all so spellbound by
the contraption and the fact it played by itself.

The distinguished painter Robert Motherwell was a student in art history
and philosophy in the Harvard Graduate School while I was a student in
musicology and we developed a close friendship. When I went to Paris on
the John Knowles Paine Traveling Fellowship he decided to make a trip
abroad at his own expense since he (or his parents) could well afford it, and
we saw each other there several times. We commiserated together on our

academic situations: he, an artist, committed to dry historical studies and I, a composer, committed to musicology. I suggested he talk to the lively art critic–historian Meyer Schapiro at Columbia. He left Harvard and under the aegis of Schapiro embarked on the cycle of study and professional life that established him as one of our foremost painters and one of the founders of the "New York School." Looking back, he later wrote in an autobiographical note that the advice I gave him in Paris had been "a most crucial external suggestion," and for the seventy-fifth birthday tribute that a Provincetown museum undertook for me, he did a collage memorializing our Paris talk.

———

It seems, though my political leanings were somewhat leftish, I always ended up on the most conservative newspapers. Also, they were all on the way to extinction and in each case folded not long after I left. The signs were palpable, as I said earlier: turn the lights off when not absolutely needed; use the phone as little as possible, even for business calls; don't mind that the floors haven't been swept for weeks and electric light bulbs have not been replaced. I never felt any pressure to toe a political line but it was a hardship that friends who did not normally read the paper I worked for felt put upon when they had to buy it to read a review of mine.

APPENDIX # From My Scrapbook

Since I have devoted space to the daily music reviewer's trade I think I should give some examples of the product, namely, how I operated in the years I was involved with that trade. Looking back at what I wrote I am impressed with the touch of a certain bravado which I doubt very much I could summon up now. The reviews are of contemporary composition since the orientation of this book has been in that direction.

Daily concert reviewing is a kind of improvisatory activity. Under pressure of time there is a minimum one can do to think things through and of course it is not possible to rewrite and rewrite. So as I look back at my reviews, at the clippings of them that I saved in my scrapbook and that have not disintegrated because of being improperly stored, I surprise myself at the things that came up, things that I let pass. It is not only through deterioration that I lack copies of much that I have written, but also because there were many times when events reviewed were so pedestrian that it scarcely seemed worth the effort to save any record of them. The habit of not cutting and pasting those reviews carried over so that for long stretches at a time I did not save any. I cannot help feeling that the many words I have written for newspapers are like ashes tossed into the sea.

From The Sun, *March 14, 1944*

Stokowski Leads Shostakovich 6th

The City Center audience last night departed from concert routine to applaud the Shostakovich Sixth Symphony after the opening Largo. At the end of the work Leopold Stokowski was repeatedly recalled. It is to be hoped that it was the suave ensemble and sensitive tone of the City Symphony that were being acknowledged. For if not for the live string quality devoted to melodies of appallingly little inventiveness, or René LeRoy's mellow rendition of the flute figures which do nothing to fill the gaping hole in the Largo, or the orchestra's buoyancy in the cheap finale, there would have been painfully little indeed to hold this listener's interest.

The ostensibly satirical objective of the Presto calls to mind Stravinsky's "Card Party," in which the commentary and the subtle cutting of analogous material make the Shostakovich seem like the most puerile venture in contrast. Even the much underestimated American composer could have easily been found who would show up this symphony. But the nearest Mr. Stokowski came to native music was the uneventful "Pacific Prayer" by Dai-Keeong Lee, the Hawaiian composer educated here and now in our armed forces.

The program also listed excerpts from Rimsky-Korsakoff's "Ivan the Terrible" and Wagner's "Tristan," and Debussy's "Afternoon of a Faun." There were, of course, fewer difficulties than last week, but the sonorous distinction of what was only the orchestra's third concert promises much for the future.

From the New York Herald Tribune, *March 8, 1949*

League of Composers

There was no dearth of creative talent and good performance at Sunday night's League of Composers concert at the Museum of Modern Art, though most of the talent seemed not quite energized in the music by which it was represented on this particular occasion, and not much of the music really came off. The work that was nearest, as a whole, to doing so was the sonata by Edmund Haines, since its proportions were attractively modest. The motoriness of the fast movements was fresh, but too much of one kind, and sustained melodies were too few.

Leon Kirchner's Duo for violin and piano strove for grand pose and "modernistic" effect, in an opaque chromatic style that kept curious company with Hungarian gypsy improvisations. But Kirchner is a newcomer of consequence, with vital music drive. John Lessard's violin work was clean in workmanship, but thin in material. Trifolium, by Betsy Jolas, started promisingly, but soon bogged down.

Shapero is a personality with musical strength enough to trouble one when he is problematic. His half-hour-long piano sonata was hissed Sunday by some because of the boldness of its frank reversion to Beethoven (the loftiest, late Beethoven). Even regarded as a stage, and a very valuable one, in his own development, it is a major effort, and it took courage to write it after contributing, in his earlier works, a personal quality that has already exerted an influence on some of his fellow musicians of his own youth. The sonata has striking inspirations, notably in the first movement before he bows so completely to Beethoven's harmonic processes. But composers use new materials not simply to avoid a new Beethoven sonata, which would be just as great now as it would have been a century ago. They do so because they need some prop to rivet them to paths allowing for adventure and surprise in the internal relations, and to avoid being carried along by their own momentum, as Shapero seems to have been carried along much of the time.

From the New York Herald Tribune, April 20, 1949

Program at Columbia

The Ditson concert offered by Columbia University at the McMillin Theater last night left one with some hope that there are still a few relatively new fields open to composers who work in an atonal direction. Milton Babbitt's Composition for Four Instruments (flute, clarinet, violin, cello) was at last music with enough profile and ingenuity of its own to take on the aspect of something more than a further exercise in the moods and disciplines so thoroughly exploited by Schoenberg, Berg and Webern. Almost any disciple of these three composers has the capacity of perplexing many listeners, because the original idiom is still unknown to a large audience. But after the indoctrination point, a listener encounters less and less surprise in each new work of the orbit.

Theodore Strongin's Septet, in its premiere last night, for example, had little that was strikingly distinct, despite the obvious musical sensitivity in its execution. And Alban Berg's early clarinet pieces, on the other hand, seemed more subtle and fresh than many a work in this idiom tossed off by our young men today. Babbitt, however, whose nearest musical relative is probably Webern, seems to realize that the problem of atonal music of all degrees is the achievement of types of abstraction. Once any given type is deployed, there it is. There is not much more to do with it than spread it on a canvas as a texture with slight ramifications of hue.

The abstraction takes the form of separating tones from their intrinsic harmonic drives and their familiar melodic profiles, giving tones, that is to say, independence. Babbitt furthers the abstraction and thus achieves a remarkable new quality, austere, piquant, and quite unlike anything one has heard before. Using twelve-tone method, he constructs a melodic line, for example, in which tones are further liberated, further differentiated, by ascribing a different loudness to each, and also a different timbre and a vastly *contrasting* pitch range. The degree of abstraction, short of relinquishing tones altogether, is now complete.

The program also included Claus Adam's Piano Sonata, a work of profound seriousness and motor drive that was reviewed not long ago in these columns.

From the New York Herald Tribune, *May 20, 1949*

Composers Forum

Final concert of the season last night at McMillin Academic Theater Columbia University; music by Leon Kirchner and Ned Rorem with John Tasker Howard as moderator. The program:

Duo for Violin and Piano (1947)—Kirchner . . . . Broadus Erle and the composer
* Piano Sonata (1948)—Kirchner . . . . Composer at the piano
* Penny Arcade (cyclical melodrama, 1948)—Rorem . . . . Nell Tangeman, mezzo
soprano, composer at the piano
Mountain Song for cello and piano (1948)—Rorem . . . . Seymour Barab and
Byron Hardin
Sonata for Piano, four hands (1943)—Rorem . . . . . . Eugene Istomin and Byron Hardin
* First performance.

Leon Kirchner and Ned Rorem, who shared the season's final Composers Forum last night at MacMillin Theater, both offered ample evidence of their musicianship in the compositions through which they were represented, but they also provided tangible confirmation of this by appearing as composer-pianists. Mr. Rorem's participation was confined to the accompaniments of his song cycle, "Penny Arcade," to which he brought the needed fleetness, nimbleness and sensitivity. Mr. Kirchner, playing his massive and uncommonly impressive Piano Sonata, naturally had more occasion to reveal his performing talents, and left us with a sense of how powerful his creative drive must be to set aside for it so much keyboard accomplishment and gift.

Power is, in fact, the word that comes first to mind in characterizing Mr. Kirchner's gifts. When he came here from California early this season on a Guggenheim fellowship, he was not long being recognized by the "arrived" composers, who keep tabs on such newcomers, as one of the most "vital young talents to invade these parts in many years." If your reporter was slower than they were in recognizing the degree of this talent from the Duo at the League of Composers, it was because the pardonably youthful forcing for effect, with all manner of violin tricks, diverted him from the many really sincere qualities in the work.

Rehearing the Duo last night I was impressed by some lyric strands that had escaped me, and was less disturbed by the gypsy style shifts, from fast to slow episodes in a chromatic idiom that seemed a bit too serious for this. But the sonata seems to me a better shaped work, with ideas of greater profile, and firmer realization of the tonal drives that seem in quite a unique way to invest material with frequently atonal leaning. Bartók is suggested as distant relative in the combination of composer and pianist, the keen ear for color, and the devices, however intellectualized in Kirchner's case, that give rhapsodic effect. It is easy, too, to recognize him as one of the Roger Sessions school. But there is considerable personality, and I am confident from his progress so far that he will, in his next few works, develop this personality to a point where he must very seriously be reckoned with.

Rorem, recent winner of the Gershwin Prize, is far less a stranger. His many works have been appearing on programs with greater and greater frequency. His enormous facility is no news, and he has become, quite inevitably, a young composer to rely upon where a job must be completed neatly and elegantly for almost any musical occasion near at hand. The four-hand sonata, composed at nineteen, indicates that the facility has been there for some time. Facility is good thing to have, but it is also a good thing to struggle with it, and last night's music seemed to have done little of this.

The first and last songs of "Penny Arcade" had intriguing figures, with their own validity, despite ancestry in Poulenc. But too much of Rorem's music was square in rhythm and phrase length, and without tension. The echoes of Satie's "Parade" may be overlooked in the four-hand sonata. But if Poulenc and Satie are admirable sources for any young composer, it seems important for Rorem now to elaborate on them more than he has, to find some dialectic for his undeniable charming and engaging languorous vein. He is a very well endowed composer, indeed, and it would be good to see him be more severe with himself, to do more to transform his rich sources of popular song.

Yesterday's forum was not only one of the best that has been given in its musical content, but it had such excellent participants as Nell Tangeman, mezzo-soprano; Broadus Erle, violinist; and Eugene Istomin, pianist, who all turned in fine performances.

From the New York Herald Tribune, *December 29, 1952*

Contemporary Music

The International Society of Contemporary Music opened its season at the Ninety-second Street Y.M.H.A. last night with a concert of major significance to those who are concerned with the evolution of music in its creative aspect. A program confined to the music of Anton Webern is not only without precedent here, but would be a rarity anywhere, and is something to be promptly noted in historical records. Even more important than this was the remarkable impression the occasion made, the wonderful sensitivity and taste that the music of the late Austrian composer maintained throughout, and the degree of satisfaction that a whole evening of his reticent, predominantly "sotto voce" miniatures was capable of offering.

More than a small part of the credit for this goes to the performers for their intimate knowledge and understanding of the music and the great pains that had obviously gone into mastering its enormous difficulties. Jacques Monod who appeared both as conductor and as piano accompanist is clearly one of the best musicians around, and he brought staggering discipline and shading to his executions. Accompanying Bethany Beardslee in two groups of songs without the aid of printed music was a sheer tour de force. The young soprano for her part maneuvered the relentless vocal skips as if they were no more challenging than scale-wise passages, and her light voice is extraordinarily suitable to the skips and gives a curve to their ostensible angularity.

The incomparable virtues of the New Music Quartet are thoroughly familiar by now, but the degrees of pianissimo it achieved last night, the precise values it gave to Webern's imaginative string coloration heightened this fine ensemble's stature. So also did the appearance as soloists of two of its members, Broadus Erle, violin, and Claus Adam, cello, each of whom played with a polish far exceeding what we expect from ensemble musicians. It was an uncommon delight, too, to hear the bass clarinet, in the hands of Sidney Keil, played quietly and soothingly, and the clarinetist, Luigi Cancellieri, is also to be complimented.

It is only through performances of last night's caliber that we may come to appreciate Webern's music, for its sparse constellations of notes are almost all about color, subtle variations of loudness and delicate balancing of tones widely removed in pitch. In traditional music such tones denoted climax, and the impulse is to play heavily. This impulse has been responsible for misrepresenting not only Webern, but also the other two members of the Viennese triumvirate, Schoenberg and Berg. This music is often not aggressive, but really as tenuous, as restrained as French Impressionism, and until the manner of playing it as such becomes more generally established, its many beauties will remain latent.

Webern is capable of making his point in as short a period as twenty seconds, as in the third of the Bagatelles for Quartet, Op. 9. It is as if a little, intensely personal confidence, rich in meaning, were whispered into our ear. The Five Canons, Op. 16, and Six Songs, Op. 14, reflected a bolder and more complex approach in Webern's middle period. The String Quartet, Op. 28, the latest work on the program, dating from 1938, had the longest movements, and lasted in all about ten minutes. Webern had obviously by this time exhausted the most minute rhythmic intricacies and had developed a style of evener note-values in which a single melody is shared in succession by several instruments to establish what is, perhaps, his most original contribution.

From the New York Herald Tribune, *April 24, 1953*

The Philharmonic

Dimitri Mitropoulos, conductor
soloist, Nathan Milstein, violinist
Passacaglia and Fugue in C minor . . . . Bach-Respighi
Violin Concerto No. 1. in D major . . . . Prokofieff (played in memory of the composer)
"Night Music" . . . . .George Rochberg (first performance) (winner of the
eighth annual Gershwin Memorial Contest)
Symphony No. 5 in C minor . . . . Beethoven

The Philharmonic–Symphony Orchestra and its musical director, Dimitri Mitropoulos, entered upon the last week end of their season at the top of their form last night in Carnegie Hall. There was also, to grace the occasion, a soloist of first rank in the violinist, Nathan Milstein, and to invest the program with more than routine musical interest there was the premiere of a work by a young American composer, "Night Music" by George Rochberg.

Mr. Rochberg, who is in his early thirties, was the 1952 winner of the Gershwin Memorial Contest which is open to young American composers. One of the substantial rewards for winners of this eight-year-old contest nowadays is performance of the prize work by the Philharmonic–Symphony, and it was thus that we came to hear "Night Music." It turned out to be a meagre ten minutes of music by a young composer who knows how to reproduce the tenuous orchestral colors of Impressionism with a fair degree of expertness.

According to the program notes provided by the composer "Night Music" was from a symphony that had one movement too many, and the name was given to the piece after it was extracted from the symphony. We are told that "night" is to be interpreted in a broad way as "a symbol of whatever is dark, unknown, awesome, mysterious or demonic." Both this program and the grotesque opening solo by contra-bassoon immediately put me in mind of the modern dance events on Fifty-second St. Valiantly as the player tried to redeem this solo in the deep dark pitch regions that seem almost below the margin of hearing, the result was a highly unprepossessing opening. It sorely cried out for some stark, expressionistic, tortured stage counterpart.

There followed a promising section that verged, in a mild way, on a valid episodic, spasmodic contemporary chromaticism. But in less than two minutes this gave way to a far too easy solution for the piece as a whole, namely, a prolonged sonority consisting largely of muted harmonies on the strings, against which the cello plays a long improvisatory solo after the fashion of Bloch's "Schelomo." Laszlo Varga's cello tone was very pretty, but the music was empty and banal.

"Night Music" dates from four years ago. The composer tells us it preceded his "first efforts in the technique of twelve-tone composition," and we may assume from this intelligence that he means to say he has gone on to higher things since. The Gershwin committee must have had very slim pickings, indeed, to have been obliged to come up with this work as the prize-winner.

Mr. Mitropoulos made the best of whatever opportunity the piece gave to make an orchestra sound lovely, lucid and sonorous. He also provided an excellent accompaniment for Mr. Milstein in Prokofieff's first concerto. The violinist for his part played with his usual suavity and superb control, and if the reading was wanting in some of its customary excitement, it had a certain ease that was nice for a change.

Notes

INTRODUCTION

1. Ned Rorem, *Knowing When to Stop* (New York: Simon and Schuster, 1994), 20.

2. E. M. Forster, "The *Raison d'être* of Criticism in the Arts," in *Music and Criticism: A Symposium,* ed. Richard F. French (Cambridge: Harvard University Press, 1948), 14.

3. Charles Jencks, *The Language of Post-Modern Architecture,* 4th ed. (New York: Rizzoli, 1984), 44.

1. COMPOSERS AND THEIR AUDIENCE IN THE THIRTIES

1. Hannah Arendt, "Society and Culture," in *Culture for the Millions? Mass Media in Modern Society,* ed. Norman Jacobs (Princeton: D. Van Nostrand, 1961), 46.

2. The lecture was called "The Irrational Element in Poetry" and was published much later in *Opus Posthumous: Poems, Plays, Prose by Wallace Stevens,* ed. Samuel French Morse (New York: Alfred A. Knopf, 1957), quotation on 225. It was the first lecture on poetry he ever gave. My brief recollection of the occasion is published in an oral biography by Peter Brazeau, *Parts of a World: Wallace Stevens Remembered* (New York: Random House, 1977), 162–65.

3. See Arthur Berger, *Aaron Copland* (New York: Oxford University Press, 1953); rpt., with introduction by Leonard Burkat (New York: Da Capo Press, 1990).

4. Aaron Copland and Vivian Perlis, *Copland since 1943* (New York: St. Martin's Press, 1989), 181–203.

5. Things have not noticeably changed in matters of this nature. The Philadelphia Orchestra was scheduled to do Milton Babbitt's *Transfigured Notes* at the weekly subscription concerts starting 7 December 1989. The players had

their parts well in advance and there were many hours of sectional rehearsals, but it still was not ready as the performance date approached and it was not even postponed, just canceled. I heard it more recently conducted by Gunther Schuller, who succeeded remarkably well with a pick-up orchestra in Boston. At mid-century some of us, Babbitt included, were optimistically anticipating a future in which our music would no longer be at the mercy of live performers and their capriciousness and we could achieve accurate performances ourselves by electronic means. But after over half a century during which electronic music has flourished, it has, however, been pretty much a separate medium or something to supplement acoustic performance, and it has been considered to be at its best when it does not imitate acoustic music but exploits the possibilities of its own sounds and forms. Some of the leading early practitioners, Babbitt and Boulez, for example, seem to have had little interest lately in pursuing it further. But there is a generation of younger composers who are active in it and are producing striking results, among them a former Brandeis student of mine, James Dashow, and a current Brandeis professor, Erik Chasalow. At the same time the extent to which it is practiced in the pop field and the state of its advancement have been sufficiently attractive to young composers to augur a future in which our dream for its replacing live performance in the execution of music of all types may yet become a reality. See Kyle Gant, "Electronic Music, Always Current," *New York Times*, 9 July 2000.

6. In the twenties there was *Gebrauchsmusik*, "music for use," a movement with Paul Hindemith as its most celebrated exponent, which was supposed to be a reaction against music that was stigmatized as being of the "art for art's sake" variety. It was on a less sophisticated level than the Copland. I remember a concert in Harvard's Sanders Theatre led by Hindemith himself at which there was a handout with a simple tune for the audience to sing along at a given point in the proceedings. It was in the thirties, but I do not have a record of the date. The only thing I recall of the event is that we were given the tune and invited to join in.

7. Berger, *Aaron Copland*, 27.

8. Berger, "Copland's Piano Sonata," *Partisan Review* 10, no. 2 (March-April, 1943): 187.

9. Aaron Copland to Arthur Berger, Hollywood, 10 April 1943, published in *Letters of Composers: An Anthology, 1903–1945*, ed. Gertrude Norman (New York: Alfred A. Knopf, 1946), 403.

10. Henry James, preface to *The Wings of the Dove* (Modern Library, 1930), xxvii–xxviii.

11. Norman Schlenoff, *Art in the Modern World* (New York: Bantam Books, 1965), 177.

12. Judith Tick, *Ruth Crawford Seeger: A Composer's Search for American Music* (New York: Oxford University Press, 1997), 192.

13. Virgil Thomson, *American Music since 1910* (New York: Holt, Rinehart, and Winston, 1971), 7.

2. NATIONALISM

1. During part of the period that this book covers, the New York Philharmonic was known as the Philharmonic–Symphony Society of New York—a reflection of its merger with Damrosch's Symphony Society. "New York Philharmonic" will be used here whether the event referred to was recent or early.

2. Edmund Wilson, *A Piece of My Mind: Reflections at Sixty* (New York: Farrar, Straus, and Cudahy, 1956), 35.

3. See Beth E. Levy, "How Roy Harris Became Western," *American Music* 19, no. 2 (summer 2001): 131–67.

4. Joseph Horowitz, "Yes, Virgil, There Were Composers," *New York Times*, 28 July 1998.

5. Roy Harris, "Problems of American Composers," in *American Composers on American Music: A Symposium*, ed. Henry Cowell (New York: F. Ungar, 1962), 151.

6. "The Rhythmic Basis of American Music," in *Elliott Carter: Collected Essays and Lectures, 1937–1995*, ed. Jonathan W. Bernard (Rochester: University of Rochester Press, 1997), 58.

7. Aaron Copland, *Music and Imagination* (Cambridge: Harvard University Press, 1952), 100.

8. Aaron Copland, "Composer from Brooklyn," in Copland, *The New Music: 1900–1960* (New York: McGraw Hill, 1941; rev. and enlarged ed., New York: W. W. Norton, 1968), 159. (Quote from revised edition.)

9. Wilfrid Mellers, *Music in a New Found Land* (New York: Alfred A. Knopf, 1964; rev. ed., New York: Oxford University Press, 1987), 92, 100.

10. Wilfrid Mellers, "American Music: An English Perspective," *Kenyon Review* 5 (summer 1943): 370–71.

11. Peter Evans, "The Thematic Technique of Copland's Recent Works," *Tempo* (spring-summer 1959): 5.

12. Alfred Kazin, "The Stillness of Light in August," in *Twelve Original Essays on Great American Novels*, ed. Charles Shapiro (Detroit: Wayne State University Press, 1958), 280.

13. See Stuart Feder, "The Veneration of Boyhood," *Annual of Psychoanalysis* 9 (1981): 265–316.

14. Henry Cowell and Sidney Cowell, *Charles Ives and His Music* (New York: Oxford University Press, 1955), 110; (rpt. New York: Da Capo Press, 1983).

15. Ibid., 102.

16. Berger, "The Young Composers Group," *Trend* (April-May-June 1933): 26–28.

17. Aaron Copland and Vivian Perlis, *Copland: 1900–1942* (New York: St. Martin's/Marek, 1984), 201. The review from which the sentence was quoted was headed "Yaddo Music Festival" and appeared with my initials (A. V. B.) in the *New York Daily Mirror*, 3 May 1933.

18. Cowell and Cowell, *Charles Ives,* 110.

19. Berger, "The Songs of Charles Ives," *Musical Mercury* 1, no. 4 (October–November 1934), 97.

20. My good friend Bernard Herrmann, destined to be one of Hollywood's most accomplished composers later on, was the person who persuaded Kalmus to undertake publication of the magazine. But Benny had not the slightest idea how to start it or even to write for it. So, in view of my experience on the *Mirror* he enlisted my help and made me coeditor. The whole venture seemed glamorous to him until he realized how much work was involved, and the third issue consequently had no Bernard Herrmann on the masthead but listed me as editor with an associate editor by the name of Dorothy Veinus. Benny had rapidly tired of it.

21. As Joseph Kerman has pointed out: "Seeger and Ives (twelve years his senior) both came from solid New England families who sent them not to conservatories but to the right colleges, where the traditional, European-based music instruction was to the taste of neither. They resisted furiously the academic 'rules' of composition. . . ." *Contemplating Music* (Cambridge: Harvard University Press, 1985), 160. Charles Seeger, by the way, never really developed his compositional skills since his interest turned to the branch of comparative musicology dealing with folk music.

22. See Arendt, "Society and Culture," in *Culture for the Millions?* 47–48.

23. Bernard Holland, "Rorem's Songs Offer a Guided Tour through Life," *Times,* 26 January 1998.

3. IS MUSIC IN DECLINE?

1. Nicholas Slonimsky, *A Lexicon of Musical Invective: Critical Assaults on Composers since Beethoven's Time* (New York: Coleman-Ross, 1965).

2. W. H. Auden, "Speaking of Books," *New York Times Book Review,* 15 May 1955.

3. Samuel Lipman, *Music after Modernism* (New York: Basic Books, 1979), 163. See my review, *Partisan Review* 48, no. 4 (1981): 624–28.

4. Harold C. Schonberg, "Can Composers Regain Their Audiences?" *New York Times,* 4 December 1977.

5. Paul Griffiths, "A Violinist's Playing Belies Her Publicity," *Times,* 17 January 2000.

6. Ernest Newman, *A Musical Critic's Holiday* (New York: Alfred A. Knopf, 1925), 160.

7. Ibid., 158.

8. See Henry Pleasants, *The Agony of Modern Music* (New York: Simon and Schuster, 1955).

9. Constant Lambert, *Music Ho! A Study of Music in Decline* (London: Faber and Faber, 1934), 231.

10. Joseph Kerman has suggested that "the turn towards nineteenth-

century studies" on the part of musicologists could be related to the circumstance "that for better or worse, the largest body of music that gains an immediate response from musicians at large is music of the nineteenth century." *Contemplating Music*, 145.

11. George Santayana, *Reason in Art* (New York: Scribner, 1942), 51.

12. Joseph Wood Krutch, "Is Our Common Man Too Common?" *Saturday Review*, 10 January 1933, 9.

4. RENDEZVOUS WITH APOLLO: FORM IS FEELING

1. Aaron Copland, "The Personality of Stravinsky," in *Igor Stravinsky: A Merle Armitage Book*, ed. Edwin Corle (New York: Duell, Sloan, and Pearce, 1949), 122.

2. Wallace Stevens, "The Relations between Poetry and Painting," undated pamphlet published by the Museum of Modern Art (New York, 1951?), 7.

3. See, for example, Berger, "The Stravinsky Panorama," in *Igor Stravinsky: A Merle Armitage Book*, 114. First published in *Listen: The Guide to Good Music* 3 (August 1943).

4. Richard Taruskin, *Stravinsky and the Russian Traditions: A Biography of the Works through* Mavra (Berkeley and Los Angeles: University of California Press, 1996), 1501.

5. Milton Babbitt in Stravinsky memorial (double issue) *PNM* 9, no. 2 (spring-summer 1971) and 10, no. 1 (fall-winter 1971): 106–7.

6. Allan Kozinn, "Transpositions and Contrasts," review of a New York Philharmonic concert, Avery Fisher Hall, *New York Times*, 26 November 1996.

7. "What is sometimes called an act of self-expression might better be termed one of self-exposure; it discloses character—or lack of character—to others. In itself it is only a spewing forth": John Dewey, *Art as Experience* (New York: G. P. Putnam, 1934; rpt., New York: Capricorn Books, G. P. Putnam, 1958), 62 (quotation is from the reprint edition).

8. Igor Stravinsky, *Chroniques de ma vie*, vol. 1 (Paris: Denöel and Steele, 1935), 116. An anonymous published translation exists: *An Autobiography* (London: Calder and Boyars, 1975).

9. Robert Craft and Igor Stravinsky, *Expositions and Developments* (Garden City, N.Y.: Doubleday, 1962), 114; (rpt. Berkeley and Los Angeles: University of California Press, 1980).

10. André Gide claimed, "Like Valéry . . . who takes the word as point of departure, Chopin, as the perfect artist, departs from the notes (and it is this fact also which makes us say that he 'improvised')": Harold A. von Arx, "André Gide on Chopin," *Musical Mercury* 3, no. 3 (September 1936): 39.

11. Ferruccio Busoni, *Entwurf einer neuen Ästhetic der Tonkunst* (Trieste: C. Schmidt, 1907), 23; trans. T. Baker, *Sketch of a New Esthetic of Music* (New York: G. Schirmer, 1911), 8.

12. The *Dominant* (London, 1927).

13. See the excellent discussion of stratification in Edward T. Cone, "Stravinsky: The Progress of a Method," in *Perspectives on Schoenberg and Stravinsky*, ed. Benjamin Boretz and Cone (New York: W. W. Norton, 1972), 155–64. First published in *PNM* 1, no. 1 (fall 1962): 18–26.

14. Stevens to L. W. Payne Jr., Hartford, Conn., 31 March 1928, *Letters of Wallace Stevens*, ed. Holly Stevens (Berkeley and Los Angeles: University of California Press, 1966), 250.

15. See William Empson, *Seven Types of Ambiguity: A Study of Its Effects on English Verse* (New York: A Meridian Book, Noonday Press, 3d ed., 1955).

5. REINVENTING THE PAST: PASTICHE, COLLAGE, OR "CRITICISM?"

1. There was no composition major at Harvard in the mid-thirties when I entered. My thesis subject was the nearest I could get to composition in musicology: a defense of Stravinsky's neoclassicism in the light of aesthetic theory, which enabled me to spend time with David Prall, the aesthetician I admired so much. Prall was a refuge for those of us at Harvard in the arts who could escape to his Leverett House quarters for relief from the stultifying academicism.

2. See Klaus George Roy, "Preview of Music by Berger," *Christian Science Monitor*, 21 January 1951.

3. "Among our younger generation it is easy to discover a Stravinsky school: Shapero, Haieff, Berger, Lessard, Foss, Fine." Aaron Copland, "Influence, Problem, Tone," in *Stravinsky: In the Theatre*, ed. Minna Lederman (New York: Pellegrini and Cudahy, 1949), 122.

4. Rudolph Elie, review of concert of the Boston Symphony Orchestra, Charles Munch conducting, program including Berger, *Ideas of Order*, Symphony Hall, Boston, *Boston Herald*, 23 January 1954.

5. *New York Review of Books*, 7 October 1999, 49.

6. Paul Henry Lang, *Music in Western Civilization* (New York: W. W. Norton, 1941), 901.

7. "'Star-Spangled Banner' Version of Stravinsky Startles Audience," unsigned, *New York Herald Tribune*, 15 January 1944.

8. See Robert Craft and Igor Stravinsky, *Memories and Commentaries* (Garden City, N.Y.: Doubleday, 1960), 93–94; (rpt. Berkeley and Los Angeles: University of California Press, 1981).

9. See Berger, "The Stravinsky Panorama," in *Igor Stravinsky: A Merle Armitage Book*, 105–14.

10. D. Rudhyar, "'Going Back' in Music: Where To?" *Pro-Musica Quarterly* 5, no. 1 (March 1927): 10–15. Rudhyar wrote some innovative music early in his career much under the influence of the Eastern tradition, but then he lapsed into a nondescript conservatism. He had too many other interests to accord music the full-time attention for making a career out of it.

11. Stravinsky's Westernization was something, as a matter of fact, that his compatriots felt was adumbrated years before the October Revolution in *Petrushka*. See Taruskin, *Stravinsky and the Russian Traditions*, 1120.

12. Ibid., 992–93.

13. Ibid., 995.

14. Taruskin, "Back to Whom? Neoclassicism as Ideology," *19th Century Music* 16, no. 3 (spring 1993): 291–93.

15. Jacques Maritain, *Art et Scholastique*, rev. and enlarged (Paris: Louis Rouart et fils, 1920), 98; Maritain, *Art and Scholasticism*, trans. J. F. Scanlan, rev. and enlarged (London: Sheed and Ward, 1934), 60.

16. Stuart Isacoff, "Remembering Stravinsky," *Keyboard Classics* (September-October, 1981): 13.

17. Ibid., 14.

18. Stravinsky and Craft, *Expositions and Developments*, 73.

19. Igor Stravinsky, *Poétique musicale sous forme de six leçons* (Cambridge: Harvard University Press, 1942), 8; *Poetics of Music: In the Form of Six Lessons*, trans. Arthur Knodel and Ingolf Dahl (Cambridge: Harvard University Press, 1947), 9–10.

20. George Perle, *Serial Composition and Atonality*, 6th ed., rev. (Berkeley and Los Angeles: University of California Press, 1991).

21. Olin Downes, review of stage performance of *Histoire du soldat* by Stravinsky, Edward Clarke, conductor, Art Theatre, London, 13 July 1927, *New York Times*, 3 July 1927.

22. John Rockwell, *All American Music: Composition in the Late Twentieth Century* (New York: Vintage Books, Random House, 1984), 76.

23. Denis Donoghue, "The Promiscuous Cool of Postmodernism," *New York Times Book Review*, 22 June 1986.

24. Stravinsky and Craft, *Dialogues and a Diary* (Garden City, N.Y.: Doubleday, 1963), 183.

25. The progression of chord-roots or tonicizations by thirds instead of fifths is a characteristic of Romantic music that has lately been getting some attention. See David Kopp, *Common-tone Tonality in Nineteenth Century Music*, forthcoming from Cambridge University Press. Taruskin cites Schubert as a composer employing this device and gives the example of "a fragment of a *circle* of minor thirds that counter-balances the major-third circle just completed" (italics mine) contending that "in its use of passing tones it foreshadows the scale of alternating whole steps and half steps—the so-called 'octatonic' scale—that looms so large in Stravinskian harmonic practice" (Taruskin, *Stravinsky and the Russian Traditions*, 257). I am somewhat concerned about the use of the locution "circle" since the members of the adjacencies in a chain of thirds have scarcely any of the special properties of harmonic relation and direction that fifths in the same position would have. That (acoustical) property is essentially what we mean by "circle." If all twelve are used, it returns to the initial member of the series, and that's what makes it a "circle."

6. SERIALISM: COMPOSER AS THEORIST

1. Quoted by Anthony Tommasini in "Babbitt's Notes Strike Colorful Continuity," report of panel (Babbitt, Berger, Robert Cogan, and Robert Seely) and review of concert, Boston's Jordan Hall, *Boston Globe*, 3 February 1993.

2. Philip Gossett, preface to Jean-Philippe Rameau, *Treatise of Harmony*, trans. Gossett (New York: Dover, 1971), vi.

3. Milton Babbitt, "Past and Present Concepts of the Nature and Limits of Music," report of the Eighth Congress of the International Musicological Society, New York (1961): 398.

4. See "Conservation of Quantities and Invariance of Wholes" in Jean Piaget, *The Child's Conception of Number*, ed. C. Gattegno and F. M. Hodgson (London: Routledge and Kegan Paul, 1952).

5. Berger, "Problems of Pitch Organization in Stravinsky," in *Perspectives on Schoenberg and Stravinsky*, ed. Boretz and Cone, 123–54. First published in *PNM* 2, no. 1 (fall-winter 1963): 11–42.

6. Music was part of the medieval quadrivium, the higher studies of the seven liberal arts along with arithmetic, astronomy, and geometry.

7. Babbitt, "Some Aspects of Twelve-Tone Composition," *Score and I.M.A. Magazine* (June 1955): 53–61, rpt. in *Twentieth Century Views of Music History*, ed. William Hays (New York: Charles Scribner's Sons, 1972), 359–74.

8. René Leibowitz, *Schoenberg and His School: The Contemporary Stage of the Language of Music* (New York: Philosophical Library, 1949).

9. I am indebted to Martin Boykan, highly accomplished composer, theorist, and pedagogue of Brandeis University, for calling to my attention the possibility that in considering the numbering of 0 to 11 a matter of counting intervals I could be construed as taking sides with Lev Kobalnykov in a view he expressed in his book on Pierre Boulez to downgrade the importance of pitch relation in Schoenberg. I have no such thing in mind. The individual pitch retains its primacy while functioning to define intervals.

10. Edward T. Cone, "A Budding Grove," *PNM* 3, no. 2 (spring-summer 1965).

11. Ernst Krenek, "Some Current Terms," *PNM* 4, no. 2 (spring-summer 1966): 82.

12. Berger, "New Linguistic Modes and the New Theory," in *Perspectives on Contemporary Music Theory*, ed. Benjamin Boretz and Edward T. Cone (New York: W. W. Norton, 1972), 22–30. First published in *PNM*, 3, no. 1 (fall-winter 1964): 1–9.

13. Theodore Chanler, from an unpublished sketchbook (1940), quoted in Edward N. Waters, "Reports on Acquisitions—Music," *Quarterly Journal of the Library of Congress* 23 (January 1966): 13.

7. RAPPROCHEMENT OR FRIENDLY TAKEOVER?

1. Stravinsky and Craft, *Conversations with Igor Stravinsky* (Garden City, N.Y. : Doubleday, 1960), 145; (rpt. Berkeley and Los Angeles: University of California Press, 1980).

2. Stravinsky and Craft, *Memories and Commentaries,* 117.

3. Quoted by Anthony Tommasini, "Boulez Gets a Chance to Make Converts," *New York Times,* 14 November 1999.

4. Stravinsky and Craft, *Retrospectives and Conclusions* (New York: Alfred A. Knopf, 1969), 196.

5. Aaron Copland, "Fantasy for Piano / Composer Explains Its Particular Problems," *New York Times,* 20 October 1957.

6. Jay S. Harrison, "Talk with Stravinsky: Composer Discusses His Music," *New York Herald Tribune,* 21 December 1952.

7. "In its emphasis on registral differentiation and intricacy of ensemble the [Cello] Duo has been justifiably characterized as 'diatonic Webern,'": Babbitt, "Musical America's Several Generations," *Saturday Review,* 13 March 1937, 36.

8. Eric Salzman, "Gunther Schuller's 3 B's Rate an 'A,'" review of a concert in Twentieth Century Innovation series, Carnegie Recital Hall, *Times,* 2 February 1964. The Los Angeles concert referred to was presented by Evenings on the Roof, 1 February 1960. Stravinsky would surely have been present since Robert Craft conducted and furthermore the composer had a piece of his own on the program. *Chamber Music* was completed in 1956, but Stravinsky, who had employed serial elements much earlier, started moving toward a more evident serialism in works like the Cantata of 1952.

9. P. Glanville-Hicks, "Arthur Berger," *American Composers Alliance Bulletin* 3, no. 1 (spring 1953): 2.

10. Milton Babbitt and Charles Wuorinen, "In Search of the Ideal Listener," in *Musically Incorrect: Conversations about Music at the End of the Twentieth Century,* ed. Hayes Biggs and Susan Orzel (New York: C. F. Peters, 1998), 26.

11. René Leibowitz, "Two Composers: A Letter from Hollywood," *Partisan Review* 15, no. 3 (March 1948): 361–65.

12. Nicolas Nabokov, "The Atonal Trail: A Communication," *Partisan Review* 15, no. 5 (May 1948): 580–85.

8. POSTMODERN MUSIC

1. The locution seems to have made more inroads in the pop field. See, for example, Andrew Dell'Antonio, "Florestan and Butt-head: A Glimpse into Postmodern Music Criticism," *American Music* 17, no. 1 (spring 1999): 65–86.

2. Bernard Holland, "Strings: Rochberg Premiere," *New York Times,* 9 February 1982.

3. Rockwell, *All American Music*, 87.

4. David Huntley, liner notes for David Del Tredici LP, *In Memory of a Summer Day: Child Alice. Part I* (New York: Nonesuch Records, 1983).

5. Donoghue, "The Promiscuous Cool of Postmodernism," *New York Times Book Review*, 22 June 1986.

6. Ibid.

7. Fluxus was a somewhat underground postmodern movement that emerged in New York among devotees of Cage around 1960. Its existence and aesthetic were not at all well known at its inception and are still considered rather offbeat. See Peter Frank, "Fluxus Music," in *Breaking the Sound Barrier: A Critical Study of the New Music*, ed. Gregory Battcock (New York: E. P. Dutton, 1981), 14.

8. See Berger, "Is There a Postmodern Music?" *Boston Review* 12, no. 2 (April 1987): 7–9, 23.

9. Jencks, *The Language of Postmodern Architecture*, 5n.

9. VIRGIL THOMSON AND THE PRESS

1. T. S. Eliot, *Collected Poems: 1909–1935* (New York: Harcourt, Brace, 1930), 32.

2. Berger, "Community of the Arts in Hartford," *Boston Evening Transcript*, 17 February 1936.

3. Thomson, *The State of Music* (New York: William Morrow, 1939), 26.

4. Thomson, *The State of Music*, rev. ed. (New York: Random House, 1961), 35.

5. Rorem, *Knowing When to Stop*, 217.

6. My review, which appeared in the *New York Herald Tribune* on 8 March 1949, two days after the concert was presented by the League of Composers at the Museum of Modern Art, will be found in the appendix, p. 233.

7. Thomson, "Fine New Works," review of League of Composers concert, New York Public Library, *Tribune*, 16 February 1942.

8. Samuel Taylor Coleridge, *Biographia Literaria*, ed. John Calvin Metcalf (New York: Macmillan, 1926), 40.

9. Kyle Gann, "It's Sound, It's Art, and Some Call It Music," *New York Times*, 9 January 2000.

10. Stravinsky and Craft, *Conversations*, 14.

11. Berger, "New Music Society," review of concert of music by John Cage, McMillin Theater, Columbia University, *Tribune*, 4 May 1951.

12. As late as 1979 when Harold C. Schonberg was senior critic at the *Times*, he talked about the "terrible spectre" of the deadline which he described as a "half-hour rush" and explained: "journalists have their talents just as musicians have theirs. Musicians can sight-read to beat the band. We can play the typewriter or computer channels just as expertly": "Some Shop Talk of Critics," *Times*, 20 May 1979.

13. This was precisely the rationalization I received from Vladimir Horo-

witz when I once met him at a cocktail party and he felt for some reason that he should explain to me why he did not program my music though I myself did not bring the subject up. He said he knew some of it and liked it, especially my little *Bagatelles*, which he received from the publisher and read through from time to time. (It seems that Horowitz besieged the publishers for every new sheet of piano music they printed because he prided himself on being a champion sight-reader and not only enjoyed going through unfamiliar music but used it to test himself and retain his sight-reading technique.)

10. MUSIC ON MY BEAT

1. I sometimes think I accomplished more at a luncheon I had with Walter W. Naumburg, head of the foundation that bears his name, than in any single review. (I should add, by the way, that it was lunch at the kind of establishment that I do not normally patronize: the Bankers Club in the Wall Street district.) It seems that the foundation's award concerts were held Tuesday afternoons at Town Hall, and I remarked in a review that it was unusual to fill a hall on weekday afternoons as these concerts did. He invited me to lunch to show his appreciation of my review and especially to tell me that his wife worked hard to achieve such excellent attendance. I thought I would take the occasion to put in a plug for contemporary music. I told him I felt a contestant should be required to have at least one twentieth-century American work on every program, and to my surprise and delight this became a convention for the contest and one that is still followed.

2. See Berger, "Bernstein Takes Walter's Place," review of concert of the New York Philharmonic, Leonard Bernstein, conductor, Carnegie Hall, *New York Sun*, 15 November 1943.

3. Concert of the New York Philharmonic, Dimitri Mitropoulos, conductor, William Kapell, pianist, Carnegie Hall, 11 April 1953.

4. Humphrey Burton, *Leonard Bernstein* (New York: Doubleday, 1994), 195.

5. Berger, "Stadium Concert: Yaysnoff Sisters Soloists / Smallens Conducts," review of concert at the Lewisohn Stadium, Alexander Smallens, conductor, Yaysnoff sisters, duo-piano soloists, *New York Herald Tribune*, 30 July 1952.

6. Current periodicals like *Fanfare* attempt to fill the same need, not always very successfully, being addressed to a less literate public than that of the old "little" magazines.

7. Quoted by Harold Schonberg, "Some Shop Talk of Critics," *New York Times*, 20 May 1979.

8. Berger, "Substitute Sings Opera Until / Train-Stalled Barytone Arrives," *Tribune*, 22 February 1947.

9. Olin Downes, "Alban Berg's 'Wozzeck' in Philadelphia," *Times*, 15 March 1931.

10. Downes, *"Rake's Progress* of Stravinsky / Makes Season's Debut at 'Met,'" *Times,* 28 January 1954.

11. *PNM* AND THE PH.D.

1. Stravinsky and Craft, *Conversations,* 120.

2. Boretz has rethought things again and has been pursuing quite a different path from the one he pursued when we founded *PNM.* His present thinking allows him to cope with the most innovative ideas that are current now at the beginning of the twenty-first century. In all fairness I should point out, though it may be immodest of me, that when what has probably been his chef d'oeuvre, his controversial *Meta-Variations: Studies in the Foundations of Musical Thought,* first published in *PNM* serially, vols. 8 to 14 (1969–74), was reprinted as a book (Red Hook, N.Y.: Open Space, 1995), it not only had minor revisions and corrections but a new preface with credits, including the tribute, "To my teacher Arthur Berger is due my first explicit realization of the possibility, scope, and nature of musical intellection, and an impressive exemplification of the 'examined traditionalism' that still seems to me the heart of my music-intellectual concerns . . ." (p. 9).

3. The other periodicals I had edited were not at all in the same league as *PNM* but they did give me experience. *Musical Mercury* has been mentioned, and *Listen* has been cited as the source of one of my articles. There was also one that I'm not particularly proud of: *Record Retailing* for the trade, which I edited to earn some cash.

4. Charles Rosen, "The Proper Study of Music," *PNM* 1, no. 1 (fall 1962): 89–98.

5. Boretz, "Meta-Variations," first installment, *PNM* 8, no. 1 (fall-winter 1969): 1–74.

6. Berger and Boretz, "A Conversation about *Perspectives,*" *PNM* (double issue) 25, nos. 1 and 2 (1987): 597.

7. J. K. Randall, "Compose Yourself—A Manual for the Young," *PNM* 10, no.2 (spring-summer, 1972): 1–12; 11, no. 1 (fall-winter 1972): 77–91; 12, nos. 1 and 2 (1973–74): 231–81; (rpt., Red Hook, N.Y.: Open Space, 1995).

8. Randall, I strongly suspect, was the scapegoat for some of the antagonisms and aggressions that had been building up. Unfortunately *PNM* was not the optimum place for his challenging experiment. It should be read and judged by people in literature as well as by musicians. I think the problem was it was something of a completely new conception that was sprung upon us without our being prepared for it. Some effort should have been made to prepare us.

9. In addition to myself, those who resigned were Elliott Carter, Lukas Foss, Andrew Imbrie, Leon Kirchner, George Perle, and Mel Powell. (I rejoined.)

10. Berger and Boretz, "A Conversation about *Perspectives,*" 607.

12. A TALE OF TWO CRITICS: ROSENFELD AND HAGGIN

1. *Musical Impressions: Selections from Paul Rosenfeld's Criticism,* ed. Herbert A. Leibowitz (New York: Hill and Wang, 1969), xv.

2. Ibid., 225.

3. Ibid., 81.

4. Paul Rosenfeld, "Concerning Schoenberg's Music," *New Republic,* 22 January 1916: 309.

5. Rosenfeld, "New German Music," in *Musical Chronicle (1917–1923)* (New York: Harcourt, Brace, 1923), 311.

6. Ibid., 311–12.

7. Ibid., 312–13.

8. Ibid., 313.

9. *An Hour with American Music* (Philadelphia: J. B. Lippincott, 1929).

10. Charles L. P. Silet, review of *False Dawn: Paul Rosenfeld and Art in America, 1916–46* by Hugh M. Potter, *American Music* 2, no. 1 (spring 1984): 105.

11. *Paul Rosenfeld: Voyager in the Arts,* ed. Jerome Mellquist and Lucie Wiese (New York: Creative Age Press, 1948).

12. B. H. Haggin, *Music on Records: A New Guide to the Music, the Performances, the Recordings,* 3d ed., rev. (New York: Alfred A. Knopf, 1943).

13. Berger, review of *Music for the Man Who Enjoys "Hamlet,"* by B. H. Haggin, *New Republic,* 4 December 1944, 758. The book was published by Alfred A. Knopf.

14. Haggin, *Music on Records,* 33–34.

13. DO WE HEAR WHAT WE SAY WE HEAR?

1. Donald Francis Tovey, *A Musician Talks: 2. Musical Textures* (London: Oxford University Press, 1941), 68.

2. Ibid., 69.

3. Edmund Gurney, *The Power of Sound* (London: Smith/Elder, 1880), 77; (New York: Basic Books, 1966), 79.

4. Hans Gal, *Johannes Brahms: His Work and Personality,* trans. Joseph Stein (London: Weidenfeld and Nicolson, 1963), 209.

5. The first of several volumes of August Wilhelm Ambros's monumental history of music appeared in 1862, the whole vast project commissioned and published by Leuckart in Breslau. However, in the course of writing the fourth volume the author died. Another edition was published subsequently and preparation of the fourth volume, which appeared in Leipzig in 1909, fell to Leichtentritt.

6. Alexander Tansman, *Igor Stravinsky: The Man and His Music* (New York: G. P. Putnam, 1949), 187.

7. Ernst Krenek, *Music Here and Now* (New York: W. W. Norton, 1939), 72.

8. See David Prall, chapter III, "The Discrimination of Surface Qualities and the Intuition of Specific Beauties," in *Aesthetic Judgment* (New York: Thomas Y. Crowell, 1929).

9. Milton Babbitt, review of *Structural Hearing* by Felix Salzer, *Journal of the American Musicological Society* 5, no. 3 (fall 1952): 261.

10. Gilbert Ryle, *The Concept of Mind*, 3d ed. (New York: Barnes and Noble, 1961), 143.

11. Anthony Tommasini, "Repeat, Repeat, Repeat, Repeat, Minimally," *New York Times*, 20 July 1999.

12. Tommasini, "The Warming of a Lucid Intellect: Boulez at Seventy-Four," *Times*, 13 June 1999.

13. I take it this is the type of musical event that David Epstein would have characterized as "ambiguous," on the order of the C-sharp in bar 5 of Beethoven's "Eroica" Symphony, surprising us by acting in the relation of D-flat and being notated as such in the recapitulation. "Ambiguity" has been rather overworked, and while Epstein made excellent use of the notion at the time he wrote, nowadays it would be better to avoid it and realize the C-sharp is ambiguous only if it is reified. It is not the note itself we are talking about but the two different relationships in which it is heard, and each of them is perfectly clear and definite. See Epstein, *Beyond Orpheus: Studies in Musical Structure* (Cambridge: MIT Press, 1979), 111, 162.

14. NEW LINGUISTIC MODES AND THE NEW THEORY

1. William Poland, "Theories of Music and Music Behavior," *Journal of Music Theory* (winter 1963): 164–65.

2. Glen Haydon, *Introduction to Musicology: A Survey of the Fields, Systematic and Historical, of Musical Knowledge and Research* (New York: Prentice-Hall, 1941), 1–5.

3. See Rudolf Reti, *The Thematic Process in Music* (New York: Macmillan, 1951).

4. Quoted by Delmore Schwartz, "Poetry as Imitation," in *Perspectives on Musical Aesthetics*, ed. John Rahn (New York: W. W. Norton, 1994), 301. Originally published in *PNM*, 24, no. 1 (fall-winter 1985): 102–6.

5. Paul Valéry, "Variété, à propos d'Adonis," *Nouvelle revue française*, 1924: 158.

6. Hugo Riemann, *History of Music Theory*, trans. Raymond H. Haggh (Lincoln: University of Nebraska Press, 1962), 125.

7. Arnold Isenberg, "Critical Communication," in *Aesthetics and Language*, ed. William Elton (Oxford: Basil Blackwell, 1959), 141.

8. Dewey, *Art as Experience*, 52.

9. Isenberg, "Critical Communication," 141–42. Note that when this text was quoted originally in *PNM* I deleted the sentence starting with "scientific explanation" and the one right after it because, as Kerman was keen to recognize, it was a "quiet article" and I was just starting to "bore from within," not

ready to make waves in my anomalous position as editor and cofounder of a magazine that favored a scientific approach with which I was not altogether comfortable.

10. Ibid., 139.

11. Stuart Hampshire, "Logic and Appreciation," in *Aesthetics and Language*, ed. Elton, 167.

15. THE OCTATONIC SCALE

1. I doubt whether anyone has to be reminded of the sound of the pentatonic since it is the mainstay of kitschy Oriental imitations in Western music. But if a reminder is needed the black keys of the piano can provide it. Incidentally, the division of the keys into seven white and five black was prescribed by tonality which dealt in seven-note scales. In a way, it is an anachronism with the advent of twelve-tone music since the latter is concerned with a dozen equal notes and does not separate out the seven of a diatonic scale.

2. Berger, "Problems of Pitch Organization in Stravinsky," *PNM* 2, no. 1.

3. Olivier Messiaen, *Technique de mon langage musical* (Paris: Leduc, 1944), 52–53.

4. Roman Vlad, *Stravinsky*, trans. Frederick Fuller and Ann Fuller (London: Oxford University Press, 1960), 7–8.

5. Rimsky-Korsakov, *My Musical Life*, 5th ed., trans. Judah A. Joffe (New York: Alfred A. Knopf, 1942), 78. He said it replaces Glinka's whole-tone scale.

6. Pieter C. van den Toorn, *The Music of Igor Stravinsky* (New Haven: Yale University Press, 1983).

7. Taruskin's thoroughgoing and scholarly treatise in its 1,756 pages gets no further than the period of *Mavra* (the early twenties).

8. Robert Craft, *Stravinsky: Glimpses of a Life* (New York: St. Martin's Press, 1993), 303.

9. Berger, "Problems of Pitch Organization," 136–38. Although C is the tone center of the tableau, the scale that I consider to be the basis of the *Petrushka* chord starts on A-sharp (or B-flat) because it is more consistent with the important registral distribution locally.

10. "I had conceived of the music in two keys in the second tableau as Petrushka's insult to the public. . . ." Stravinsky and Craft, *Expositions and Developments*, 156.

11. Berger, "Problems of Pitch Organization," 148.

12. The "referential" scale, a concept often misinterpreted, is an abstraction deduced from the pitch relationships of a concrete musical work. As an analytic device it allows us to assign more than one scale to a musical work or passage. Stravinsky's interpretation of his *Petrushka* chord was not wrong. But to my way of thinking the C-major chord is not enough to establish the key of C major, or the F-sharp chord, the key of F-sharp major. The leading tone is missing.

13. Taruskin, *Stravinsky and the Russian Traditions*, 269.

14. Berger, "Problems of Pitch Organization," 137–38.

15. What I had to say about the octatonic in "Problems of Pitch Organization" was essentially introductory. For further discussion see van den Toorn, *The Music of Igor Stravinsky*. There is also an interesting approach on a more modest level by a former graduate student of mine, Joel Eric Suben, in "Debussy and Octatonic Pitch Structure," Ph.D. dissertation, Brandeis University, 1979. Suben presents a neat diagram showing the absolute pitch content of the three possible octatonic collections available as segments of the total chromatic. If we call the three diminished seventh chords I, II, and III, the collection of pitches of any given octatonic scale will consist of I and II, II and III, or I and III.

16. Joseph Straus, "Stravinsky's Tonal Axis," *Journal of Music Theory* 26, no. 2 (fall 1982): 264.

17. When I referred to four possible pitch priorities that could be tone centers of equal weight perhaps I should have made it clearer that I didn't mean that they all functioned necessarily in the same piece. What I meant was that they stood in symmetrical positions like G and C in the major which have symmetry in that each note is, intervallically, in the same position as the first note in a tetrachord which has the form tone-tone-semitone. As far as symmetry is concerned, nothing is changed by the fact that the diatonic tetrachords are discrete and the octatonic trichords are conjunct (overlapping).

16. BACKSTAGE AT THE OPERA

1. Berger, "Spotlight on the Moderns," *Saturday Review*, 25 November 1950.

2. Berger, "Bing Wins a Test Case," *New York Herald Tribune*, 6 January 1952.

17. A TALE OF TWO CONDUCTORS: KOUSSEVITZKY AND MITROPOULOS

1. Leonard Bernstein, *The Unanswered Question* (Cambridge: Harvard University Press, 1975). The title is borrowed from Ives, who used it for an orchestra piece.

2. Fred Lerdahl and Ray Jackendoff, *A Generative Theory of Tonal Music* (Cambridge: M.I.T. Press, 1983).

3. Moses Smith, *Koussevitzky* (New York: Allen, Towne, and Heath, 1947), 256.

Index

absolute music, 161
Abstract Expressionism, 101
academic music, modern music as,
    100, 101
Adam, Claus, 237; Piano Sonata, 234
Adler, Guido, 175
aesthetic surface, 167
Afternoon of a Faun (Debussy), 232
Agon (Stravinsky), 93
Aida (Verdi), 207
All Set (Babbitt), 33
Ambros, August Wilhelm, *Geschichte
    der Musik*, 164, 253n5
American Composers Alliance, 229
American Composers Orchestra, 36
The American Mercury, 140
Apollinaire, Guillaume, 162
Apollon musagète (Stravinsky), 50, 77
Appalachian Spring (Copland), 47,
    210
Aristoxenos, 89
Art et Scolastique (Art and Scholasti-
    cism) (Maritain), 74
atonality, 185–86
Auden, W. H., 35, 141, 203
avant-garde composers, 36–37, 45
Averino, Olga, 216

Babbitt, Irving, 74, 173
Babbitt, Milton, 84–85, 88–91, 139,
    148–49, 167, 174, 212, 242n5,

248n9; *All Set*, 33; Boretz's agree-
    ment with theories of, 142; *Com-
    position for Four Instruments*, 98,
    234; conversation with Stravinsky
    on "returning to" past, 51–52;
    led movement to establish Ph.D.
    in music composition, 143; *Trans-
    figured Notes*, 241n5; as twelve-
    tone composer, 95; wrote "album
    notes" for Columbia's recording of
    Moses and Aaron (Schoenberg),
    207
Bach, J. S., 50–51, 70, 71–73, 107,
    131, 154, 157; "English" Suite
    No. 3, 193, 194; *Passions*, 162
Baiser de la fée (The Fairy's Kiss)
    (Stravinsky), 75
Balanchine, George, 48, 154
Ballade No. 4 in A-flat major
    (Chopin), 190–92, 194
Bard College, 147
Barenboim, Daniel, 46
Barkin, Elaine, 148
Bartók, Béla, 15, 32, 34; Sonata for
    two pianos, 113
"Basle" Concerto (Stravinsky), 79
Batstone, Philip, 88, 145
Beardslee, Bethany, 237
Beatles, 32
Beecham, Thomas, 19
Beethoven, Ludwig van, 45, 56–57,

Symphony in E minor (Sessions), 216
Symphony on a Hymn Tune (Thomson), 21
symphony orchestras, 19–20, 46–47
Szell, George, 229

Talma, Louise, 70, 97
Tangeman, Nell, 236
Tansman, Alexander, 165
Taruskin, Richard, 51; on octatonic scale, 187, 192, 193, 194, 196; on progression of chord-roots by thirds, 247n25; *Stravinsky and the Russian Traditions*, 187, 192; on Stravinsky's return to the past, 73–74, 247n11
Taubman, Howard, 122, 134, 137
Taylor, Deems, 133
Tchaikovsky, Pyotr Ilyich, 17, 75
Telegram, 123
terminology: difficulty of, used with serialism, 88–91, 248n9; for music analysis, 177–78; new, proposed by Princeton school, 85–86, 89–90
theory: relationship between criticism and, 173–74, 182–84; scientific method as endemic to, 176–77; as verbal explanation of composers' works, 178–79
Third Symphony (Copland), 217
Third Symphony (Harris), 22, 23
Thomas, Michael Tilson, 46–47, 75
Thomson, Virgil, 19–20, 22, 24, 120, 125, 225, 233, 250n6; as composer, 153, 162; contents of reviews desired by, 115–17, 124, 133; contributions of, as music critic, 119–21, 132; on "fifty pieces" as commonplace music repertory, 44; "neoromanticism" used by, 78; at *New York Herald Tribune*, 112–15, 121, 129, 154; *Sonata da Chiesa*, 112; *The State of Music*, 113; supported delayed appearance of concert reviews, 119; supported Stravinsky's neoclassical works, 48–49; *Sym-

phony on a Hymn Tune, 21; on Toscanini's perfectionism, 210
Three Pieces (Berg), 212–13
Three Satires (Schoenberg), 51
Tick, Judith, 16, 46
Tommasini, Anthony, 129, 169
tonality: application of terminology, 177; as approach to *Rite*, 166; beginnings of, 84; composers' study of theory of, 87, 90; as more than traditional scales and triads, 186; Schenker's illumination of, 88
tone clusters, 16, 34, 133
Toscanini, Arturo, 12, 210
Tovey, Sir Donald Francis, 149, 161
Traité d'Harmonie (Treatise on Harmony) (Rameau), 84
Transfigured Night (Schoenberg), 78
Transfigured Notes (Babbitt), 241n5
Tristan (Wagner), 53, 232
Trotsky, Leon, 10
Tuyl, Marian van, 103
twelve-tone composition, 39, 97–98, 203; Bernstein's antagonism toward, 45; international spread of, 95–96; necessity of studying theory underlying, 87, 90; prior to Princeton school, 86. *See also* atonality; serialism

University of California at Berkeley, 144
Untermeyer, Jeanne Starr, 205

Valéry, Paul, 178
van den Toorn, Pieter, 187, 196
Van Wyck, Brooks, 26
Varèse, Edgard, 30, 153
Veinus, Dorothy, 244n20
Verdi, Giuseppe: *Aida*, 207; *Falstaff*, 205
Verklärte Nacht (Schoenberg), 152
Vivaldi, Antonio, 38
Vlad, Roman, 186–87

Wagner, Richard, 74, 56, 78, 121, 152; Hindemith and, 53; on "music of